Roman Comedy

Five Plays by
Plautus and Terence

Roman Comedy

Five Plays by
Plautus and Terence

TRANSLATED WITH
INTRODUCTION AND NOTES BY
David Christenson

an imprint of
Hackett Publishing Company, Inc.
Indianapolis/Cambridge

THE FOCUS CLASSICAL LIBRARY
Series Editors • James Clauss and Stephen Esposito

Copyright © 2010 David Christenson

Cover: Theatrical masks, mosaic, Roman, from Villa Adriana, Rome, Italy. Location: Museo Capitolino Rome. © The Art Archive / Museo Capitolino Rome / Gianni Dagli Orti.

Previously published by Focus Publishing/R. Pullins Company

Focus an imprint of
Hackett Publishing Company, Inc.
P.O. Box 44937
Indianapolis, Indiana 46244-0937

www.hackettpublishing.com

ISBN 13: 978-1-58510-319-5

20 19 18 17 16   4 5 6 7 8

Table of Contents

Introduction

Plautus (*ca* 254-184 BCE) and Terence (fl. 166-60 BCE) are enormously important figures in western comedy. As Rome began to establish its hegemony over the ancient Mediterranean basin, these two popular comic poets entertained Roman audiences in successive generations. Latin literature was still in its formative years, and Rome was in an early stage of becoming a cosmopolitan city. Plautus' plays continued to be performed for centuries after his death. Revivals of Terence's plays were less common, though their survival was ensured by their central position in the educational curriculum, thanks to the simple elegance of Terence's Latin and his plays' perceived morally upright content. Plautus' more boisterous comedies, despite their linguistic extravagances and their portrayals of dubious morality, likewise survived through continuous copying down to the Renaissance, where they enjoyed a great revival of interest. The works of Plautus and Terence went on to influence scores of dramatists in the European tradition, including such luminaries as Shakespeare and Molière. The extremely successful Broadway musical and film *A Funny Thing Happened on the Way to the Forum* is a pastiche of several Plautine plays, and the entire television sit-com genre is much indebted to the tradition of Greek and Roman New Comedy as it is represented chiefly by Plautus and Terence.[1]

The five plays translated here provide a representative sample of the rich and varied comedy in Latin that delighted audiences in Rome during the culturally tumultuous first half of the 2nd century BCE.

The World(s) of Plautus and Terence

Latin literature begins in 240 BCE, when Livius Andronicus produced a comedy and a tragedy translated from Greek at a religious festival (*Ludi Romani*) in honor of the god Jupiter. In the 3rd century BCE, the Romans had seized control of Italy, and they had begun to set their sights beyond the Italian peninsula. The first phase of this process that eventually led to Roman domination throughout Europe and beyond was conflict with Carthage, a powerful Phoenician colony and trade center located in what is now Tunisia. The First Punic War (261-241 BCE) ended in a Roman victory over the Carthaginians. Many citizen-soldiers had been exposed to Greek-style drama while on campaign in southern Italy, and it is no coincidence that Livius, said to be a freed slave from the Greek colony of Tarentum (now Taranto) there, staged his plays in Rome in the year following the war's end. The Carthaginians, under Hannibal's leadership, were soundly defeated in the Second Punic War (218-

---

1   See further Grote (1983).

201 BCE). The protracted wars with Carthage also brought the Romans into conflict with various kings and city-states of Greece. A series of wars with the Macedonians, the remnants of Alexander the Great (d. 323 BCE) and his short-lived, now fractured empire, ended with a Roman victory at Pydna on the northeast coast of Greece in 168 BCE. This decisive battle effectively negated the possibility of a Greek resurgence in Mediterranean politics, and signaled a new phase in the Roman appropriation of Greek culture. These wars with the Carthaginians and the Greeks finally came to a conclusion with the destruction of Carthage and the sack of Corinth (marking the final relegation of Greece to a Roman province) in 146 BCE. During this period of military expansionism, Roman generals competed fiercely with each other for public acclaim and the cherished right (granted by the senate) to celebrate a formal triumph in Rome. Roman playwrights had inherited the stock figure of the braggart soldier from Greek comedy, but characters such as Stratophanes in Plautus' *Truculentus* and Thraso in Terence's *Eunuchus* perhaps also resonated with Roman audiences as grotesque parodies of these ambitious, celebrity-seeking aristocrats.

The plays of Plautus and Terence thus were produced during a dynamic period of the Roman Republic. Rome at the peak of both Plautus' and Terence's careers was experiencing a major cultural revolution. Soldiers stationed abroad and other Roman travelers had fallen under the spell of Greece, and many had learned Greek. Greek culture was now exerting enormous influence on Roman life, and Greek philosophers, rhetoricians, artists, poets and teachers were ubiquitous in the city. The years *ca* 240-160 BCE in fact mark the first major epoch of Latin literature. While the Romans' literature essentially was a derivative product and so always a kind of homage to the Greeks, it also proved to be a forum in which they would increasingly assert their own cultural and national identity.

The process of establishing a distinctly Latin literature thus unfolded in the midst of considerable cultural upheaval. The successful wars with Carthage and her allies had introduced unprecedented new wealth to Rome, an influx of foreigners, and many exotic new customs. Though there was much demand in Rome for (esp.) things Greek, there was also a conservative backlash. Moral traditionalists such as Cato the Elder (239-149 BCE) publicly railed against the decadence and dangerousness they saw in the new wave of outside influences, while also sometimes enjoying aspects of it in their private lives. In particular, conservatives depicted the infusion of Greek culture as a serious threat to the traditional homogeneity of Roman institutions, and to the national character itself, which they idealized as rooted in such values as practicality, perseverance, frugality and parsimony. The Greek cultural invasion nonetheless rolled on in Rome, though with considerable tension. The introduction of the eastern cult of the god Bacchus (= Greek Dionysus), for example, resulted in major scandal, and by an emergency decree in 186 BCE, the senate declared it a threat to public morality and order. In 161 BCE, Greek rhetoricians were universally banished from Rome.

But even the most traditionalist members of the elite ranks of society gradually saw the utility in creating a national literature to rival that of the Greeks as a means of enhancing Roman prestige in the Mediterranean world. Drama received generous state-sponsorship in Rome, and it flourished in this period. After all, the Greek source plays that playwrights such as Plautus and Terence adapted for the Roman stage came with a built-in "safety-net:" all were set in Greece (usually Athens) or some other non-Roman locale (e.g., North Africa in the case of Plautus' *Rudens*), and so their shady characters and depictions of immoral action could be dismissed as foreign imports. But both comic playwrights—Plautus to a much greater extent than Terence—Romanized their plays by mixing in distinct references to Roman institutions, customs, laws, public officials, the geography and topography of Italy and Rome, and to contemporary events and issues. Far from being purely escapist entertainments, the comedies of Plautus and Terence engage directly with the ongoing 2nd century BCE culture wars. As the five plays in this volume collectively demonstrate, complex contemporary issues such as the effect of wealth upon morality, the possibilities for social mobility/rebirth, the integrity of the family, personal and group identity, gender, sexuality and otherness figure prominently in the comic drama of this period. The comedies of Plautus and Terence brought the Roman populace together to participate in what amounted to a dramatic evaluation of the cultural process unfolding outside the theater.

The Tradition of Ancient Comedy

The extant comedies of Plautus and Terence are based on plays belonging to the genre of New Comedy, which flourished in Greece from *ca* 325 to 250 BCE. This was the third phase of Greek comedy after Old Comedy, which is now represented primarily by the bawdy, fantastical, and quintessentially Athenian plays of Aristophanes that were originally performed in the late 5th and early 4th centuries BCE. Middle Comedy, which survives only in fragments (mostly dating to the 4th century) and through titles of plays, marks the period of transition to the better-attested New Comedy. Greek New Comedy no longer focused so squarely on contemporary Athenian politics and the prominent individuals involved in them, but was cosmopolitan and featured more universal themes and plots. It depicted the more mundane social lives of upper- and upper-middle class families in Athens (or in reality any Hellenistic urban center). New Comedy did away with the pervasive obscenity, elaborate costumes, exuberant music and choruses, and the satire and personal invective that had defined Greek Old Comedy. Comedies became more domestic than political, and were now built around stock characters such as clever slaves, greedy pimps and prostitutes, parasites, young men hopelessly in love, saucy cooks, and egotistical soldiers.

The only plays of Greek New Comedy whose remains are substantial are those of Menander (*ca* 344/3-292/1 BCE). The extant plays—or parts of plays, as no single play survives wholly intact—consist of five-acts, and feature stereotypical and often highly coincidental situations involving, e.g., the reunion of children separated at birth with their families. Despite the unrealistic character of his plots, already in antiquity Menander was praised for his subtlety in capturing human psychology and realistically depicting the complexities of social life; the ancient scholar Aristophanes of Byzantium (*ca* 257-180 BCE) is said to have exclaimed: "O Menander and Life, which of you imitated the other?" Menander's plays are very much in keeping with the still predominant modern trend toward theatrical realism or naturalism. Menander provided the source plays for Terence's *Adelphoe* and *Eunuchus*.

Menander died well before the beginnings of Roman drama in 240 BCE. But his plays and those of other New Comedy playwrights such as Diphilus (b. *ca* 360-350 BCE), who provided the source play for Plautus' *Rudens*, enjoyed frequent revivals in Athens. They were also performed throughout the Hellenistic world by itinerant acting companies such as the famed "Artists of Dionysus." Parts of southern Italy and Sicily, though under Roman control, had been colonized by Greeks centuries earlier, and the earliest Roman playwrights, such as Livius Andronicus, were probably exposed to Greek comedy there. Though the genre they created came to be known as the *fabula palliata*, or "play in Greek costume," Roman playwrights did not slavishly "translate" Greek New Comedy, but, rather, adapted it for the Roman stage and for their Roman audiences. The extant fragments of the earliest Roman playwrights, for instance, reveal the addition of musically elaborate songs, or *cantica*, which do not correspond to anything in Greek New Comedy.

Native forms of Italian comedy[2] were also instrumental in this process that is best described as creative adaptation, and seem to have had a major influence on Plautus. These forms of popular Italian drama were unscripted in Plautus' and Terence's day, and so we only know of them through later testimony or the fragments of much later scripted versions. One popular form of comedy was Atellan farce, so named because of its origin in Atella in Campania. These performances were short, largely improvised skits involving masked, stock characters such as Bucco ("Fool"), Maccus ("Clown"), Manducus ("Chomper-Man"), and Pappus ("Grandpappy"). There were certain fixed routines and situations, which were probably full of slapstick and vaudeville-like comic banter, traces of which are not infrequently found in Plautus. Mime was another form of popular Roman entertainment, also unscripted in the early period, and nothing like mime today. Mime actors and actresses (a rare example of the use of female performers in European theater before relatively recent modern times) had a reputation for bawdiness. They were nicknamed "flat-foots" because they performed barefoot. The actors' costumes sported large phalli and the actresses sometimes appeared in the nude. Mime troupes likewise performed stock scenes calling for improvisation, and they seemed to have favored short, bawdy skits, including those featuring adultery. Another form of highly farcical comedy called *phlyax* drama, which survives primarily through 4th century BCE depictions of scenes on vases, flourished in southern Italy. Mythical burlesques, especially plays featuring the figure of Herakles/Hercules, seem to have been very popular in *phlyax* drama.[3]

Roman Theater

Roman plays were primarily performed in connection with state-sponsored religious festivals, and, like the other entertainments that took place in this festival context, were referred to as *ludi* ("games"). They were also sometimes performed in

---

2   For these, see further Panayotakis (2005b).

3   For the *phlyax* plays, see further Bieber (1961): 129-46.

connection with funeral games (*ludi funebres*), grand public occasions to acknowledge the life and death of a distinguished Roman aristocrat, such as those put on by the sons of Lucius Aemilius Paullus in 160 BCE, at which Terence's *Adelphoe* debuted. In the early period of Roman theater, festivals associated with drama were held in honor of the gods Jupiter, Apollo, Ceres, Flora (an Italian goddess of flowers/flowering), and the Magna Mater ("The Great Mother"), an Anatolian fertility goddess introduced to Roman cult in 204 BCE. The temple of the Magna Mater on the Palatine Hill was the setting for the performance of Terence's *Eunuchus* in 161 BCE.

The festivals featured grand processions, the sacrifice of animals, and public feasts. Various events and sideshows took place during them, e.g., boxing matches and gladiator contests.[4] The plays were performed either in the Roman forum, a circus (the venue for chariot racing), or in front of a god's temple. State funds allocated by the elite Roman senate financed the festivals. It was the direct responsibility of Roman magistrates called *aediles* to administer the festivals and oversee the entertainments that took place during them. As this Republican magistracy was held by ambitious politicians, the *aediles* also contributed some of their private funds to finance special entertainments for the *ludi* as a means of cultivating political support from the Roman populace. As the festivals approached, their specific duties included contracting for plays with producers, playwrights and acting troupes. The male actors that made up these troupes typically were slaves or free persons of low status, such as freedman (i.e., former slaves). It was considered disgraceful for a freeborn citizen to perform as an actor, and one who did normally forfeited his citizen's rights.

Though the Romans possessed the architectural expertise to build grand stone theaters after the manner of the Greeks, no permanent theater was constructed in Rome until Pompey the Great's in 55 BCE. Later writers moralized that the senatorial elite regarded the theater as a locus of decadence with the potential to foment civic unrest, and so had fiercely resisted all attempts to build permanent theaters. Pompey crowned his theater with a temple of Venus (Victrix), probably to justify the unprecedented structure by continuing the tradition of dramatic performances before a temple, and so also drama's religious associations. A more practical explanation for the ban on stone theaters is that the senate and the ambitious sponsors of the *ludi* viewed the construction of temporary structures for each festival as a visible reminder to the Roman people that the *ludi* depended on their personal munificence; they took great pains to advertise their public benefactions through inscriptions and other public notices.

Consequently, nothing survives of the theaters in which Plautus' and Terence's plays were performed. There is little written testimony as to the nature of these temporary theaters and no contemporary visual evidence, and so we mostly rely on the plays themselves to reconstruct only a general layout. The stage was a simple platform (*proscaenium*). The action there usually takes place on what is supposed to be a street in front of a wooden backdrop (*scaena*) with up to three doors, which can

---

4   For a glimpse into the full festive atmosphere, see the prologues of Terence's *Hecyra* ("The Mother-in-law").

represent up to three houses depending on the play.[5] Much later artistic representations of Roman theaters depict partially enclosed porches in front of these houses, but there is nothing in the texts of the plays to verify their existence in early, temporary theater. Nor is there evidence for the use of a curtain in early Roman theater, and the audience sat on benches constructed for the occasion. The best seats directly in front of what was probably only a slightly raised stage were reserved for the senatorial elite from 194 BCE on.

The texts of the plays are transmitted without stage directions, though the characters provide most of these through their own words, e.g., in describing their movements. There were two side wings to the stage, one of which is usually assumed to lead to the forum/center of town, the other to the country and/or harbor (though some plays have alternative requirements). There was also an altar somewhere in front of the stage-backdrop. Props were used sparingly, but effectively, as in the case of the stolen pashmina (an expensive woolen shawl) that passes through various hands in Plautus' *Menaechmi*. There is no definitive way to calculate the precise capacity of such theaters,[6] but references to the crowd in prologues indicate a diverse and densely packed audience, whose members comprised the broad socio-economic spectrum of Roman Republican society.[7] Such a physical layout suggests a high degree of theatrical minimalism and stylization. Most significantly, and in stark contrast with Greek stone theaters that featured a large orchestra (i.e., dancing area for the chorus) between the stage and the audience, temporary Roman theater encouraged close interaction between actors and audience, an intimacy that Plautus especially exploited.

All the actors wore masks, as also had been the case in Greek New Comedy and Atellan farce. No definitive visual representations of the masks used in early Roman comedy survive, and so we lack detailed understanding of these. Stereotypical masks were used to immediately identify a character-type to the audience, e.g., a pimp vs. a soldier, etc. The evidence of the plays themselves, however, is ambiguous as to whether each character-type allowed for the use of multiple masks, e.g., did all comic slaves always wear the same mask? Masks do not, as is sometimes assumed by those unfamiliar with masked performances, severely restrict an actor's expressive capabilities and lend a static quality to performance. An actor skilled in masked drama can subtly animate his mask through gestures and careful control of his body. An audience familiar with a form of masked drama featuring stock characters brings certain expectations regarding each character's behavior to the performance, a factor which only further piques their interest when a character diverges from the expected, as Plautine and Terentian characters sometimes do. Very few details are known about costumes, except that they too were codified to sharply distinguish character-types, e.g., an old man (*senex*) wore

---

5   The setting of Plautus' *Rudens* is unusual: see pp. 16-18.

6   Goldberg (1998) estimates that only *ca* 1,600 spectators could have attended plays staged before the temple of the Magna Mater on the Palatine Hill in Rome. Other venues could have accommodated much larger crowds.

7   See especially the prologue of Plautus' *Poenulus*.

a white wig and cloak and held a walking stick, old women wore green or light blue, while the cloak of a young man (*adulescens*) was darkly colored (crimson or red).[8]

Plautus and his Work

Virtually nothing certain is known about Plautus' life. He is said to have been born in Sarsina in northern Umbria in 254 BCE, though the sources for this are not entirely credible. The twenty-one Plautine plays that survive (not all are complete) were probably first performed between *ca* 200 and 184 BCE. Of the three Plautine plays translated here, only *Truculentus* can be dated with some security to *ca* 190 BCE (see pp. 19-20 below). The playwright's name itself—Titus Maccius Plautus—is suspicious. Titus may have been Latin slang for "Phallus" (cf. "Dick" in English), Maccius means "Son of Clown" (the clown is a stock character in Italian farce) and Plautus or "Flat(foot)" is a nickname for an actor in Roman Mime.[9] It is unlikely that this tripartite, seemingly mock-grandiose name was bestowed upon the playwright at birth, but rather, he probably took it on after working in theater in multiple capacities and eventually achieving fame in Roman comic theater. Plautus most likely then was by birth a slave or free person of low social status who only acquired a social identity through his success in the theater.

Given Plautus' apparent experience in Roman mime and Atellan farce, the native Italian comic tradition can in Plautus' case be viewed as a transitional bridge between Greek New Comedy and Roman theater that provided his comedy with some of its unique flavor. The 1968 discovery of a short section (on papyrus) of Menander's *The Double Deceiver*, the source play for Plautus' extant *Bacchides*, allows us to see how far Plautus departs from his Greek source play. The parallel texts reveal that Plautus has added much musical accompaniment to the scene; obscured an act-division and distorted his source-play's dramatic pace by combining what had been separate speeches in separate acts; and he has freely removed or added entire speeches.[10] Where Menander is focused on his characters' psychological motivations and realism in general, Plautus opts for a swift joke and delineates character in only the broadest strokes. He also changes the names of Menander's characters and in fact makes them more exotic, and he superimposes an entirely different and characteristically Plautine linguistic style. Plautus' characters, while generally speaking in what could pass for everyday "street Latin," also frequently engage in language that is artificially baroque, especially in its exuberant puns, abundant terms of abuse, and its relentless sound effects (e.g., alliteration and assonance).

Roman comedy (not just Plautus) did away with the five-act structure and choral interludes of Greek New Comedy, and replaced these with continuous action, while also greatly enhancing the element of music and song. In Plautus in particular, Greek New Comedy's focus on character, characterization, and careful structuring of plot

---

8 For masks and costumes in New Comedy in general, see Wiles (1991); a short account of the limited evidence for these can be found in Duckworth (1994): 88-94.

9 For Plautus' name, see further Gratwick (1973).

10 For detailed comparison of the parallel texts, see Anderson (1993): 3-29.

gives way to immediate verbal banter and a steady barrage of jokes, and to more elastic and often unbalanced plots in which characters at times appear to be improvising. Another of the distinctive features of Plautine comedy is the unusual degree to which the actors speak directly to the audience, from the opening prologues to the asides and the monologues or monodies (solo songs) in which they may address the audience in the second-person plural ("you") or refer to them as "spectators." Plautine characters thus acknowledge that the audience is an essential player in theatrical spectacle, and they often appear to be in a fervent competition with each other to persuade the audience over to their own points of view.

Another pervasive feature of Plautine comedy is the phenomenon of metatheater (or metadrama), which here refers to any self-reflexive means used by actors/characters to refer to the production of the play or simply to remind an audience that it is watching a play.[11] *Rudens*, for example, engages in continuous byplay with the genre of tragedy. Immediately following the prologue, the gruff, rustic slave Sceparnio inaugurates this quasi-running dialogue between the genres of tragedy and comedy:

> Immortal gods! What a storm
> Neptune let loose upon us this past night!
> The wind unroofed the cottage. Did I say "wind?"
> Hardly a wind, but it must have been an *Alkmene* of Euripides
> That blew every last tile off the roof
> And created all new light and windows for us! (83-88)

The *Alkmene* of Euripides was a 5th century BCE tragedy that featured a dramatic storm scene,[12] and to give the reference special point here, an adaptation of the Greek play probably had appeared recently on the Roman stage. The characters of *Rudens* frequently employ mock-tragic language (the precise source for which is usually lacking, owing to the fragmentary state of early Roman tragedy), as when Venus' priestess Ptolemacratia, instead of simply acknowledging that Palaestra and Ampelisca have reached North Africa by sea, asserts that they have been carried "Over greenish-blue paths on a wooden steed" (268; cf. similarly paratragic language at 332-3 and 942). Even the pimp Labrax and his ex-friend Charmides affect lofty tragic language (cf. 513, 523-24) as they clownishly trade insults in assigning blame for the shipwreck to each other in Scene 11. In that same scene, the wet and shivering Labrax quips that he "should go get a job as Chomper-Man at a festival" (535), thereby metatheatrically referring to the figure of Manducus (see p. 4 above) in Italian farce and also calling to mind the type of theater to which a "low-brow" character like himself properly belongs. Gripus similarly uses metatheatrical play to deflate Daemones' serious, didactic speech about greed (1235-48):

> I've seen comic actors speak words of wisdom like that
> And win all sorts of applause for

---

11 For excellent treatments of metatheater in Plautus, see Slater (1985) and Moore (1998).
12 See further n. 16 of the translation of *Rudens*.

Enlightening the folks in the crowd.
But when the show was over and people made their way home,
To judge by their behavior anyway, they all forgot those lines. (1249-53)

All this paratragedy and byplay with tragedy perhaps serves to underscore the fact that *Rudens* features many serious themes (see pp. 16-19 below), but other types of metatheater abound in the play as well, as when, e.g., Gripus tells the audience they have no chance of claiming the lost trunk (1296), and when Daemones jokes about (not) inviting the spectators to dinner at the play's end (1418-22).

Closely akin to metatheater in its effect in Plautine comedy is Romanization (cf. p. 3 above). When, for example, Menaechmus I complains that his planned day of festivity has been compromised by what is a pointedly Roman patron-client legal scenario (*Menaechmi* 571ff.), the audience is reminded that they are not simply viewing foreign characters and events in faraway Epidamnus, but a play very much about themselves and their own socio-political world. Plautine metatheater works in much the same way, by so frequently reminding the audience that they are not merely watching a comically distorted slice of life, but a theatrical construction, built as it is on accepted conventions and the assumption of conventional roles. It thus brings home to the audience the idea that they are watching a play designed for them as Roman theatergoers and Romans. Persistent metatheater can even invite audiences to examine the roles they assume in their own complex lives as the social constructs they ultimately are: all the world's a stage.

Terence and his Work

Though an extensive ancient biography of Terence dating back to *ca* 100 CE survives, few of the details it provides are accepted as historical. His full name is Publius Terentius Afer, the last element of which suggests some personal or familial connection with (North) Africa. The biography states that Terence was born at Carthage and originally came to Rome as a prisoner of war/slave, but his date of birth, 184 BCE, if correct (it suspiciously matches the year given for Plautus' death), does not correspond with any of the Punic Wars between Rome and Carthage. Terence is said to have died while on a cultural tour of Greece in 159 BCE, which is at least consistent with the dates given for his floruit (his six extant plays all date to the 160s BCE). Whatever his origins, Terence was well-connected in Rome, and his association with distinguished aristocrats seems to have provoked some jealousy and charges of unethical collaboration (cf. the prologue of *Adelphoe*, 15-21). He is especially associated with the preeminent Roman clan of the Scipios, best known for their military exploits and philhellenism. *Adelphoe* was commissioned for the funeral games of Lucius Aemilius Paullus Macedonicus, the general who triumphed at the Battle of Pydna (cf. p. 2 above). While there is no reason to doubt Terence's association with the most socially prominent figures of his day (they probably provided him with patronage), Terence's membership in, and the very existence of, a philhellenic "Scipionic Circle" dedicated to advancing enlightened humanistic ideals as part of a progressive cultural-political program, is now largely dismissed as a fantasy of idealizing 19th century scholars.

To succinctly describe the general character of Terence's comedy, comparison with Plautus is instructive. Since antiquity, critics of Terence have noted a relative lack of verbal fanfare in his characters' diction. It is true that much of the exuberance of Plautine language is muted in Terence. There are few scenes in which characters trade seemingly endless insults and pile on colorful terms of abuse. Terentian language generally occupies a less imaginative and innovative register than Plautus', and so is relatively free of the racy slang, bold new phrases, rich metaphors, sprawling conceits, puns, exclamations and seemingly non-stop sound-effects that distinguish the elder playwright's style. In Terence there is much less direct colloquy between actors and audience than in Plautus, far fewer examples of Romanization, and, while metatheatrical devices are not entirely lacking in Terence, they are employed rarely and with greater subtlety.[13] But what Terence foregoes in linguistic fireworks, he compensates for in giving his characters smoother and more naturalistic discourse. Characters deliver, for example, simple but elegant monologues that neatly capture their thoughts, or they speak to each other in realistically broken and elliptical dialogue. All this reflects a priority on delineating character and exploring themes, motivations and the complexity of human relationships that is far less in evidence in (most of) Plautus. Overall, Terence seems to have adhered more closely to the style and ethos of his Greek sources than had his Roman predecessors (such as Plautus).

Terence's prologues have drawn special attention as marking a new direction in the comic tradition. While their status as specimens of early Roman rhetoric has been overrated (there is much rhetorical strategizing already in Plautus' prologues), it is the case that their almost exclusive focus on literary and theatrical issues strictly extraneous to the performance at hand is something new. Terence altogether eschews what in New Comedy is the main purpose of the prologue, i.e, to provide necessary plot background. As the prologist explicitly states in *Adelphoe*:

> Now don't expect to hear the plot of the play at this point.
> The old men who appear in the opening scene will divulge some of it;
> The rest you'll get from the action. (22-24)

Rightly or wrongly, Terence assumes considerable sophistication on the part of his audience, and thus that they do not need to be given any background prior to the opening scene and instead are necessarily interested in the esoteric literary matters his prologues address.

We cannot say for certain whether the critical issues raised by Terence in the prologues represent contemporary controversies in Roman theater and that the recurrent figure of the adversarial "old poet,"[14] identified as Luscius of Lanuvium[15] is just a rhetorical straw man, or if the polemics expressed in the prologues actually reflect a personal feud between Terence and a rival. Regardless, the main charges

---

13 Cf. *Adelphoe* n. 16 and *Eunuchus* n. 29.

14 I.e., *poeta vetus*, as he is called at, e.g., Terence, *Phormio* 1. Regardless of Luscius' actual age, by dubbing him "old," Terence, in accordance with a common rhetorical technique in literary polemics, is indirectly casting his own practices and work as "fresh," "novel," etc.

15 For Luscius, see *Eunuchus* n. 2.

against which Terence repeatedly feels compelled to defend himself are that he plagiarizes earlier Roman playwrights and that his methods of composition are somehow "impure" and unprecedented. As to the charge of literary "theft:" at *Eunuchus* 19ff., the prologist recounts how the "old poet" has accused Terence of stealing his characters of the parasite and the soldier from previous plays of Plautus and Naevius (a late 3rd century BCE Roman playwright), both of which were based on a Greek original by Menander. The prologist counters (33-34) that Terence had no knowledge of the earlier Roman plays (we have no way of knowing if this claim is accurate) and took the two characters directly from Menander. Furthermore, the prologist argues (35ff.), these are stock characters of a comic tradition built around conventional characters and situations, and so "you can't say anything that's never been said before" (41). So much for the charge of plagiarism, at least as this one-sided argument would have it.

The more interesting persistent claim is that Terence, from a literary purist's point of view, wrongfully "contaminates"[16] his source plays when he takes plot elements or entire scenes from multiple Greek plays and combines them into a single composition. In the prologue to his *Andria*, Terence asserts that he is not the first Roman playwright to do so, and cites the examples of his predecessors Naevius and Plautus (17-21), a claim we again cannot confirm or refute. While we may reasonably infer from Terence's defensiveness that this recombining of Greek texts was still regarded by some as controversial, the process he describes goes right to the heart of what Latin literature was to become. As noted above (pp. 2-3), Latin literature from its inception was overwhelmingly derivative, and seldom involved the creation of entirely new narratives, characters, and modes of expression. The development of Latin literature was essentially a mass appropriation of previous Greek texts.[17] To take a famous example from a later period, Dido in Book 4 of Vergil's *Aeneid* is a rich composite of Sophocles' Ajax and Euripides' Medea (i.e., from the 5th century BCE tragedies of the same name), the Medea of the 3rd century BCE Greek epic poet Apollonius of Rhodes (as portrayed in Book 3 of his *Argonautica*), Ariadna in the 1st century BCE Roman poet Catullus' epyllion on the marriage of Peleus and Thetis (i.e., *Poem 64*), and various other literary figures. Constructed as she is through this complex web of literary appropriation(s) and verbal allusion(s), Dido nonetheless emerges as one of Vergil's most memorable creations. Terence here defends the practice— still in its formative years so far as Latin literature is concerned—of marshalling together previous literary texts in the service of creative adaptation. The charge of *contaminatio*, when viewed more positively in this light, marks the beginnings of the intertextual play that gives Latin literature so much of its richness and lends to it its uniquely creative stamp. Fortunately, the complaints of critics such as Luscius of Lanuvium seem not to have been heeded.

---

16 Terence uses the verb *contaminare* ("to debase by the addition of other elements") to describe this charge; modern critics refer to it by the corresponding (rare) noun *contaminatio*.

17 For intertextuality in Latin literature, see further Hinds (1998).

The Five Plays

MENAECHMI ("The Menaechmus Brothers")[18]

Like the Shakespearean drama it inspired, *The Comedy of Errors* (1592), Plautus' *Menaechmi* is indeed a comedy of confusion, mistaken identity, and reunion. As is the case for any "doubles" comedy, the play is structured around the errors that result when two characters who to all appearances are the same individual alternately interact with the other characters. To maximize the confusion, every possible combination of characters is brought together (cf. Scenes 6-7, 9-10, 12-15, 19, 21-22) until the doubles come face to face in a climactic encounter (Scene 23) to resolve all. As such a play moves toward its inevitable conclusion, the tension between appearance and reality builds, and characters typically exchange charges of insanity (cf. 288ff., 310ff., 325, 510ff., 818-19), drunkenness (373-74), or even imagine that they or others have lapsed into a dream- or sleep-like state (395, 503, 1047). As insecurities about the uniqueness of personal identity increase, the notion of mirroring may come into play (cf. 1062, 1088-90). Mirroring is a notion that goes to the core of theater, a medium in which actors seek to assume/usurp the identities of their characters, as Menaechmus II does with metatheatrical flair when he successfully plays the role of a madman (831ff.) to frighten off Matrona and Senex. According to an old theory of comedy, audiences enjoy observing characters bungle their way through a confused tangle of appearances and realities because their position of superior knowledge bears psychological benefits.[19] Such, then, is a schematic approach to a doubles comedy like *Menaechmi*, but Plautus' play proves to be richer than what first meets the eye.

Menaechmus I of Epidamnus is the central figure of *Menaechmi*. He gradually experiences a kind of (social) death, i.e., of his Epidamnian identity, and rebirth, i.e., as the Syracusan he was destined to be before being kidnapped as a boy, and ultimately is to be reintegrated into his long-lost family. But at the beginning of the play he is far from ready to make such a liberating break. There he makes a loud entrance in song (110ff.) as he exits his house while still arguing with his wife inside. He then triumphantly boasts to his parasite Peniculus waiting outside of a military-like conquest (129-34), claims that the personification of Convenience (or Opportunity, 137) has volunteered her services to him, that his Roman *genius* or "Guiding Spirit" (138) is right at his side, and that his accomplishments rival those of Jupiter and Venus (143-44)![20] The occasion for all of this bluster? He has successfully purloined his wife's pashmina, which he plans to give to his prostitute-girlfriend next door! Such bravado in Plautus is almost exclusively the property of clever slaves, who by play's end usually can claim at least a temporary defeat of the once seemingly all-powerful *paterfamilias* (the father of the household who in Roman comedy more often is the "blocking character") in their aiding and abetting of his son in a forbidden love affair. But the grandiose boasts of Menaechmus I—who is himself the *paterfamilias*

---

18 My interpretation of *Menaechmi* here is much indebted to McCarthy (2000): 35-76.
19 For an historical outline of the "superiority theory," see Stott (2005): 131-37.
20 For the ironies in this mythical comparison, see n. 30 of the translation.

and should have the upper-hand over his wife in a traditional Roman family—here only underscore his uxoriousness. As the later testimony of Senex confirms (Scene 15, esp. 764a-67, 787-97), Menaechmus I's wife, owing to her status as a "dowered wife,"[21] clearly "wears the pants" in this household, and the spouses' relationship is terminally acrimonious. It is primarily against his wife's domineering vigilance that Menaechmus I's "day of play" (596) is launched.

No less flawed and fractured are Menaechmus I's relationships with his other social subordinates in the play, Peniculus and his mistress Erotium. Erotium is the quintessentially avaricious comic prostitute (cf. Phronesium in *Truculentus* and pp. 19-26 below), as is made most clear in her song addressed to her slaves preparing the luncheon for Menaechmus I:

> *Leave the doors open, just as they are. Go back in,*
> *See everything's done that needs to be done.*
> *Deck out the couches, fire up the incense:*
> *Elegance lures and entices a lover's heart.*
> *Our charm brings them pain—and us gain!*
> *But where is he? The cook said he was out by the door. Oh, he's over there:*
> *My finest and foremost source of income!*
> *As long as his cash keeps pouring in, he reigns supreme in this house!*
> (351-59)

Menaechmus I mistakes Erotium's solicitousness on his behalf for genuine affection, and declares her to be "the only woman in the world who knows what I like" (202).[22] Menaechmus II, by contrast, though a newcomer to Epidamnus, muses: "I'll know soon enough whether it's me or the wallet she wants" (386). The true superficiality of Menaechmus I's purely economic relationship with Erotium is best captured when (Scenes 7, 9) she has an intimate lunch followed by sex with the drastically differ-ent Menaechmus II without ever suspecting he is not Menaechmus I. Conversely, Menaechmus I mistakenly believes he can curb his wife's domineering behavior merely by providing her with gifts, as if she were a prostitute:

> *It's clear I've spoiled you, so here's the new program:*
> *Seeing as I lavish you with personal slaves, household provisions,*
> *Wool, a wardrobe, cash, and fancy accessories, the smart thing for you to do*
> *Is to stop spying on your husband. So get with it now! (119-22)*

The pashmina, originally an expensive gift from Menaechmus I to his wife, but now the latest in what appears to be a non-stop parade of his gifts to Erotium, emblema-tizes Menaechmus I's confusion of the roles of wife and prostitute.[23] Menaechmus I's failure to find satisfaction in either of these confused relationships neatly comes to a

---

21 I.e., *uxor dotata*: see n. 17 of the translation.

22 See further n. 37 of the translation.

23 Cf. the bracelet that has migrated from Matrona's to Erotium's jewelry box (531-32).

head when in the middle of the play he finds himself simultaneously shut out of both
his own house (661ff.) and Erotium's (688ff.).

Menaechmus I similarly misjudges his relationship with Peniculus. A misplaced
belief in Peniculus' role as trusted confidante leads Menaechmus I to divulge his entire
plan for his "day of play" to the parasite (Scenes 2-3). One missed lunch, however, is
enough to shatter Peniculus' presumed loyalty to his patron:

> That's it! I swear, no one will ever talk me out of divulging
> Every last detail that's happened here to your wife,
> And every last insult of yours is coming right back at you!
> Oh, you'll pay, and pay dearly for eating that lunch—*my* lunch! (518-21)

The revenge Peniculus earns by revealing all to Matrona, whose resulting con-
frontation of Menaechmus I is exceedingly discomfiting (Scene 12), is entirely
disproportionate with the offense.

Enter Menaechmus II of Syracuse into this jumble of dysfunctional relationships.
Though he is in reality Menaechmus I's identical twin, he is also in many respects
his polar opposite. Despite being firmly rooted back in Syracuse, he has spent the
last six years of his life at sea, scouring the Mediterranean in search of his lost twin.
He has no wife (399) and, in contrast to his Epidamnian twin (cf. 571ff.), apparently
bears no pressing (and irritating) civic responsibilities back home that would deter
his determined search. And in sharp contrast to his ever-harried twin, his daily life,
consisting as it does of searching, has a clear purpose:

> Well then I'll keep searching until I know that [he's dead] for certain
> And I find someone who knows that he's dead.
> Once that happens, I'll never again expend an ounce of energy in search
>   of him.
> But in the meantime, I'll never stop looking for him as long as I'm
>   breathing.
> I'm the only one who understands the place he holds in my heart. (242-46)

Through what amounts to dumb luck, Menaechmus II reaps all the benefits of
Menaechmus I's planned day of festivity—and does so without the emotional and
commercial entanglements that mark his brother's flawed relationships in Epidamnus.
Perhaps the starkest contrast of all between the twin brothers lies in Menaechmus II's
ideal(ized) relationship with his slave Messenio. Reflecting what probably was more
often a fantasy of slave owners than a reality, Menaechmus II has secured Messenio's
absolute obedience and respect for his authority as master. As Messenio himself puts
it:

> *This is the trademark of a good slave: his eyes are fixed*
> *On his master's affairs (watching, gauging, arranging them*
> *So that when Master's away, his orders still hold sway)*
>   *And then some, just as if he were there.*
>   *A slave with horse-sense respects his back more than his craw,*
>   *His shanks more than his belly.*

> *And he must always be mindful of what masters*
> *Mete out to wicked and utterly worthless slaves:*
> > *Whips, chains*
> > *Millstones, fatigue, famine, piercing frost—*
> > *These are the wages of slacking!*
> *This is just the sort of trouble I take pains to escape: ergo, I'll be good, not*
> > *bad this time.*
> *I can stand a tongue-lashing, but my back just can't hack that type of*
> > *treatment.*
> *I like my bread ground, but I'd rather not be part of that grind.*
> *That's why I follow Master's orders calmly and carefully,*
> > *That's what works best for me.*
> *Others can do as they think is best for them; I'll be as I ought to be.*
> *That's my rule: to be blameless and always at Master's beck and call.*
> *The best slaves are afraid of their masters even when they've nothing to*
> > *fear.* (966-83a)

Whereas such set-pieces extolling "the good slave" in Plautus are usually under-cut, Messenio's allegiance to his master is genuine. After he rescues Menaechmus I from Senex's slaves, the Epidamnian brother ironically comments: "No slave of mine has ever done what you just did for me" (1027). Messenio then states his wish to continue serving his real master after he is (illegitimately) freed by his faux-master, Menaechmus I:

> Please continue to give me orders just as when I was your slave.
> I'd like to live at your house, and when you leave for home I'll go with you.
> > (1033-34)

Messenio plays the central role (Scene 23) in sorting out the brothers' true identities and effecting their reunion. The contrast between the genuine loyalty of Messenio and the tenuous and conditional loyalties of a Peniculus or Erotium could not be sharper.

Menaechmus II thus functions as his twin's alter-ego. He seems naturally blessed with psychologically liberating qualities and a penchant for avoiding unhealthy relationships—that is, he has just what Menaechmus I sorely lacks. Their reunion not only fills an emotional void felt deeply by any separated twins, but also marks the possibility for a new psychological wholeness in Menaechmus I's life. The confused events of this day result in Menaechmus I's complete liberation from his debilitating life in Epidamnus. In the end, all his assets are to be liquidated and his unhappy (and fortunately childless) marriage is to be dissolved (1157-61). The *paterfamilias* in this unusual play thus achieves what promises to be permanent separation from his oppressive subordinates, namely Matrona, Peniculus, and Erotium. The twins will leave Epidamnus behind, a port of call that has been confirmed to be the land of the lost/damned.[24] Beyond the time frame of the play, a happier future marked by

---

24 See further n. 16 of the translation.

the restoration of his blood relations and the absence of his destructive Epidamnian entanglements looms romantically ahead in Syracuse for a reinvigorated and socially reborn Menaechmus I. Menaechmus I could not have imagined that his narrowly conceived plans for a day of play would turn out so successfully. Sometimes—in a utopian comedy such as Plautus' *Menaechmi*, anyway—you get even more than you wished for.

RUDENS ("The Rope")

Rudens is one of Plautus' most unusual and enduringly popular plays. It is set on the North African coast somewhere near Cyrene (in Libya), a Greek colony dating back to the 7th century BCE that was famed for its products derived from the silphium plant.[25] In contrast to the usual urban setting of Roman comedy, the action takes place near the seashore in a mostly uncultivated and deserted area, save for the modest cottage and farm of Daemones and a small temple of Venus staffed by a single priestess. There is thus an atmosphere of wildness, exoticism and romance not present in Plautus' other plays.

Nothing definitively dates *Rudens*, but it is usually assumed to be one of Plautus' later plays (i.e., debuting in *ca* 190-185 BCE), owing to its musical and dramaturgical sophistication. We know nothing about Plautus' Greek source-play, apart from the fact that it was by Diphilus. The play is named for the highly entertaining Scene 21, in which Trachalio encounters Gripus using a fisherman's rope to drag the trunk he has extracted from the sea during the stormy night. The rope becomes part of a tug-a-war for the treasure the trunk contains, as the two slaves delightfully advance mock-philosophical and legal arguments regarding its rightful ownership. Though most of their banter is absurd and self-serving, some of the issues they raise—in particular, the applicability of the laws of civilization (i.e., land/property law) to the aquatic realm, especially as regards what emerges from the wild, natural domain of the sea—bear serious significance for the play as a whole.

The sea, and the motif of water in general, are inextricably enmeshed with the central theme(s) of *Rudens*. In addition to the omnipresent seashore and the central shipwreck-plot, characters make frequent references to submersion, bathing, and fundamental rituals associated with water. When Daemones and Sceparnio first catch sight of the shipwrecked pimp and his friend, they jokingly cast their plight in terms of ritual bathing and feasting:

> **Daemones**
> By the immortal gods, Sceparnio! What do you make
> Of those men alongside the shore over there?
> **Sceparnio**
>   If I had to make a guess,
> I'd say they've been invited to a bon-voyage feast.
> **Daemones**
> Why's that?

---

25 Cf. nn. 7 and 55 of the translation.

Sceparnio
Because they took quite a bath last night,[26] it seems. (148-51)

Sceparnio then spots Palaestra and Ampelisca in a similar plight, and exclaims by
Palaemon (160), an obscure mythical figure originally named Melicertes who was
thrown into the sea by his mother Ino, rescued by a dolphin, in essence reborn, and
finally renamed Palaemon.[27] Two separate jests (382-85, 527-28) refer to public baths
and the prospect of having one's clothes stolen there, and so comically highlight the
ritualistic elements of bathing as a form of rebirth: nudity and the shedding of clothes,
i.e., the social integuments used to mark status, gender, etc.; submersion and purification in water; and re-emergence from a watery, womb-like realm. Most significantly,
when Palaestra and Ampelisca seek sanctuary again from the pimp, this time at
Venus' altar (689ff.), and apologize for what they fear is their lack of the requisite
ritual cleanliness, Trachalio jests:

Trachalio
A fair request, Venus, and one you should grant.
You should forgive them—fear has driven them to these extremes.
They say you were born from a shell, so please don't turn your back on
    these two tacos. (702-4)

Trachalio here clearly refers—albeit obscenely[28]—to an ancient version of the birth of
Venus (= Greek Aphrodite), in which she emerges from a seashell, the seashell being
suggestive of the vulva and so pointing to Venus' role as (earthy and profane) goddess
of sex. An extant version of the myth in which Aphrodite/Venus is depicted as rid-
ing or reclining on a shell as she emerges from the sea (as in Botticelli's famous 15th
century painting) is first attested in ancient art after Plautus, but that does not mean
that this story was not already in circulation. And at least part of a Roman audience
would be aware of an extremely old literary version of the myth of Aphrodite's birth,
whereby Kronos castrates his father Uranus and tosses the severed genitals into the
sea, whereupon the goddess is born from the surrounding sea-foam.[29]

    This polyvalent reference to the primordial birth of the goddess Venus/Aphrodite
holds special relevance for Palaestra and Ampelisca. As the rest of the crew is paralyzed
by fear (365-71), the two girls manage to escape the sinking ship in a lifeboat—a
shell-shaped vessel (Latin *scapha*: 163, 367). In the lifeboat, they spend a trying, but
less perilous night than do the scoundrels Labrax and Charmides. In the morning,
they tumble out of the skiff and finally reach land on the coast near Cyrene. There
they discover Venus' temple and immediately are granted protection by the goddess'
priestess. Their "bath" in the sea and subsequent delivery to Venus' guardianship
thus commences a purification process culminating in their social rebirth as freeborn
persons.

---

26 For the different senses of "bath" here, see n. 22 of the translation.
27 For the myth, see further n. 23 of the translation.
28 Cf. n. 59 of the translation.
29 See further Leach (1974).

Separated from each other and the lives they have known to this point, and terrified at their strange new circumstances on the wild and desolate coast, Palaestra (209) and Ampelisca (222) initially despair of life altogether. But ultimately, and again only as the result of the storm at sea that throws their former life on land into chaos, Labrax must surrender his previous claim of ownership over Palaestra and Ampelisca, and the two girls are liberated from their slavery to the pimp. While the details of Ampelisca's freeborn status are glossed over, Palaestra proves to be Daemones' long-lost daughter and so is reunited with the family of which she has been deprived since childhood. Palaestra is also eligible for marriage with her suitor Plesidippus, who is an Athenian citizen and related to Daemones. Ampelisca, who in contrast to Palaestra may have already served as a prostitute in Labrax's employ,[30] will marry Trachalio, who is to be emancipated from his slavery to Plesidippus (1220) for his role in establishing Palaestra's identity. Both girls are to be freed from a life of prostitution, i.e., a life that dooms them to serve—in the crudest sexual sense—as metonymic shells. Thanks to the confusing, yet cleansing properties of the sea, and, by inference, the beneficent influence of Venus, the two girls are permanently liberated from Labrax's contaminating influence.

The world of the play thus proves to be one in which the providential justice of an ever-vigilant Jupiter prevails, just as Arcturus had asserted to be the case in the prologue:

> He keeps a separate list of the names of the good,
> Though this doesn't keep the scumbags from supposing
> That they can win Jupiter over with gifts and sacrifices.
> They're just wasting both their energy and expense,
> Seeing that he accepts no offerings from perjurers.
> A righteous person who prays to the gods
> Is more likely to be liked by them than a scumbag.
> My advice for all of you fine folks
> Who lead your lives with conviction and honor
> Is to continue on that course—you'll be glad for it later. (21-30)

Daemones, who, under circumstances not elaborated on by Arcturus (33-40), years ago unjustly lost his daughter, fortune, and Athenian citizenship, is ultimately rewarded for his righteousness. So too, Palaestra's initial protests (194-97a) that neither she nor her parents have done anything to offend the gods so as to deserve their miserable lives are in the end seemingly answered by divine providence when she is reintegrated into her family. By contrast, the pimp Labrax and his greedy friend Charmides, who originally advised the ill-conceived voyage at sea in search of greater profits abroad, are punished by the loss of a significant portion of their respective fortunes. Charmides fades from the play when he is no longer useful to the plot (891), but, as comic society tends to reintegrate rather than banish its members in the end, Labrax is generously invited to enjoy a post-dramatic feast with Daemones, along

---

30 See further nn. 8 and 38 of the translation.

with Daemones' slave Gripus, who apparently will be manumitted for his role in re-
trieving the trunk that proves to be essential in establishing Palaestra's identity.

Not all characters, however, in the world of *Rudens* are meted out their just
desserts. We hear nothing more about Venus' priestess Ptolemocratia after she is
physically assaulted by Labrax (644ff.), but given her generosity toward the girls and
austere piety in the service of the goddess, we can accept with some confidence that
Ampelisca's assertion that "she deserves to be showered with goods by both gods and
men" (407) will come to fruition. More mysterious are the Piscatores or anonymous
"Fishermen," who appear briefly only to complain of their difficult and poverty-
laden life (Scene 6-7). The Piscatores fish with rods and hooks from the shore and
apparently do not venture out into the sea in search of larger catch. Unskilled as they
are, their entire days are consumed in (haphazard) subsistence fishing, and due to a
lack of leisure time and probably social status, find themselves excluded from athletic
training in the gymnasium and wrestling school, the social and cultural centers of
Greek male life.[31] Apart from perhaps foreshadowing (by contrast with their own
sorry situation) the success of their colleague Gripus, who embraces a "no risk, no
gain" philosophy of fishing (906ff.), the Piscatores do not advance the plot and simply
disappear without a trace.

While this account of *Rudens* has focused on its more serious themes, the play is
in many ways also a typical Plautine comedy, and so outfitted with the usual comic
tropes and techniques. In Scene 11, for example, Labrax and Charmides, freshly
expelled from the sea as they are, engage in a lively verbal competition about which
of them is responsible for their ill fate that is replete with mutual curses, taunts, name-
calling, comic appropriation of myth (508-9), and parody of tragedy (see p. 8 above).
Sceparnio in Scene 9 engages in highly sexualized (and probably very physical)
humor when Ampelisca asks him to fill her urn with well water. And the debate
between Gripus and Trachalio about the laws of ownership as they relate to produce
of the sea, while thematically important, is one of the most hilarious in Plautus.

Rudens, in both its comic and more serious elements, is a play that seemingly
has something to offer to everyone. Shakespeare appreciated its complexities and in
it found fertile ground for his masterful *Tempest* (1611).[32]

TRUCULENTUS ("The Fierce One")

According to the orator Cicero (106-43 BCE),[33] *Truculentus* was a product of
Plautus' latter years and taken as evidence that the playwright's creative juices were
still flowing then. The notice about *Truculentus* in Cicero is brief, and does not elaborate
on the play's presumed merits. In this same passage, *Truculentus* is lumped together
with Plautus' *Pseudolus*, which is dated securely to 191 BCE, and so we may safely
assign an approximate date of *ca* 190 BCE for the debut of *Truculentus*.[34] The play

---

31 See further n. 30 of the translation.

32 See further Louden (1999).

33 *De Senectute* ("*On Old Age*") 50.

34 For the internal evidence that helps to date the play, see nn. 9, 26 and 46 of the translation.

thus was performed about ten years after the defeat of Hannibal and the Carthaginians in the Second Punic War. Its debut then falls within a period of unprecedented wealth and cultural expansion in Rome, to where, along with other spoils of war, there had been an influx of captives, many of which would be doomed to prostitution. *Truculentus* is a biting satire about a clever prostitute exotically named Phronesium,[35] who acknowledges no bounds in her manipulation of her customers. Much wealth is redistributed to her in that process, and underneath the play's gross caricature and exaggeration lies a serious, contemporary concern with personal expenditures and their perceived connection with morality in traditional Roman thinking.

First, some background on the place of prostitution in Roman society is necessary. The use of prostitutes by men for sexual gratification seems generally not to have been viewed as a moral shortcoming. A well-attested tradition has none other than Cato the Elder (cf. p. 2 above), the arch-defender of traditional Roman values, recommending such liaisons to men (married or unmarried) as a healthy alternative to seducing married women or preying on freeborn virgins. The satirist Horace (65-8 BCE) preserves the following anecdote:

> When Cato saw a man he knew coming out of a brothel,
> He says, in all his god-like wisdom, "Congratulations!
> The instant that foul lust expands the veins of young men,
> It's right for them to come down here,
> And not to grind other men's wives." (*Satires* 2.31-35)

Another version of the anecdote preserved by a scholiast on Horace has Cato quip to his acquaintance, after seeing him exiting the brothel on multiple occasions, "I praised you on the grounds that you were a visitor here, not that you lived here." Cicero, in his famously obfuscating speech in defense of Caelius (apparently a notorious "player" among the young Roman elite of his time) similarly argues:

> If anyone thinks there is a prohibition against young men having affairs
> with prostitutes, he is extremely stern—I can't deny it. In fact, such a
> person is out of step with not just the liberality of contemporary times,
> but also with the customary allowances of our ancestors.
>
> (*In Defense of Caelius* 48)

Frequenting prostitutes, as Cicero makes abundantly clear elsewhere in the speech, becomes a matter of concern only when it drains one's finances. While liaisons with prostitutes are to be encouraged in so far as they may help prevent sexual crimes (adultery, rape) against free women, they can pose a serious threat to wealth, especially inherited aristocratic wealth,[36] if they become longstanding economic exchanges.

Truculentus is built around the successive manipulations of Phronesium's three best customers, each of whom represents an established comic stereotype: (1) Diniarchus, a hopelessly infatuated young urban sophisticate whom the relationship

---

35 For the meaning (and formation) of her name, see n. 28 of the translation.

36 I.e., one's *patrimonium*. Cf. *In Defense of Caelius* 42 for this particular concern.

has impoverished; (2) Stratophanes, a braggart soldier from abroad who is laden
with the spoils of war; and (3) Strabax, an Athenian raised in the countryside who
is a simpleton. As representatives of the city, country and places abroad, the three
collectively represent all the young lovers in the universe of New Comedy. The scenes
of *Truculentus* may seem repetitive in their focus on the lovers' gullibility, but that
repetition goes straight to the point of this cynical satire.

Diniarchus is immediately distinguishable from his two rivals in that he is so
self-consciously aware that he is a stereotypical comic lover and dupe:

> Do you know what makes falling in love our greatest downfall?
> When we're told what we want to hear, even when it's an outrageous lie,
> We're foolish enough to take it as the truth, and we foolishly stay calm.
>
> (190-92)

Nonetheless, in Roman comedy hope springs eternal for a foolish young man in
love. When Phronesium, always seeking to maximize profits on all fronts, informs
Diniarchus of her false pregnancy and the scheme against the soldier, he reacts as
follows:

> By the immortal gods! For her to do what she just did for me!
> That was not the act of a mistress,
> But the sort of thing only a close confidante or a soul mate does!
> She confided in me about passing a child off as her own!
> That's something not even a sister tells her very own sister!
> She's revealed the innermost part of her heart to me!
> She'll never be unfaithful to me, as long as she lives!
> How could I not be in love with her? How could I not want the best for her?
> I'd sooner stop loving myself than I would her.
> Why shouldn't I send her a gift? Yes!
> I'll have five minae sent over to her in honor of the occasion,
> And at least another mina's worth of food.
> Why shouldn't she have the best when she wants only the best for me?
> Better her than me—seeing that I'm my own worst enemy. (434-47)

Phronesium's revelation here earns her a net gain of six minae. Even after Diniarchus'
rape of Callicles' daughter is revealed, and it turns out that the baby Phronesium is
passing off as her own is the product of that rape, Phronesium is able to manipulate
Diniarchus into allowing her to keep his newborn son for three more days so that she
can extort the maximum from Stratophanes. And their relationship, entirely dictated
as it is on Phronesium's terms, will not end with Diniarchus' imminent marriage to
Callicles' daughter. Whenever things go sour in the marriage, Phronesium assures
Diniarchus, he can still enjoy her as a "booty-buddy" (880),[37] by which she means he
can bestow gifts upon her in exchange for sex and the affection he foolishly imagines
is genuine.

---

37 For this phrase, see n. 71 of the translation.

Stratophanes is depicted as an even bigger, if less sympathetic dupe. In his first appearance (Scene 8), he instantly aligns himself with the stereotypical braggart soldier of Greek and Roman comedy. Astaphium, as she informs him of the suppositious baby's birth, skillfully plays upon his monstrous egotism:

Stratophanes
                    … But tell me, has Phronesium had the baby?
Phronesium
Yes, a beautiful baby boy.
Stratophanes
                    Aha! So, does he take after me at all?
Astaphium
                                        You have to ask?
He shouted for a shield and a sword the instant he was born!
Stratophanes
That's proof he's mine!
Astaphium
                    Yes, he's your spitting image.
Stratophanes
                                        Woohoo!
Is he big? Has he joined the army already? Did he return from battle laden
    with spoils?
Astaphium
He was only born five days ago.
Stratophanes
                    So what?
By Hercules, he should have accomplished something after so many days!
Why'd he leave his mother's uterus if he wasn't ready for battle? (504-11)

The only spoils to be won here are those Phronesium will collect as she successively cons Stratophanes out of an endless stream of gifts. Stratophanes is forced to surrender even more cash to support his faux-son (Scene 16) and to share Phronesium's sexual favors with Strabax (958ff.). The duping of a braggadocio such as Stratophanes probably held special significance for a Roman audience living in an era of unprecedented aristocratic self-assertion (cf. p. 2 above).

Finally, there is Strabax. The son of an Athenian citizen, Strabax has been raised on the family's country estate and so, hypothetically at least, has steered clear of the corruptions traditionally associated with urban life. Roman moralists idealized the country as a locus of pristine character, where a deep reverence for *mos maiorum* ("the way of the ancestors") was naturally cultivated. Foremost among the traditional virtues was *pietas*, a broader concept than modern notions of (religious) piety, in that it demanded absolute obedience towards, and reverence for the gods, parents and ancestors, and the Roman state itself. In his first appearance (Scene 10), Strabax, with a festive and typically Plautine disdain for *pietas*, announces that he has intercepted twenty minae intended for his father, which he intends to apply to the competition with his rivals for Phronesium. His plans for financing his tryst include bamboozling even his mother:

> My plan is to rip up my father by the roots first
> And then proceed to rip off my mother too.
> Now I'll deliver this money to the woman I love more than my own mother.
> (660-62)

Laden with spoils from pillaging his father, Strabax is admitted into the house of Phronesium. We next see him in the final scene when he exits from the house with (apparently) a painful case of testicular vasocongestion (916), as he has been waiting for Phronesium's promised services inside for some time. A verbal skirmish with Stratophanes follows, but in the end Phronesium coaxes Strabax into accepting Stratophanes' role as her co-lover.

The character who lends his name to the play, Strabax's family's slave Truculentus, further reinforces the notion that even the sternest traditional morality is defenseless in the face of the prostitutes' charms. In his initial encounter with Astaphium (Scene 4), Truculentus appears to be the uncompromising representative of good old-fashioned rustic values, resolutely opposed to the prostitutes and their decadent life as he is, and cognizant of the possible deleterious effects on the family fortune:

> ... Me touch you? I solemnly swear by this little hoe of mine
> That I'd rather canoodle with a broad-horned cow out in the country
> And spend the whole night long lying in the straw with her
> Than receive a hundred free nights with the likes of you, dinner included!
> You think country-living's disgraceful? I'm ashamed to even think of your
>   way of life!
> But just what business do you have at our house, woman?
> Why do you run over here every time we come to the city? (276-82)

But despite all his obstinate support for traditional parsimony (309-13), Truculentus too ultimately succumbs to Astaphium's alluring charm—and readily surrenders his cash (Scene 11) to her.[38]

At the core of Strabax's plan to fleece his parents out of money in order to support his affair is a common Plautine plot. In a play such as Plautus' *Pseudolus*, a clever slave typically controls the plot and in the end wins the day for his lovesick young master at the expense of his elder master, the *paterfamilias*. The slave exults in his skills as a trickster, and confides his plans to the audience at every stage. In *Truculentus*, however, the main intrigue is directed at the lover(s), and the self-conscious delight in malignant deception usually enjoyed by the clever slave is transferred to Phronesium and her able assistant Astaphium. The two prostitutes openly proclaim their professional creed, that is, their relentless dedication to greed and profit, e.g.:

---

38 Consistent with the play's broadly satirical mode, Truculentus' transformation is swift (though see 289-90, where he first shows a hint of vulnerability to Astaphium).

Now when a lover and his gifts are barren,
We take him on his word alone that it's so,
And when he has nothing to give, it's not as if we have enough.
And so we're always seeking new donors
Who have untapped treasures to donate. (241-45)

That saying, "your wealth is where your friends are," sure rings true.
Thanks to him, there's still hope of swindling the soldier today.
Oh, I do love that soldier more than I do myself—that is, while I get
    what I want from him. (885-87)

Running imagery reinforces the idea of the dangerous power swirling about Chez
Phronesium. Diniarchus characterizes the house as a kind of whirlpool that consumes
everything that comes its way (350-51). His slave Cyamus, as he delivers Diniarchus'
gifts to Phronesium's house, similarly muses:

> *A prostitute is just like the sea:*
> *She absorbs all the gifts you give her, but never overflows.* (568-69)

The semi-articulate Stratophanes regards Phronesium's brothel as some sort of anthropomorphic creature, and in a fit of anger when he is shut out from it pledges to
"shatter this damn house's ankles to bits" (638).

Male characters such as Callicles, the father of the girl Diniarchus has raped,
misogynistically chalk up the prostitutes' rapacity and intrigue to "the nature of female
behavior" (809), and Phronesium herself asserts that "We [= women] are given far too
little credit for being as wicked as we naturally are!" (452; cf. 465-71). But counter
claims that it is the foolish men who are ultimately responsible for their entrapment are
equally, if not more compelling, as when Diniarchus' slave Cyamus comments:

> *A man in love can't help but be worthless and pillage himself in*
>   *disgraceful ways.*
> > *How do I know this, you ask?*
> *At our place there's a lover doing disgraceful things*
> > *By treating his property like pooh*
> > *To be promptly removed from the house.*
> > *He's quite clean, or maybe he just fears an inspection.*
> *But he clearly wants his house clean—or should I say cleaned out?* (553-58)

Or, in his master's own words: "We [= men in love] voluntarily destroy our finances, our credibility and ourselves" (57); or, as Astaphium puts it, "No man is ever
ruined here in our house. The men destroy themselves" (300). There is thus much
credibility in Callicles' Maid's assertion that Diniarchus and his male tendencies for
sexual violence are ultimately responsible for the current chaos surrounding Callicles'
household:

Maid
Surely the blame here belongs to men much more than women:
A man, not a woman, got her pregnant.

Callicles

I understand that too.

Fine chaperone you were!

Maid

"Where there's greater strength, there's greater power."
He's a man, he's stronger. He overtook her and took what he wanted.

(810-13)

Whereas this thoroughly satirical play is nominally set in Athens, Plautus is clear about its particular relevance for his Roman audience. The prologist opens by emphasizing that the setting in Athens is merely an arbitrary theatrical construct:

Plautus seeks a small slice of your city,
Just a section of your enormous and glorious edifices,
Where he can construct Athens without a construction crew (1-3)

This stage you see is set up to be Athens,
At least for as long as we're putting on this comedy. (10-11)

There he also playfully flatters his audience as "pillars of our good-old fashioned values" (7) and invites them to distance themselves from the morality of Phronesium by viewing her as emblematic of degraded contemporary morality (13-15). But in a highly Romanized passage in the opening scene that follows, Diniarchus frames his own bankrupting behavior in terms of typically Roman generational conflict (57-61), and characterizes the forum, Rome's business center, as swarming with pimps and prostitutes (62a-73). And in sharp contrast to the prologist who praises the audience for their alleged respect for *mos maiorum*, Diniarchus invites his contemporaries to join in the financially destructive festivities:

Bottom line: in this great nation of ours,
Made up of so many men living in leisure following the defeat
   of our foes,
It behooves all who have the wherewithal to buy themselves some lovin'.

(74-76)

Phronesium speaks even more directly to these citizen warriors—and potential dupes—in what serves as the play's epilogue:

What a lovely day of hunting, with everything done just the way I wanted!
All my business has turned out so fine! I'll try to do the same for you:
If anyone's in the mood for love, be sure to let me know. (964-66)

The fiscal danger of redistributing family wealth on projects such as the House of Phronesium is thus made very real and immediate for Plautus' Roman audience. Behind the gross caricatures of this Plautine comedy lies a didactic message for a society currently grappling with the effects of newfound wealth and luxuries. Plautine comedy is rightly characterized as (mostly) light-hearted, amoral and farcical, but *Truculentus* serves up an acrid satire on fiscal folly that seems to extend beyond the immediate topic of expenditures on prostitution.

ADELPHOE ("The Brothers")

Every culture engages in debate about how best to raise children. Roman tradition granted virtually absolute power to the eldest living male, the *paterfamilias*, over his legal offspring (the mother of the family had no corresponding power). The *paterfamilias* only relinquished this power over his descendents at death, unless he agreed to do so voluntarily beforehand by, e.g., transferring his power (= *manus*, the Latin word for "hand") over a daughter to her husband upon the occasion of her marriage. Until the descendants of the *paterfamilias* were liberated from his power, they technically owned no property. His word was final in all matters of marriage and divorce, and the *paterfamilias* could disown or even execute his children with impunity (such extreme measures were probably rare and enacted only after consultation with a family council of male elders). Thus, the legal status of Roman children in many respects differed little from that of slaves.[39]

Not surprisingly, much of extant Roman comedy reflects the tensions that must have existed between patriarchs and their offspring. Within the festive and fictional confines of Roman comedy, lovesick young males and their slave accomplices often dupe the *paterfamilias* to finance a liaison with a prostitute. Still, natural affection and individual temperament no doubt allowed for wider scope in parenting philosophies than this grim outline of Roman family structure suggests. A play such a Terence's *Adelphoe*—performed in 160 BCE at funeral games held in honor of the Roman general Lucius Aemilius Paullus by his sons—suggests the existence of a rich and timely debate on childrearing in this socially dynamic period of Roman history.

The differences in character and parenting styles between the two brothers Demea and Micio could not be starker. Demea, the champion of traditional rustic values, devotes himself to his ideal vision of familial responsibility: he works hard, makes self-sacrifices, is financially acquisitive and is always making provisions for the future. Micio, who has never married and has adopted the elder of Demea's sons, is known for his affability and indulgence. He mostly lives in the moment and encourages his adopted son Aeschinus to do the same, and represents a more liberal outlook on things that is conventionally associated with urban life. Micio lays out his philosophy of parenting, and how it diverges from his brother's, in the clearest terms:

> I've raised him since he was a child and loved him as my own.
> I take sheer joy in him, and he's the most precious thing in my life.
> I also take pains to see that he feels the same way about me.
> I provide well for him, I look the other way, and I don't impose
> My paternal authority all the time; I've actually trained my son
> To keep me in the loop about just the sorts of things
> Youngsters are always trying to hide from their fathers.
> To my thinking, a boy who's been trained to con his father,
> And dares to do it, has no qualms about snowing others.

---

39 Perhaps (in origin) to distinguish them from the offspring of household slaves, the legitimate children of the *paterfamilias* were referred to as *liberi* (lit., "the free ones").

I believe we can discipline our children best by generosity,
And by cultivating a sense of respect—not just fear.
My brother disagrees with me on that and has no stomach whatsoever
For my views: "What are you doing, Micio?
Why are you ruining the boy we both care so much for?
Why's he whoring about? Why's he out drinking? Why give him
So much spending money for that, and for a wardrobe? You're such a fool!"
He's far too strict, and goes way beyond what's reasonable.
Now in my opinion, he's making a big mistake in assuming
That authority based on intimidation has more weight
Or lasts longer than when it's rooted in friendliness. (48-67)

Proper paternal training results in a son who does what's right on his own,
And not just because someone else threatens him
That's the difference between a father and a master. If a father can't do this,
He should own up to the fact that he has no true authority over his children.
                                                                (74-77)

Much of this strikes a resoundingly modern chord. Whereas Demea asserts his traditional paternal authority over his son on ideological grounds, Micio wants to be his son Aeschinus' best friend, and asserts that by cultivating mutual trust and respect with his son, Aeschinus will turn out to be a better human being. Some may pause to question Micio's motivation here: is his liberality toward Aeschines perhaps the result of his insecurity over his status as adoptive father? Regardless, given the primary position of Micio's monologue here and the fact that comedy usually shows little tolerance for cantankerous puritans like Demea (as he immediately shows himself to be in Scene 2), at this point we probably expect Micio's more liberal views to ultimately prevail in *Adelphoe*. But Terence's play will take a surprising turn, and by the end it is unclear which, if either, of the two brothers' views, in their initial extreme formulations at least, merits an absolute claim on our sympathies.

For the bulk of the play, the dour Demea assumes the expected role of spoilsport and is the butt of almost everyone's joke. Demea is at first blissfully ignorant that it was on behalf of Ctesipho (the son he has raised in the country) that Aeschinus has broken into Sannio's house, roughed up the pimp and absconded with a stripper:[40]

He ripped off the door of someone's house and broke right in.
He practically beat the owner and his entire household to death,
And he snatched a woman out of there that he's hot for!
Everyone's saying his behavior is utterly disgraceful!
Everyone I run into tells me about it, Micio!
It's the talk of the whole town! If he needs a role model,
Hasn't he noticed how his brother keeps his nose to the grindstone
Out there on the farm, and shows proper respect for frugal and sober living?

---

40 For my translation of the unnamed harp-playing prostitute as a "stripper," see n. 25 of the translation.

> He's nothing like Aeschinus! And what I say about him
> Really applies to you, Micio: you're the one that's spoiled him! (88-97)

Demea is ironically mocked and manipulated by Micio's clever slave Syrus (Scene 9), who later sends him on a wild-goose chase (573ff.) in search of Micio, a form of treatment to which other unsympathetic patriarchs are subjected in Roman comedy. Meanwhile, events proceed smoothly enough for Micio as he deals with the aftermath of Aeschinus' actions. He appears unfazed by news of the larceny and assault at Sannio's house and adopts a "boys will be boys" attitude in the face of Demea's protests:

> Catered parties, booze, scented hair-gels—it's all out of my pocket.
> He has an affair? I'll finance it for as long as I can;
> When I can't, he'll probably be locked out of her house.
> He broke some doors? They can be fixed.
> He tore some clothing? I'll see it's mended. (117-21)

Still, once Demea exits, Micio reveals that he harbors some anxieties about Aeschinus (141-54), and thus, indirectly, about the effects of his own parenting. We subsequently learn that one of Micio's chief parental objectives—that his son keep him in the loop about his youthful indiscretions—has failed, as Aeschinus has not told Micio about his rape of Pamphila several months earlier. Nevertheless, Micio retains his calm self-assurance about all and playfully coaxes out a confession about the rape from his son (Scene 16), at which point his goal of becoming his son's best friend seems to have been realized when Aeschinus exclaims:

> What do you make of this? Is this what it means to be a father or a son?
> If he were my brother or a close buddy, he couldn't have done any more
>   for me!
> How can you not love him? And don't you just want to hug him? (707-9)

The play, however, is far from over. Demea eventually learns the truth about Ctesipho's role in all, and so must face the reality that his authoritarian style of parenting has not been successful. Left alone on stage, Demea reviews and assesses his experience as a parent:

> No one has ever plotted out his life's plan so successfully that he never
>   faces
> New challenges and discoveries brought about by circumstances, the
>   passing of time,
> Or experience itself. Inevitably, you discover you don't know what you
>   thought you did,
> And the principles we first formed don't hold up in the face of everyday
>   practice.
> That's where I am. As I approach my life's home stretch,
> I have decided to renounce the frugal life I've lived up to this very moment.
> Why? The realities of human life have taught me to place nonchalance
> And leniency above all else. To see the wisdom in this, just compare my

brother and me.
For him, life is a leisurely and endless stream of parties.
He's generous, easy-going, never offensive and has a smile for everybody.
His prime responsibility is to himself, he spends money on himself,
And everyone respects and likes him. Me? I'm the typical farmer:
Boorish, gloomy, cheap, fierce, stubborn—and married. And what misery
    that has been!
The birth of my sons? More stress. Phew! I wore myself down wanting
    to earn
As much as I could for them, and ground my life away in search of more
    stuff.
And now at the end of my life what are the fruits of all my labors?
Their contempt! Meanwhile, my polar opposite enjoys the benefits of
    fatherhood
Without lifting a finger. (855-72)

> ... All right then, I'm up for a little experiment.
I'll be the anti-me, and see if I can talk a smooth game and act generously
    like him.
He's challenged me after all.
I want to be loved and respected by my children as much as he does.
If the path to that is generosity and indulgence, don't count me out!
Bankruptcy? That's of least concern to the person who's oldest. (876-81)

Demea here unveils an unforeseen flexibility in choosing to learn from experience rather than merely preach from ideology, and he emerges with a newfound pragmatism and a new strategy. Demea, as is shortly confirmed, does not plan to fully embrace Micio's laissez-faire philosophy of parenting, but he nonetheless seems to experience a genuine transformation of character. He acknowledges that his extreme rigidity has alienated him from his sons, and decides to cast aside or at least temper his obsession with the acquisition of property in favor of winning their affection in his old age.

But while his outlook has softened some, Demea proceeds to brutally expose, in terms especially meaningful for Roman slave owners and heads of households, the practical shortcomings of Micio's extreme liberality. With each suggestion Demea makes for further expenditure in connection with Aeschinus' wedding (Scenes 25-27), he clearly increases Micio's discomfiture. We can easily imagine every *paterfamilias* in the audience cringing as Micio's generosity is taken to its financial *reductio ad absurdum*: the garden wall delimiting Sostrata's and Micio's households is to be torn down so as to "make one house out of two" (909), a clear indication that Micio is to absorb his less fortunate neighbors and all their expenses; Micio is made to agree to marry the elderly and destitute Sostrata sans dowry (929-45), and to relinquish an apparently valuable plot of land to her relative Hegio (947-56); and as perhaps the most absurd of all these blows to his finances, Micio is to free his saucy slave Syrus. The sardonic nature of Demea's newfound hyper-generosity is clearest in the rationale he offers for freeing Syrus for his services as a typically scheming clever slave to Aeschinus and Ctesipho:

Syrus
　　　　　Oh Demea! You really are a gentleman!
I've devoted my life to taking care of the both of them since they were
　　children.
Teacher, advisor, mentor—I've done it all to the best of my ability.
Demea
And the proof is in the pudding! Yes, shopping on credit,
Rounding up whores, and throwing a party in the middle of the day!
These are not the accomplishments of the average person.
Syrus
　　　　　　　　　　　　　　You are a delightful man!
Demea
And on top of that, he was an accomplice in buying the stripper today.
He took care of everything. He should be rewarded, and it'll inspire
The other slaves to do better. Aeschinus wants it too. (961-69)

Demea's sarcastic remarks here are completely in character, but they also seem to offer bluntly realistic commentary on an aspect of Roman—and especially Plautine—comedy: why should the type of clever slave who amorally aids and abets his young master in an affair with a prostitute against the wishes of the young man's father be rewarded at all, whether with manumission or, as typically happens in Plautine comedy, by assuming comically heroic status and control of the play? In addition to granting Syrus his freedom, Micio is forced to provide him with some cash for the road (980-83)!

Though there obviously is calculated cynicism (cf. 911-15) in his plan to force Micio to spend more money than he wants to, Demea's ultimate goals nonetheless hint at the possibility of a compromise somewhere between Micio's philosophy and his own formerly uncompromising views. As Demea tells his brother:

It was to show that the reason the boys consider you to be so approachable
And jovial is not because your life is truly just and good at the core,
But only because you agree with whatever they want, spoil them,
And lavish money on them, Micio. Now if my way of living is so repulsive
　　to you,
Aeschinus, just because I don't indulge you in whatever you do, regardless
　　of
Whether it's right or wrong—I'm through here. Buy, squander, do whatever
　　you want!
But when you're not seeing things clearly because of your age,
Or pulled along too much by your desires and too little by your brains,
If you want me to grab hold of you and straighten you out or provide some
　　support
When it's needed, I'll be there for you. (986-95)

Demea believes he has demonstrated that Micio's laissez-faire approach to parenting is without solid moral foundation, and merely reflects his brother's strong desire—perhaps rising from his insecurity as a non-biological parent—to be liked by the boys. That both Aeschinus immediately accepts this new arrangement and Demea demonstrates a new willingness to compromise by allowing Ctesipho to enjoy the stripper's company on the farm (996-97) suggests the viability of a middle course between the two extremes initially represented by the brothers. The hitherto stereotypically impetuous boys themselves seem to be ready to assume more socially responsible, adult roles, a transformation that will entail—perhaps paradoxically to modern readers—greater obedience to Demea, i.e., their biological father. Micio presumably has learned that he must acknowledge some boundaries in both his expenditures and his liberality toward the boys. That Demea coaxes Micio into marrying Sostrata suggests some sort of acknowledgment that the bachelor brother's urban and libertine ways require some reining in. Granted, none of this is explicitly communicated at the play's end: Terence's method is more dialectical and suggestive than it is prescriptive. Plays seldom serve up recipes for how we should live, but are as complex as our own everyday social dramas. In a dynamic and increasingly cosmopolitan city such as Rome in 160 BCE, in an epoch where new wealth, new ideas, and outside influences were increasingly making their mark, blanket validation of a philosophy of parenting such as that held by either brother at the opening of the play might seem out of place. A truly great play such as Terence's *Adelphoe* will engage its audience in continued discussion of the questions it poses, both after they leave a debut performance, and maybe even centuries later following a reading of it in translation.

EUNUCHUS ("The Eunuch")

According to the ancient biographical tradition, *Eunuchus* was Terence's most successful play and earned him (or its producer) unprecedented revenue. Our sources for this information do not offer explanations for the play's popularity, and we do not know enough details about current events at the time of its premiere (161 BCE) to speculate about the play's particular appeal. The subject matter of *Eunuchus* is especially appropriate to the context in which we know it was performed, i.e., the Megalesian festival held in April in honor of Cybele. Cybele, or the Magna Mater ("Great Mother") as the Romans called her, was an eastern goddess who was incorporated into Roman worship in 204 BCE. It is likely that the ecstatic nature of her cult simultaneously fascinated and repulsed many Romans (for the Roman senate's emergency decree of 186 BCE outlawing the cult of Dionysus/Bacchus, see p. 2 above). The priests of Cybele no doubt drew special attention, as they were required to castrate themselves, and, once initiated into her eunuch priesthood, wore women's clothing. Thus, by Terence's floruit, these eunuch priests had become a highly visible feature of Roman religious life, and their sexual ambiguity probably generated much speculation, curiosity, and anxiety. In *Eunuchus*, frequent reference is made to the "flashy outfit" (683) the sexually aggressive Chaerea wears while disguised as Dorus the eunuch (and is extremely ashamed of once his ruse is over), and perhaps a good part of the audience's fascination with the play was centered on this costume and the latent sexual possibilities it suggested to them. *Eunuchus* has certainly generated much critical interest in recent years, largely because of the provocative issues it raises in regard to transvestitism, gender-bending, sexual predation, and sexuality in general.

The central character of *Eunuchus*, and the character most in control of her emotions and personal life in general, is Thais. She is a twenty-something (527) foreigner living in Athens, where she makes her living as a prostitute and brothel-operator. As such, she is not eligible for marriage with an Athenian citizen, and is in a socially and legally vulnerable position. Currently she maintains simultaneous, longstanding relationships with a soldier named Thraso and with Phaedria, a young and typically infatuated (cf. Scene 1) Athenian citizen who lives next door. As the play opens, the two suitors are engaged in a battle for Thais' affections, which currently takes the form of competitive gift-giving. In her relationship with the foolish and deluded Thraso, Thais displays the stereotypically detached and mercenary character of the comic prostitute (cf. Phronesium in Plautus' *Truculentus*). But, while she necessarily accepts gifts and other payments from Phaedria, she reveals in an early monologue that she also has sincere feelings for him:

> Oh dear! Maybe he doesn't put much faith in me
> And gauges me by the character of the other women here.
> I can say with absolute certainty and honesty
> That I haven't lied to Phaedria
> And no man is closer to my heart than he is. (197-201)

Such an admission defies the comic stereotype, whereby the *meretrix* is absurdly greedy, callously dishonest, openly manipulative and devoid of any genuine affection for her clients. Thais might better be associated with the stock figure—pervasive in literature and film—of the "hooker with a heart of gold."

The particular gifts Thais' suitors bring have enormous consequences for the plot of *Eunuchus* and what it "has to say" (45). By an extraordinary coincidence not atypical in New Comedy, Thraso has given Thais a beautiful sixteen-year-old girl named Pamphila. As an infant, Pamphila, who is actually the daughter of an Athenian citizen, had been abducted by pirates and then purchased by a merchant who gave her as a gift to Thais' mother (apparently in the same profession as her daughter). The girl had been raised by Thais' mother as if she were her own daughter, and Thais regards her as a sister. Following the death of Thais' mother, Thais' greedy brother sold Pamphila back into slavery, whereupon Thraso has fortuitously purchased her. To Phaedria Thais confides her plan to reunite Pamphila with her Athenian family, represented in the play by Pamphila's brother Chremes, whom Thais is trying to befriend for this purpose. Thraso initially withholds the girl from Thais, who openly admits to Phaedria that she is acting out of motives of both sisterly affection and self-interest in seeking possession of the girl:

> ... Now I have many reasons, my dear Phaedria,
> For wanting to take the girl away from him.
> First of all, she's virtually my sister. Second, I might be able

> To reunite her with her family. I'm alone here,
> And I don't have any friends or relatives, Phaedria,
> And that's why I want to win some allies by doing a favor like that.
>
> (144-49)

As an independent woman and alien lacking citizen's rights and the protection of male relatives, Thais is deeply aware of her vulnerability in Athens, and her dual motivations here should not be viewed as mutually exclusive. For her plan to succeed, she will need to manipulate the thoroughly unsympathetic Thraso, and that also calls for Phaedria to stay clear of her house for two days. While various male characters—Phaedria (Scenes 1-2), Chremes (Scene 8), Parmeno (Scene 21)—throughout misjudge Thais and her motivations in assuming that she acts purely out of greed, she perseveres in her plan to restore Pamphila to her family and her freeborn status.

Phaedria's choice of a eunuch that he has purchased on the slave market as a gift for Thais has no less significant ramifications. Phaedria's impetuous younger brother Chaerea glimpses Pamphila as she is being taken to Thais' house and experiences a terrible case of lust at first sight. The infatuated Chaerea loses track of Pamphila when he is detained by an elderly relative, but luckily meets up with Parmeno (Scene 5), a trusted family slave who immediately grasps that Chaerea is seeking Thraso's gift-girl. Parmeno has been charged with delivering the elderly eunuch (described as a "geriatric she-man" in 357) to Thais. The two launch the plot to dress Chaerea up in the eunuch's costume, so that he may be admitted to Thais' all-female household in the hope that he may then gain intimate access to Pamphila.

The eighteen year-old Chaerea, who has begun his mandatory military training and so is in peak athletic condition, cuts an alluring figure costumed as the eunuch Dorus, in the eyes of both males and females (472ff; cf. 686-87). He is admitted into the house of Thais and put in charge of Pamphila. Chaerea triumphantly relays his own shocking account (Scene 10) of his rape of Pamphila to his friend Antipho. Obviously elated, Chaerea begins by boasting of his connoisseurship of feminine beauty (564-66), and, without a trace of remorse or concern for Pamphila, details what happened once he was left alone with her after Thais and most of her attendants left for a dinner engagement:

> The girl sits in her room looking up at a painting. The subject of it
> Was the story of how Jupiter shot a shower of gold into Danaë's lap.
> I started to gaze at it too. The fact that so long ago *he* had pulled off
> The very same trick made me even more excited.
> A god had made himself into a man and secretly penetrated
> Another man's roof, and a woman was tricked via a skylight!
> And what a god it was: "He whose thunder rattles the lofty foundations of
>   the sky."
> Could I, a mere mortal, possibly do the same? I could … and I did it gladly!
>
> (584-91)

Terence here provides a disturbing glimpse into the mind of a sexual predator about to pounce. Through the description of the painting and its mythic subject matter, and the quotation of a line of high poetry (590) from (probably) a Roman tragedy, aestheticism and imminent sexual violence are conflated here in a dissonant, eerily modern way, as in a David Lynch film. We are also guided through the process of rationalization as the rapist musters his courage: if Jupiter, the sexually omnipotent king of the gods, could adopt a disguise to secretly infiltrate a home where a virgin is being sequestered and rape her, why shouldn't he do the same? The actual rape is described with stark brevity (601-5), and Chaerea crudely quips that he "would have been a eunuch for real" (606) if he had passed up such a golden opportunity.

Once Chaerea finishes his narrative, the two friends, with shocking casualness, turn to finalizing arrangements for a party they have planned with some of their fellow military trainees. Terence, however, makes sure that we learn how traumatizing the rape has been for Pamphila, first through the reports of Thais' (female) slave Pythias:

> The scumbag! It just wasn't enough for him to have his way with her!
> He had to rip up the poor girl's clothes and tear her hair out on top of it all!
>   (645-46)

> The girl's all in tears, and can't even say what happened when you ask her.
>   (659)

Thais herself later attests (820) that Pamphila's clothing is torn, and that she is weeping and uncommunicative. Recognition of a rape victim's anguish is most unusual in ancient literature, and especially so in Roman comedy, where rape usually is part of the play's remote prehistory (cf. the rape of Pamphila in *Adelphoe*), and the rapist's actions are portrayed as partially justified by the fact that he was intoxicated.

The rape of a free citizen or even a slave, in both Athens and Rome, was a serious offense—i.e., against the victim's male family members or owner—that might result in a substantial fine or in some circumstances the death of the offender. One possible resolution was for the rapist to marry his victim (this is still an option in some cultures today!) if she was a free citizen, as typically happens in Roman comedy. Chaerea insists that he did not commit the rape to insult Thais (i.e., as Pamphila's owner), but acted "out of love" (878), and agrees to marry Pamphila, once she is shown to be a citizen and so eligible for marriage. But what might in other comedies more easily pass for a case of "all's well that ends well" is problematized in *Eunuchus* by the fact that the audience has been informed of Pamphila's trauma and emotional devastation, and so might have wondered—as modern audiences do—about the prospects for a marriage whose foundation is a violent sexual crime such as Chaerea's.

Critics have also long debated the roles of the braggart soldier Thraso and his fawning parasite Gnatho, in part because Terence in the prologue admits (31-33) that he has incorporated them into *Eunuchus* from a second Menandrian play (see pp. 3-4 above). Some have found the prominent inclusion of one or both of these buffoonish characters in no less than seven scenes (4, 6-7, 17, 24-26) to be largely "inorganic," and intended chiefly to provide comic relief in what is mostly a serious play. But Thraso in fact serves as a sharp foil to his rival Phaedria—who is seeking a relationship with Thais based on sincere affection—in that he can even be gulled into equating Thais' love with the reception of his gifts:

Thraso
That would be the right strategy, Gnatho—if she actually loved me.
Gnatho
Seeing as she's quite eager for your gifts and loves them,
She's been in love with you for quite a while, and for some time now you've
Been able to yank her chain without much effort.
She's so afraid you'll get mad at her and transfer the bounty she now
receives elsewhere.
Thraso
So true. I hadn't thought of that myself.
Gnatho
Nonsense! You just hadn't applied your gifted intellect to it.
If you had, you would have put it so much better yourself, Thraso! (446-53)

Others have convincingly argued that the unifying theme of *Eunuch* is self-interest, and that all the main characters are, with varying degrees of success, striving to achieve their own selfish ends, none more so than the deluded Thraso and his opportunistic parasite Gnatho, who proclaims self-interest to be his personal creed (1070).

Self-interest and the necessary compromises that accompany it do in fact ultimately win the day. Thais' plan to reunite Pamphila with her family succeeds, and she can expect a reward (750) from them, and, most importantly, she wins the social and legal protections she initially sought from the family of Chaerea and Phaedria (1039-40). Phaedria is convinced by Gnatho of the utility of allowing Thraso to hang around and bankroll Thais:

... Think on it now. It's clear how much you enjoy living with her, Phaedria—
Or perhaps I should say *living it up* with her—
But you have so little to offer her, and Thais is someone who needs a lot.
What could be better than financing your love affair in full at no expense to
yourself?
And who in the world's more readily available for this purpose than Thraso?
First of all he's got the means and loves to lavish it.
On top of that, he's a fatheaded, dimwitted dolt who snores his way through
life.
Thais could never fall in love with him, and he's easy to boot out when you
want to. (1073-80)

For convincing Phaedria and Chaerea to accept Thraso, Gnatho himself will be allowed to partake in festivities at Thais' house (1084ff.), and granted free meals for life at Thraso's (1058-60). The final compromise benefits Thais as well, and not just financially, as it allows her to retain the company of Phaedria, with whom she genuinely seems to desire something more than fiscal, in so far as the circumstances of her profession allow for this. This arrangement probably does not conform with any modern concept of romantic love, and the disturbing account of Pamphila's rape still lingers, but a quintessential, if sometimes arbitrary and insecure, ending is achieved in which all adversaries are incorporated into one harmonious comic society.[41]

Translator's Note

As was the case for my 2008 Focus edition, *Plautus: Four Plays (Casina, Amphitryon, Captivi, Pseudolus)*, my goal in these translations is to strike a satisfactory balance between faithfulness and liveliness. This applies not just to diction, style and idiom, but also to cultural beliefs, values, assumptions, ideologies, etc. Accordingly, I have mostly avoided references and expressions currently in vogue that seem destined for the ever-expanding linguistic landfill. In an attempt not to elide or over-familiarize the distant and strange culture(s) behind the Latin texts, I have preserved much of their foreignness by not modernizing the names of the characters, and by leaving in references to Roman and Greek places, persons, deities, institutions, currency, etc. These are explained in the notes at the bottom of the page or in the appendices, which assume a readership with no prior experience of Plautus and Terence or ancient literature, history and culture in general.

As a reflection of my wish to stay close to the originals, I have translated line by line. The vast majority of Plautus and Terence is composed in spoken (i.e., iambic) and chanted or recitative (i.e., chiefly trochaic) verse based on the quantity of syllables or, more precisely, the relative time it took to pronounce them (i.e., "long" vs. "short"). These early Latin verse forms were remarkably free and allowed for many metrical licenses, with the result that it is very difficult for English ears to follow the rhythm of the Latin verse without artificially imposing stress accents at regular intervals— which by translating into prose I intentionally have avoided. In addition, about 14% of Plautus is in lyric meters meant to be sung (we know virtually nothing about the nature of how these were performed). These sung sections (*cantica*), which signal a bold departure from the mostly spoken verse forms of Greek New Comedy, are so marked at the beginnings of scenes in the translations and the (italicized) lines are arranged so as to mostly follow how they appear in modern Latin editions. Terence, however, who has just about 30 lines of song in his six extant plays, broke from the Plautine and early Roman trend toward a more boisterous form of musical comedy.

The translations of the plays are not here divided into acts and scenes,[42] as this was only first done in the Renaissance. Similarly, there are no stage directions in the manuscripts in which Plautus and Terence are preserved, and I have added these sparingly, and only where it seemed necessary in order to avoid possible confusions. The characters of the comedies themselves overwhelmingly explain what is taking place on stage. In the translation, asterisks (****) are used to indicate where a line has been lost in the transmission of the text.

---

41 Cf. Aristotle *Poetics* 1453a36ff.: "… [in comedy] the most bitter enemies in the plot, such as Orestes and Aegisthus, walk off as friends in the end and nobody is killed by anyone."

42 For the correspondence of the scene numbers used in this edition with the traditional act and scene numbers, see Appendix III, pp. 339-42.

For Plautus, I have most closely consulted the Latin texts of Lindsay (Oxford 1910) and Leo (Berlin 1895-6); for Terence, the Latin text of Kauer-Lindsay (Oxford 1926). For the individual plays, I have made extensive use of the following editions: for *Menaechmi*, Gratwick (Cambridge 1993); *Rudens*, Sonnenschein (Oxford 1901) and Fay (repr. New Rochelle, NY 1983); *Truculentus*, Enk (repr. New York 1979); *Adelphoe*, Martin (Cambridge 1976) and Gratwick (Warminster 1987); *Eunuchus*, Barsby (Cambridge 1999).

It is my hope that these translations will serve the needs of students and teachers in literature in translation courses, as well as the general reader. While they are not primarily designed as scripts for performance, it is also my hope that they could be adapted for use on the stage with relative ease.

Suggestions for Further Reading

GREEK NEW COMEDY

Arnott, W. G. 1975. *Menander, Plautus, and Terence*. Oxford.

Goldberg, S. M. 1980. *The Making of Menander's Comedy*. Berkeley.

Hunter, R. L. 1985. *The New Comedy of Greece and Rome*. Cambridge.

Lape, S. 2003. *Reproducing Athens*: *Menander's Comedy, Democratic Culture, and the Hellenistic City*. Princeton.

Lowe, N. J. 2007. *Comedy. Greece & Rome*: New Surveys in the Classics, no. 37. Cambridge.

McDonald, M. and Walton, J. M., eds. 2007. *The Cambridge Companion to Greek and Roman Theater*. Cambridge.

Wiles, D. 1991. *The Masks of Menander: Sign and Meaning in Greek and Roman Performance*. Cambridge.

Zagagi, N. 1994. *The Comedy of Menander*. London.

ROMAN COMEDY

Anderson, W. S. 1993. *Barbarian Play: Plautus' Roman Comedy*. Toronto.

Beacham, R. C. 1992. *The Roman Theatre and its Audience*. Cambridge, MA.

Beare, W. 1964. *The Roman Stage*. 3rd edn. London.

Bieber, M. 1961. *The History of the Greek and Roman Theatre*. 2nd edn. Princeton.

Chalmers, W. R. 1965. "Plautus and his Audience." In *Roman Drama*, ed. T. A. Dorey and D. R. Dudley, pp. 21-50. London.

Csapo, E. G. 1993. "A Case Study in the Use of Theatre Iconography as Evidence for Ancient Acting." *Antike Kunst* 36: 41-58.

Duckworth, G. 1994. *The Nature of Roman Comedy*. 2nd edn. Norman, OK.

Dutsch, D. M. 2008. *Feminine Discourse in Roman Comedy: On Echoes and Voices*. Oxford.

Forehand, W. E. 1985. *Terence*. Boston.

Fraenkel, E. 2007. *Plautine Elements in Plautus*, trs. T. Drevikovsky and F. Muecke. Oxford.

Garton, C. 1972. *Personal Aspects of the Roman Theatre*. Toronto.

Gentili, B. 1979. *Theatrical Performances in the Ancient World: Hellenistic and Early Roman Theatre*. Amsterdam.

Gratwick, A. S. 1982. "Drama." In *The Cambridge History of Classical Literature II: Latin Literature*, ed. E. J. Kenney and W. V. Clausen, pp. 77-137. Cambridge.

Goldberg, S. M. 1986. *Understanding Terence*. Princeton.

Goldberg, S. M. 1998. "Plautus on the Palatine." *Journal of Roman Studies* 88: 1-20.

Handley, E. W. 1968. *Menander and Plautus: A Study in Comparison*. London.

Konstan, D. 1983. *Roman Comedy*. Ithaca and London.
Leigh, M. 2004. *Comedy and the Rise of Rome*. Oxford.
Marshall, C. W. 2006. *The Stagecraft and Performance of Roman Comedy*. Cambridge.
McCarthy, K. 2000. *Slaves, Masters, and the Art of Authority in Plautine Comedy*. Princeton.
Moore, T. J. 1998. *The Theater of Plautus: Playing to the Audience*. Austin, TX.
Panayotakis, C. 2005a. "Non-verbal Behaviour on the Roman Comic Stage." In *Body Language in the Greek and Roman Worlds*, ed. D. Cairns, pp. 175-93. Swansea.
Panayotakis, C. 2005b. "Comedy, Atellan Farce, and Mime." In *A Companion to Latin Literature*, ed. S. J. Harrison, pp. 130-47. Oxford.
Parker, H. N. 1996. "Plautus vs. Terence: Audience and Popularity Re-examined." *American Journal of Philology* 117: 585-617.
Segal, E. 1987. *Roman Laughter*. 2nd edn. Oxford.
Slater, N. W. 1985. *Plautus in Performance: the Theatre of the Mind*. Princeton.
Wright, J. 1974. *Dancing in Chains: The Stylistic Unity of the Comoedia Palliata*. Rome.

MENAECHMI

Gratwick, A. S. 1993. *Plautus: Menaechmi*. Cambridge.
Leach, E. W. 1969. "*Meam quom formam noscito*: Language and Characterization in the *Menaechmi*." *Arethusa* 2: 30-45.
McCarthy, K. 2000. *Slaves, Masters, and the Art of Authority in Plautine Comedy*. Princeton. [Chapter II, "The Ties That Bind: *Menaechmi*." Pp. 35-76]
Segal, E. 1969. "The *Menaechmi*: Roman Comedy of Errors." *Yale Classical Studies* 21: 75-93.

RUDENS

Connors, C. 2004. "Monkey Business: Imitation, Authenticity, and Identity from Pithekoussai to Plautus." *Classical Antiquity* 23: 179-207.
Fay, H. C. 1983. *Plautus: Rudens*. Repr. New Rochelle, NY.
Konstan, D. 1983. *Roman Comedy*. Ithaca and London. ["*Rudens*: City-State Utopia." Pp. 73-95]
Leach, E. W. 1974. "Plautus' *Rudens*: Venus Born from a Shell." *Texas Studies in Literature and Language* 15: 915-32.
Louden, B. 1999. "*The Tempest*, Plautus, and the *Rudens*," *Comparative Drama* 33: 199-223.
Sonnenschein, E. A. 1901. *T. Macci Plauti Rudens*. Oxford.

TRUCULENTUS

Dessen, C. S. 1977. "Plautus' Satiric Comedy: The *Truculentus*." *Philological Quarterly* 56: 145-68.
Enk, P. J. 1979. *Plauti Truculentus*, vols I-II. Repr. New York.
Konstan, D. 1983. *Roman Comedy*. Ithaca and London. ["*Truculentus*: Satiric Comedy." Pp. 142-64]
Moore, T. J. 1998. *The Theater of Plautus: Playing to the Audience*. Austin, TX. [Chapter 8, "Prostitutes and Lovers: *Truculentus*." Pp. 140-57]

ADELPHOE

Fantham, E. 1971. "*Hautontimorumenos* and *Adelphoe*: A Study of Fatherhood in Terence and Menander." *Latomus* 30: 970-98.
Grant, J. N. 1975. "The Ending of Terence's *Adelphoe* and the Menandrian Original." *American Journal of Philology* 96: 42-60.
Gratwick, A. S. 1987. *The Brothers*. Warminster.
Lape, S. 2004. "The Terentian Marriage Plot: Reproducing Fathers and Sons." *Ramus* 33: 35-52.

Leigh, M. 2004. *Comedy and the Rise of Rome.* Oxford. [Chapter 5: "Fatherhood and the Habit of Command: L. Aemilius Paullus and the *Adelphoe.*" Pp. 158-91]

Lowe, J. C. B. 1998. "Terence, *Adelphoe*: Problems of Dramatic Space and Time." *Classical Quarterly* 48: 470-86.

Martin, R. H. 1976. *Terence: Adelphoe.* Cambridge.

EUNUCHUS

Barsby, J. 1999. *Terence: Eunuchus.* Cambridge.

Dessen, C. S. 1995. "The Figure of the Eunuch in Terence's *Eunuchus.*" *Helios* 22: 123-39.

James, S. L. 1998. "From Boys to Men: Rape and Developing Masculinity in Terence's *Hecyra* and *Eunuchus.*" *Helios* 25: 31-47.

Konstan, D. 1986. "Love in Terence's *Eunuch*: The Origins of Erotic Subjectivity." *American Journal of Philology* 107: 369-93.

Philippides, K. 1995. "Terence's *Eunuchus*: Elements of the Marriage Ritual in the Rape Scene." *Mnemosyne* 48: 272-84.

Smith, L. P. 1994. "Audience Response to Rape: Chaerea in Terence's *Eunuchus.*" *Helios* 21: 21-38.

MISCELLANEOUS

Astin, A. E. 1967. *Scipio Aemilianus.* Oxford.

Beard, M., North, J. and Price, S. 1998. *Religions of Rome*, vols. I-II. Cambridge.

Bradley, K. R. 1994. *Slavery and Society at Rome.* Cambridge.

Corbeill, A. 2004. *Nature Embodied: Gesture in Ancient Rome.* Princeton.

Crook, J. A. 1967. *Law and Life of Rome.* London.

Dixon, S. 1992. *The Roman Family.* Baltimore and London.

Earl, D. 1967. *The Moral and Political Tradition of Rome.* Ithaca.

Easterling, O. and E. Hall, eds. 2002. *Greek and Roman Actors: Aspects of an Ancient Profession.* Cambridge.

Edwards, C. 1993. *The Politics of Immorality in Ancient Rome.* Cambridge.

Fitzgerald, W. 2000. *Slavery and the Roman Literary Imagination.* Cambridge.

Goldberg, S. M. 2005. *Constructing Literature in the Roman Republic.* Cambridge.

Gowers, E. 1993. *The Loaded Table: Representations of Food in Roman Literature.* Oxford.

Gratwick, A.S. 1973. "Titus Maccius Plautus." *Classical Quarterly* 23: 78-84.

Grote, D. 1983. *The End of Comedy: the Sit-Com and the Comedic Tradition.* Hamden, CT.

Gruen, E. S. 1984. *The Hellenistic World and the Coming of Rome.* Berkeley.

Gruen, E. S. 1990. *Studies in Greek Culture and Roman Policy.* Leiden.

Gruen, E. S. 1992. *Culture and National Identity in Republican Rome.* Ithaca.

Harris, W. V. 1979. *War and Imperialism in Republican Rome.* Oxford.

Hinds, S. 1998. *Allusion and Intertext: Dynamics of Appropriation in Roman Poetry.* Cambridge.

Hornblower, S. and Spawforth, A., eds. 1996. *The Oxford Classical Dictionary*, 3rd edn. Oxford.

Moore, T. J. 1994. "Seats and Social Status in the Plautine Theater." *Classical Journal* 90: 113-23.

Nelson, T. G. A. 1990. *Comedy.* Oxford.

Saller, R. P. 1994. *Patriarchy, Property, and Death in the Roman Family.* Cambridge.

Slater, W. J., ed. 1996. *Roman Theater and Society.* Ann Arbor.

Stott, A. 2005. *Comedy.* New York.

Taplin, O. 1993. *Comic Angels.* Oxford.

Treggiari, S. 1991. *Roman Marriage.* Oxford.

Menaechmi
("The Menaechmus Brothers")

CHARACTERS WITH SPEAKING PARTS

PENICULUS, *a parasite, i.e., a glutton and professional dinner-guest*
MENAECHMUS I, *lost twin of Menaechmus II, currently living in Epidamnus*
EROTIUM, *a prostitute/brothel owner who lives next door to Menaechmus I*
CYLINDRUS, *a cook and slave of Erotium*
MENAECHMUS II, *Syracusan twin of Menaechmus I, originally named*
     Sosicles
MESSENIO, *slave of Menaechmus II*
MAID, *a slave (i.e., "maidservant") of Erotium*
MATRONA, *the unnamed wife of Menaechmus I*
SENEX, *unnamed elderly father of Menaechmus I's wife*
DOCTOR, *an unnamed doctor of Epidamnus*
SLAVE, *one of the unnamed slaves of Senex brought on to take Menaechmus to*
     the Doctor

SCENE

*Epidamnus: the action takes place in front of the houses of Menaechmus I
and Erotium. One stage wing leads to the forum/ city-center, the other to the
harbor.*

PROLOGUE[1]

Greetings, spectators! First and foremost I'm here to announce
That Safety[2] herself is smiling on both you and me.
I'm also here to present Plautus[3] to you—with my voice, not my hands, that is!
I only ask that you and your ears be kind to this play and give it a fair hearing.
Pay careful attention now and I'll provide all the details of the plot   5

---

1   The Roman comic playwrights introduced the use of an impersonal prologist (perhaps the head of the
    acting troupe) to ancient comedy to speak on behalf of the play and playwright.

2   Many personified abstractions were worshipped in Roman religion. There were temples and shrines of
    the personified deity *Salus*, "Salvation" or "Safety" (especially in relation to the welfare of the state), in
    Rome and elsewhere.

3   For the life and career of Plautus, see Introduction pp. 7-9.

In as few words as a prologist possibly can.
Comic playwrights have this habit of pretending
That everything on stage is taking place at Athens.[4]
Why? So you think it's in Greece, not Rome.
Me? I won't pretend it takes place anywhere except where it happened.   10
Yes indeed, this play will have a genuinely Greek atmosphere,
Though it's really more of a Sicilian air than the aura of Athens about it.[5]
Well, that's the prologue to my prologue.
Time for me to shovel out the entire plot of this play to you
(Okay, it's really more like a barn-load than a shovel-full):   15
I'm *so* generous when it comes to giving away the story![6]
Now there was an old merchant from Syracuse[7]
Who had a couple of kids, twin boys in fact.
They looked so much alike that the woman who breast-fed them,
Their own wet-nurse, couldn't tell them apart,   20
And neither could the woman who gave birth to them, their own mother!
At least that's what somebody who saw them told me.
So don't go supposing that I saw them myself.[8]
Now when the boys were seven years old,
Their father loaded up a ship with a load of goods.   25
He took one of the twin boys onboard with him,
And set off for Tarentum[9] to conduct his business.
The other boy stayed home with his mother.
It just so happened that there was a festival going on in Tarentum,
And like at any festival, flocks of folks assembled.   30
The boy wandered off from his father and into the crowd.
A merchant from Epidamnus[10] was celebrating there,
And he grabbed the boy and carried him off to his home.
Now the unlucky loss of the lad
Sent his father into a funk so deep and deadly   35
That the old merchant died just a few days afterwards right there in Tarentum.
News of what happened reached the boys' grandfather back in Syracuse.
When he learned of the death

---

4   Athens is the nominal setting for the majority of extant comedies, but Plautus' Athens is a jumble of
    Roman and Greek places, persons, and institutions. See Introduction p. 3.

5   Plautus coins new words here, perhaps to suggest that the play will feature a more farcical Sicilian
    brand of humor (*sicilicissitare*) rather than that associated with the relatively "high-brow" New Comedy
    of Athens (*atticissare*).

6   A reference to the Roman practice of publicly distributing grain underlies the prologist's humor here.

7   The chief city of Sicily and one of the great cities of classical antiquity. Cf. n. 52 below.

8   Ancient narrators are often careful to distinguish events they have only heard about from others with
    those they have personally observed (i.e., by "autopsy").

9   The modern city of Taranto (in southern Italy), colonized by Spartans in the 8th century BCE.

10 A Greek colony and important trade center on the Adriatic Sea, now part of Albania.

Of his son and the theft of his grandson,
He decided to change the name of the other twin   40
Because he loved the grandson he'd lost so much.
This is how the twin who'd stayed at home
Came to be named "Menaechmus,"[11]
The name of his abducted brother and the name of the grandfather too.[12]
How do I know this?[13] Simple: I distinctly remember hearing the name   45
Shouted over and over again—by debt-collectors![14]
Got it? Just so there's no confusion later, I repeat:
BOTH BROTHERS HAVE THE SAME NAME.
Now I must measure my way back to Epidamnus on foot,[15]
To explain all of this to you down to the very last detail.   50
If any one of you wants some *damned* business of yours done there,[16] speak up now.
There's no need to fear as long as I'm taken care of—
With cash up front, that is!
No cash, you say? Well, you're screwed.
Have the cash for me? See you later, then—and screw you!   55
So let me go back to where I started, that is, right where I'm standing.
Now back to that Epidamnian I started to talk about,
The guy who snatched the one twin.
The only fruits of his loins were his assets,
So he adopted the kid he'd kidnapped,   60
Found him a wife endowed with a dowry,[17]
And had the decency to die and make him his heir.[18]
Seems he happened to go out to the country after a big rain

---

11 The lead characters in this doubles comedy are cleverly named after a 4th century BCE Syracusan
    mathematician and geometer who solved the problem of "doubling the cube." The name may very well
    be Plautus' invention; where direct comparison with Greek source plays is available, Plautus jazzes up
    the names of the Greek characters. Cf. Introduction p. 7.

12 Naming the child after the grandfather was the usual Greek practice.

13 For autopsy in narration, see n. 8 above.

14 A reference to the ancient Italian practice (*flagitatio*) of publicly shaming a debtor into payment.

15 Latin verse (such as Plautus' here) is measured in metrical feet, and so there is a metapoetic pun here.
    For the prologist's emphasis on the arbitrariness and fictionality of the setting, see 72-76. Cf. also
    Truculentus 1-11 and Introduction p. 25.

16 The prologist plays on *Epidamnum* (= accusative case of *Epidamnus* in Latin) here, as if it were a
    hybrid of the Greek preposition *epi* ("to," "toward" + accusative case) and Latin *damnum* ("financial
    loss"). The bilingual pun and the idea that Epidamnus harbors con-artists who doom visitors to
    financial catastrophe is even more explicit in Messenio's warning to Menaechmus II at 257-64.

17 Under Roman marriage law, a dowry remained a husband's property only as long as the marriage
    lasted. Thus, a woman whose husband had squandered her dowry might gain the upper-hand in the
    marriage—such a situation at any rate is the basis for the Roman comic stereotype of the "dowered
    wife" (*uxor dotata*), who in comedy is unsympathetically portrayed as a "shrew" at war with her
    husband and his pursuit of pleasure.

18 Under Roman inheritance law, an adopted child who was not recognized as a Roman citizen could
    inherit property; the same was not true in ancient Athens.

And tried to cross a raging river not far from town.
The river snatched up the boy-snatcher's feet,   65
And escorted the creep off on a one-way trip to hell.
His adopted son nets his net-worth—
That is, the kidnapped twin who lives right over there.
Now the twin who lives in Syracuse
Will arrive in Epidamnus today with his slave,   70
In search of his long-lost identical twin.
While this play is being staged, this city's going to be Epidamnus;
When it's time to stage another play, it'll be another town.
The same thing happens with houses and households:
One minute a pimp lives here, another minute a young man does,   75
Or an old man, a pauper, a beggar, a king, a parasite, a fortune-teller ...[19]

SCENE 1

Peniculus enters from the wing leading to the forum/city-center.
Peniculus[20]
The young men have nicknamed me Peniculus
Because I always wipe the dinner table clean.
To my way of thinking, it's extremely foolish
To put prisoners of war in chains   80
Or to bind up runaway slaves in shackles.
How so? If you double an unfortunate fellow's trouble,
You'll just make him all the hungrier to act up and cut out.
They'll always find a way to remove their chains.
Fetter them and they file away a link,   85
Or take a rock to the lock and flee. Waste of time!
Why, what's the right and proper way to keep a man from fleeing?
Why, chains of food and drink of course!
Let him clamp his jaws down on a full table,
Keep serving him his favorite edibles and potables each and every day,   90
And you'll wear him down with satisfaction.
He'll never escape, not even if he's facing capital punishment.
It's really that simple. There's no stronger chain
Than the food-chain: the looser you let it out,
The tighter it ties a criminal down.   95

---

19 Stock characters from both comic and serious drama: the pimp (*leno*), the typically lovesick young man
    (*adulescens*), old man (*senex*) and parasite (*parasitus*) belong to New Comedy; the pauper (*pauper*),
    beggar (*mendicus*) and king (*rex*) to tragedy. The prologist describes a markedly theatrical world.

20 As Peniculus is a diminutive form of Latin *penis* ("tail," "penis"), the audience probably expects a
    sexual joke to follow (the parasite Ergasilus makes a strikingly similar entrance at Plautus, *Captivi*
    69, where he asserts that the young men call him *scortum*, i.e., "whore"). Instead, in 78 he relates his
    nickname to the word *peniculus* meaning "brush" or "sponge." Cf. 286 and 391.

Case in point: myself. I'm off to Menaechmus' house here,
Where I've been a prisoner for years. Bring on the chains, yum, yum!
He doesn't just feed you, he treats you like you're family,
He refreshes you with refreshments! There's no sweeter medicine in the world!
That's the type of young man he is. He serves feasts fit for Ceres,[21]   100
His helpings are huge, veritable mountains of food!
He concocts culinary monuments so lofty,
You have to stand on your couch[22] to trim a tasty morsel off the summit!
But there's been quite a hiatus since I last ate here,
And I've been resigned to dine at home with my precious little ones.   105
I'm the kind of consumer who consumes only what's precious;
Problem is, I have precious little left at home to consume.
So it's time to pay him a visit. Ah, the door's opening.
Look, there's Menaechmus coming out right now!

SCENE 2

Menaechmus enters from his house, yelling back at his wife inside.
(SONG through 134)

Menachmus I[23]
If you weren't so nasty, stupid, bitchy and just plain nuts,   110
You'd pick your likes and dislikes with an eye to pleasing me—your husband!
If after today you keep treating me this way, I guarantee
I'll see you're escorted straight out of this house and home to Daddy.[24]
Every time I step out of the house, you're in my face with impositions and inquisitions:
"Where are you going?" "What are you doing?" "What business do you have?"
"What are you up to?" "What's that you've got?" "What were you doing?"   116
I have to declare every little thing I've done or am doing:
It's like I brought a customs officer into my house, not a wife!
It's clear I've spoiled you, so here's the new program:
Seeing as I lavish you with personal slaves, household provisions,   120
Wool, a wardrobe, cash, and fancy accessories, the smart thing for you to do
Is to stop spying on your husband. So get with it now!
And do you know what? To reward you for all your spying,
I'll be having dinner out today—with my favorite whore!

---

21 For the goddess Ceres, see Appendix I p. 335. In addition to the fact that Ceres is the goddess of grain (= food by metonymy), the joke here turns on the conception of the anthropomorphic Greek and Roman gods as living their lives on an exaggeratedly human scale.

22 Greeks and Romans usually ate while reclining on couches with trays of food and drink placed before them.

23 For the meaning of the name Menaechmus, see n. 11 above.

24 Roman marriages could be easily dissolved (in some cases at the initiative of the woman) by a mere speech-act followed by an appropriate division of property.

Peniculus (*aside*)

He may think he's bad-mouthing his wife, but I'm the one taking it in the jaw.   125
If he dines out, he punishes my stomach, not his wife.

Menaechmus I

Booyah! By Hercules,[25] *I've successfully derided her right away from the door!*
Where are the guys who know the only marital bliss is extramarital?[26]
And how about some props for my bold defeat of that battle-axe?   129
Take a look at this pashmina I "kidnapped" from the wife. It's soon to be my whore's.
How apt is that? I've so smartly outsmarted my clever guard!
What a work of sheer beauty, a moral triumph, craftsmanship of the highest
      caliber!
I'll be sorry I stole it from that sorry excuse for a woman, and I'll take a hit,
But at least for now I've won the spoils and our side's safe and sound!

Peniculus

Hey, soldier! Any of that booty there for me?   135

Menaechmus I

Damn! I'm trapped!

Peniculus

                    No, it's not a trap! I'm one of your troops. No need to fear.

Menaechmus I

Who's there?

Peniculus

              Me.

Menaechmus I

              Convenience,[27] no Opportunity herself is knocking at my door!
Hey!

Peniculus

          Hey.

Menaechmus I

              What you up to?

Peniculus

                        I'm holding my Guiding Spirit[28] in my right hand!

---

25 For the god Hercules, see Appendix I p. 335.

26 As the opening formula *ubi sunt* … ("Where are the …") shows, this is a direct and characteristically
    Plautine appeal to the males in the audience, who perhaps were expected to vociferously identify
    themselves. Roman males' extra-marital liaisons were largely tolerated (and expected), as long as they
    did not incur significant financial loss or involve a married woman. See further Introduction p. 20.

27 The personification of abstractions is a feature of Roman religion (cf. n. 2 above), but the comic
    personification of Convenience (*Commoditas*) and Opportunity (*Opportunitas*) here is Plautus' own
    doing.

28 Every Roman male was thought to have been born with a divine "Guiding Spirit" or "Second-Self"
    (*genius*) that dwelt within him throughout his life. The *genius* of the male head of the household, i.e.,
    the *paterfamilias*, was worshipped by the entire household.

Menaechmus I

You couldn't have come at a more convenient time than right now.

Peniculus

That's my specialty. Convenience and I go back a long ways. 140

Menaechmus I

Want to see a really fine piece of work?

Peniculus

Who cooked it up?
Just show me the leftovers and I'll tell you if he messed up.

Menaechmus I

Have you ever seen the scene on a wall-painting where an eagle
Snatches Ganymede, or the one where Venus takes Adonis? [29]

Peniculus

Lots of times. But what do those have to do with me?

Menaechmus I

Check this out: 145
Remind you of anything (*models the pashmina*)? [30]

Peniculus

What's with the get-up?

Menaechmus I

Aren't I just the most charming fellow you've ever seen?

Peniculus

When's dinner?

Menaechmus I

Didn't I just ask you a question?

Peniculus

Yes, yes, you're the most charming fellow ever.

Menaechmus I

And? Anything else?

Peniculus

Yeah. You're a hoot. Absolutely hilarious.

Menaechmus I

And?

Peniculus

Please, no more "And?"'s! … until I know what's in it for me. 150
You and your wife are back at it again. All the more reason to watch my back.

---

29 Jupiter (see Appendix I p. 335.), sometimes in the form of an eagle, snatched up the handsome young
Trojan prince Ganymede and took him to Olympus to serve as a cupbearer for the gods and as his
eternal "beloved" in a typically Greek pederastic relationship. Venus (see Appendix I p. 335.) became
sexually enamored of the youthful eastern divinity Adonis, though no other extant source refers to her
seizing him in the manner of the eagle that seized Ganymede. Cf. n. 30 below.

30 Menaechmus grandiosely suggests that his theft of the pashmina rivals the gods' (see n. 29 above)
abductions of their mortal lovers. But given his wife's apparent domination (cf. 110ff.) of him in
their marriage, there is irony in the reference to the powerful gods' subordinate lovers, as also in his
effeminate modeling of the pashmina here. Cf. 511-14 and n. 56 below.

Menaechmus I
We're going to seize the day and burn it right up in a place   152-3
My wife doesn't know about.
Peniculus
                              Oh, well put! So how soon do I light the pyre?
The day's already half-dead-right down to its belly-button!   155
Menaechmus I
Your interruptions just make it deader.
Peniculus
                              You can scrape my eye out of its socket, Menaechmus,
If I so much as say one word you don't want me to.
Menaechmus I
Now move away from the door.
Peniculus
                              Done.
Menaechmus I
                              More over here.
Peniculus
                              Okay.
Menaechmus I
Stay cool. A little farther away from that lioness's den.
Peniculus
You know, I'm pretty damn sure you'd make a great chariot racer.   160
Menaechmus I
Come again?
Peniculus
                              You know, the way you keep looking back for your wife.
Menaechmus I
But what do you think …
Peniculus
                              Me? Whatever you want me to—or don't want me—to think.
Menaechmus I
How's your sense of smell? If you just take a whiff of something,
Can you make a good guess at what it is?
Peniculus
                              Absolutely! I could ferret out
A scent that stumped the entire State Board of Sniffers.   165
Menaechmus I
Then take a whiff of this pashmina. What do you smell? Why're you backin' off?
Peniculus
Only the upper region of a woman's garment should be sniffed:
What's been *down there* scars a sensitive nose for life!
Menaechmus I
Quite the connoisseur of scents, I see. Take a whiff of this part then.

Peniculus

All right.

Menaechmus I
Well? What do you smell?

Peniculus

A steal, copping a feel, a free meal. 170

Menaechmus I
Well put!

****
****

And now to transfer its ownership to my favorite neighborhood prostitute, Erotium.
I'll see she has a luncheon prepared for the three of us.

Peniculus

Perfect!

Menaechmus I
And we'll be drinking, non-stop, all the way til' the morning star![31] 175

Peniculus
Perfect! Well-put! Time for me to batter down the door?

Menaechmus I

Batter away.

Er, hold on a second.

Peniculus

What? That second will put a hold on my drinking cup!

Menaechmus I
Knock nicely.

Peniculus

What? You think her door's made out of Dixie Ware?[32]
****

Menaechmus I
Hold it, by Hercules! Look, she's coming out on her own! 180
How the sun pales in comparison with her beautiful body!

---

31 As Venus is both the morning star and the goddess of sex, Menaechmus here points to a long night of sexual activity.

32 Literally "Samian Ware." Samos, a Greek island off the coast of Asia Minor (modern Turkey), produced a cheap and brittle type of pottery. In New Comedy, prostitutes are often said to hail from Samos, as Thais in Terence's *Eunuchus* (cf. 107); thus, the joke here may also turn on the assumption that the brothel's door might (by metonymy) also be Samian.

SCENE 3

Erotium enters from her house.

Erotium[33]
Menaechmus! Hello, dearest darling!

Peniculus

And what about me?

Erotium

You're not on my list.

Peniculus
You know, that's not the first time an enlisted man like me has heard that.

Menaechmus I
I'd like to propose a little encounter at your house today.   184-5

Erotium
Today it is.

Menaechmus I
I'm proposing a duel, a war of wine if you like.
Whichever warrior manages to win the drinking contest
Becomes an enlisted man in your commission for one night. You decide.
When I gaze upon you, my darling, I can only think of … how much I despise
    my wife!

Erotium
Though that doesn't seem to stop you from wearing her clothing.   190
What is that?

Menaechmus I

Something right off her rack—for your rack, my flower!

Erotium
You're the best! You outrank all the other johns who want to infiltrate my unit!

Peniculus *(aside)*
Aw, there's nothing sweeter than a prostitute with a target in her sights.
But if you really loved him, you'd already have bitten his nose off.[34]   194-5

Menaechmus I
Help me with my cloak here, Peniculus. I've got spoils to dedicate.

Peniculus
Hand it over. But please do a little dance in your wife's pashmina.

Menaechmus I
Me dance?[35] Damn! Are you nuts?

Peniculus

I'm the one who's nuts?

---

33 Her name means "Love-Thing" in Greek. Prostitutes' names often have the neuter Latin suffix *-ium*,
    though they are usually treated as feminine. Cf. *Truculentus* n. 28.

34 As is also indicated in other sources, biting was a regular feature of Roman erotic kissing.

35 Romans—or at least the elite, conservative Roman moral tradition—in contrast to Greeks, generally
    scorned dancing as an exotic and decadent activity.

Either dance or take it off.

Menaechmus I

I absconded with this at great personal risk today.

Peniculus

Why, I don't believe Hercules ever ventured such a risk   200
When he took off with Hippolyta's girdle![36]

Menaechmus I

Take it, it's yours,
Since you're the only woman in the world who knows what I like.[37]

Erotium

That's the spirit! If only all my clients were just like you!

Peniculus

That's the spirit, all right—if they're set on a life of poverty!

Menaechmus I

Cost me four minae[38] last year when I bought it for my wife.   205

Peniculus (*aside*)

By my accounting, those four minae just lost their lives.

Menaechmus I

There's something I want you to do.

Erotium

Your wish is my command.

Menaechmus I

Good. I'd like you to arrange a luncheon for three at your house.

Peniculus

Yes, and no scrimping on delicacies from the forum:
Go get some pork glands and bacon, the lardy offspring of Ham,   210
A slab of hog's head—something along those porcine lines,[39]
Served up piping hot to make me as ravenous as a raptor.
And make it snappy!

Erotium

Not a problem.

Menaechmus I

We've got some business in the forum,
But we'll be back soon for a drink before our feast.

---

36 One of the canonical labors of Hercules was to retrieve the girdle of the Amazon warrior-queen
   Hippolyta. Peniculus here ironically hints at Menaechmus I's effeminence/subordination to his wife: cf.
   n. 30 above and n. 56 below.

37 By asserting that only Erotium "is indulgent (*morigera*) to [his] ways," Menaechmus I evokes a
   commonplace Roman marriage ideal. For Menaechmus I's over-rating of his relationship with Erotium,
   see Introduction pp. 13-14.

38 For the value of a mina, see Appendix II p. 337. Clothing was usually produced in the ancient
   household, and the purchase of clothes from outside was considered a luxury. Four minae for the
   purchase of the pashmina is a significant sum.

39 Peniculus' grandiose obsession with pork reflects Roman, not Greek, taste.

Erotium

Come whenever you want. I'll be ready for you.

Menaechmus I

                         And none too soon.   215

And you: follow me!

Peniculus

                I won't just follow you, I'll shadow you. I'd sooner
Lose all the gods' riches than lose sight of you today!

Erotium (*to slaves within*)

Someone bring out Cylindrus, my cook—and right now!

SCENE 4

Cylindrus enters from Erotium's house.

Erotium

Take a shopping basket and some money. Got some?

Cylindrus[40]

Yes.

Erotium

         Off you go! Get exactly enough for three: 220
No more, no less.

Cylindrus

             Just who are you expecting?

Erotium

Besides me, there'll be Menaechmus and his parasite.

Cylindrus

                        That'd make it enough for ten:
That parasite eats as much as eight normal human beings!

Erotium

That's the guest-list. You'll take care of the rest?

Cylindrus

                      Okay.
The meal's as good as done. Tell them to take their places.

Erotium

                    Hurry back. (*goes inside*)

Cylindrus

                        Will do.   225

---

40 His name means "cylinder" or "roller" in Greek.

SCENE 5

Menaechmus II and Messenio, accompanied by slaves carrying their baggage, enter from the wing leading to the harbor.

Menaechmus II

Ah, Messenio! For an old sea dog,
What pleasure could ever possibly surpass
The glimpse of dry land from the deep?

Messenio

        To tell you the truth,
I'd prefer catching a glimpse of my own land and setting foot on it.
But please tell me why we've put in at Epidamnus.   230
Are we going to go around every island—like the sea itself does?

Menaechmus II

We are searching for my identical twin brother.

Messenio

Yes, but will there ever be an end to that search?
We've been at this for the last six years now:
Istria,[41] Spain, Marseilles, Illyria,[42]   235
Up and down the Adriatic, Sicily, the Greek colonies—
Everywhere the sea laps the shore along the entire Italian peninsula,
We've been there! If you were searching for a needle in a haystack,
You'd have found it long ago—if it was anywhere to be found at all.
We're searching for a dead man among the living;   240
If he were alive, we'd have found him a long time ago.

Menaechmus II

Well then I'll keep searching until I know that for certain,
And I find someone who knows that he's dead.
Once that happens, I'll never again expend an ounce of energy in search of him.
But in the meantime, I'll never stop looking for him as long as I'm breathing. 245
I'm the only one who understands the place he holds in my heart.

Messenio

Well, you're looking for a peck of pears on an elm tree.
We should just go back home—unless we're planning to write a travelogue.

Menaechmus II

Do what you're told, eat what you're given, and watch out for trouble!
Stop bothering me: it's my way or the highway.   250

Messenio

Ouch! That's cutting to the chase! Okay, I'M A SLAVE.
No one's ever said that so loudly and clearly before, and in so few words!
But I won't bite my tongue about one thing.
Listening? As I look over the ol' wallet here,

---

41 A Greek colony on the Black Sea near the estuary of the Danube.

42 The (Indo-European) Illyrians occupied the Balkan Peninsula.

It's damn clear our travel fund is fast unraveling.   255
If you don't cease and desist from this search for your brother,
You won't just be short of cash—you'll have to cash it in.
You do know about this damn nation of Epidamnians, don't you?[43]
Why it's decadence galore here! They've got loafers and slackers,
Dipsomaniacs, kleptomaniacs, swindlers and chiselers everywhere!   260
And surely you've heard about the local hookers?
They're the most stunning *and* the most cunning in the world!
It's a place for *damnation*, not a vacation (hence the name)!
Drop in anytime—if you want to do some serious *dam*age to your wallet!

Menaechmus II

Yes, yes, I'll be careful. Now give me that wallet.   265

Messenio

Why?

Menaechmus II

I worry about you after what you just said.

Messenio

You're worried about me?

Menaechmus II

Yes, worried about you and the wallet:
You see, you're a great lover of the ladies, Messenio,
And I've a nasty tendency for anger and general excitability.
So by keeping the money myself we avoid two things we don't want: 270
The money won't escape from your hands and you'll escape my rage.

Messenio

Fine. Take it, guard it. It's all yours.

SCENE 6

Cylindrus returns from the forum-wing with provisions.

Cylindrus

A fine job of shopping! I got just what I wanted,
And it'll be a fine luncheon I serve up to these luncheoneers.
But look! There's Menaechmus! Damn, my back's already sore![44]   275
The guests are strolling outside the door and I haven't even unpacked the groceries.
I'd better go up and speak with them.
Menaechmus! Hi!

Menaechmus II

Good afternoon, whoever you are.

Cylindrus

Whoever I am? You know who I am, don't you?

---

43 For the pun on Epidamnus as the land of the financially damned, see n. 16 above.

44 I.e., in anticipation of a beating for being late.

Menaechmus II

I sure as hell don't.

Cylindrus

Where are the other guests? 280

Menaechmus II

Guests? What other guests?

Cylindrus

Your parasite—

Menaechmus II

My parasite? (*to Messenio*) This guy is absolutely nuts!

Messenio

Didn't I tell you the place is crawling with con-artists?

****

Menaechmus II

Which parasite of mine do you mean, young man? 285

Cylindrus

Peniculus, your sponge.[45]

Messenio

Look: I've got one of those right here in the bag.

Cylindrus

Menaechmus, you're a bit early for the luncheon.

I just got back with the groceries.

Menaechmus II

Answer me this, young man:

What are pigs going for here? The unblemished ones for sacrifice,[46] that is.

Cylindrus

Two drachmas each.[47]

Menaechmus II

Here's two drachmas. 290

Go get yourself cured. It's on me.

Whoever you are, I have no doubt you're utterly mad,

Seeing that you're bothering a complete stranger like me.

Cylindrus

I'm Cylindrus! You know my name, don't you?

Menaechmus II

I don't care if you're Cylinder or Coreander—I just want you to get lost! 295

I don't know you, and I don't want to know you!

Cylindrus

Is your name Menaechmus?

---

45 Cf. n. 20 above.

46 Pigs were sacrificed in the ancient world to expiate insanity believed to have been brought on by a deity.

47 For the value of two drachmas, see Appendix II p. 337.

Menaechmus II
                    So far as I know.
You're talking sense now, at least when you call me by that name.
But where do you know me from?

Cylindrus
                         Where do I know you from?
I believe you have a girlfriend, none other than my owner Erotium here?   300

Menaechmus II
I damn well don't have a girlfriend and I have no idea who you are!

Cylindrus
You don't know who I am?
Have you forgotten who serves your drinks here?

Menaechmus II
Damn! If only I had something to knock his brains out with!
So *you* serve *me* drinks here—when I've never laid eyes on this place   305
Or set foot here before today?

Cylindrus
                         Yep. You denying it?

Menaechmus II
Damn right I am!

Cylindrus
                    And I suppose you don't live in that house there?

Menaechmus II
Nope! And the gods can curse whoever does!

Cylindrus (*aside*)
He's cursing himself! Sheer insanity!
Listen to me, Menaechmus.

Menaechmus II
                         What?

Cylindrus
                         If you don't mind my advice: 310
You should take that two drachmas you offered me a while back
And get that pig you were talking about for yourself.
You clearly are not in your right mind, Menaechmus,
Seeing as you're now calling down curses upon yourself.   314-5

Menaechmus II
My god, you're tedious and annoying!

Cylindrus (*aside*)
Oh, that's just his way, always joking with me!
He's an absolute card when his wife isn't around.
But hey, now what do you say?
Is this enough food here for the three of you or should I get some more?   320
There's you, the parasite and the lady—

Menaechmus II

Ladies?
Parasites? What are you talking about?

Messenio

Just what's gotten into you,
To make you bother him like this?

Cylindrus

I've got no business with you:
I don't even know you! I'm talking to someone I actually know.

Messenio

I do know for certain that you're completely insane.   325

Cylindrus

I'll see everything's cooked to perfection. It won't be long,
So don't go too far off from the house here.
Want anything else?

Menaechmus II

No—except for you to go straight to hell!

Cylindrus

And you should just go ... straight in and take your place at the table
While these victuals wend their way to Vulcan's violence.[48]   330
I'll go in and tell Erotium you're out here.
She'll come out and take you inside.

Menaechmus II

Has he finally gone? By god, I now understand
That you were telling the truth about this place!

Messenio

Well, watch your step!
My guess is that one of the local prostitutes lives here,   335
At least judging by what that crazy person who just left said.

Menaechmus II

I wonder how that guy knew my name.

Messenio

No need to wonder about that at all: it's an old hooker's trick.
Every time a ship comes in from abroad,
They station their little slave boys and girls at the harbor,   340
To find out the captain's name and where he's from.
Then they glom right on to him like glue.
Once they get their hooks into him, he's sunk for good.
Right now I say we should proceed with extreme caution:
There's a pirate ship on the prowl in that port right over there.   345

Menaechmus II

That's damn good advice.

---

48 For the god Vulcan (= fire by metonymy), see Appendix I p. 335. Cooks in Plautus often spice things up
    by being grandiloquent, and Cylindrus' language here parodies that of tragedy.

Messenio
>   Oh it's damn good advice
> All right—and you damn well better follow it!

Menaechmus II
> Hush up for a second! The door just creaked.
> Let's see who's coming out here.

Messenio
>   I'll just set this down for now.
> Hey you human ships (*to slaves*)! Watch these now, will you? (*pointing to*
>   *the luggage*)   350

SCENE 7

Erotium enters from her house.
(SONG through 368)

Erotium (*to slaves inside*)
> *Leave the doors open, just as they are. Go back in,*
> *See everything's done that needs to be done.*
> *Deck out the couches, fire up the incense:*
> *Elegance lures and entices a lover's heart.*   354-5
> *Our charm brings them pain—and us gain!*
> *But where is he? The cook said he was out by the door. Oh, he's over there:*
> *My finest and foremost source of income!*
> *As long as his cash keeps pouring in, he reigns supreme in this house!*
> *Now I'll run up and shower him with greetings.*   360
> *My dearest darling! I'm so surprised you're standing outside.*
> *For you my door's wide open:*
> *My house is yours more than your house is yours.*
> *Everything's ready, just as you ordered,*
> *Just as you like it. Once you're inside,*   365
> *   Don't expect a second's delay.*
> *Lunch is served, precisely to order: if you hanker for a feast that's*
> *   Sure to sate, your couch awaits.*

Menaechmus II
> Who's this woman talking to?

Erotium
>   To you of course!

Menaechmus II
>   What dealings
> Have I ever had with you?

Erotium
>   My goodness! You're well aware it's Venus' will   370
> That I adore you beyond all my other lovers. And you certainly deserve it,

Seeing that I flourish because of you and your gifts alone!

Menaechmus II

This woman's obviously either drunk or insane, Messenio!

Calling me by name, speaking on such intimate terms to a stranger!

Messenio

Didn't I tell you that's how they do things here? Leaves are falling now,   375

But stay here another three days and a whole forest will crash on you!

Magnets that strip you of your cash—that's what the hookers are here!

Let me have a word with her. Hey, lady! I'm talking to you.

Erotium

                                                              Yes, what is it?

Messenio

Where do you know this man from?

Erotium

                                      From the same place he's known me

For a long time: Epidamnus.

Messenio

                                      Epidamnus? He's never ever set foot   380

In this place until today.

Erotium

                              Now, now, you're just being silly.

Menaechmus dear, please come on in. You'll like it better in there.

Menaechmus II

Damn! This woman called me by the right name.

I really wonder what's up here.

Messenio

                              She got a whiff of that wallet

You're holding there.

Menaechmus II

                              Yes, you sure were right about that.   385

Here—take it. I'll know soon enough whether it's me or the wallet she wants.

Erotium

Let's go in and have our lunch.

Menaechmus II

                              Thanks, but no thanks.

Erotium

Why'd you tell me to prepare the luncheon a little while ago?

Menaechmus II

I told you to prepare lunch?

Erotium

                              You certainly did. For yourself and your parasite.

Menaechmus II

What parasite, damn it? This woman is clearly nuts!   390

Erotium

Your sponge, Peniculus.

Menaechmus II

What sponge? One to clean my sandals off with?[49]

Erotium

No, obviously the one who was with you

When you brought me the full-length pashmina you stole from your wife.

Menaechmus II

Huh?

I GAVE YOU A PASHMINA THAT I STOLE FROM MY WIFE? Are you nuts?

This woman's a horse—she dreams while standing up straight!   395

Erotium

Do you get your jollies out of mocking me and pretending

What happened didn't?

Menaechmus II

Just what am I pretending didn't happen?

Erotium

That you gave me your wife's pashmina today.

Menaechmus II

Well, I didn't!

And I don't even have a wife and I've never had one!

And since the day I was born, I have never, ever stuck my foot inside your city's

gates!   400

I already ate on my ship and then came here and met you.

Erotium

Oh, dear!

This spells trouble—what ship[50] is it you're talking about?

Menaechmus II

One made of wood,

A veteran of many knocks, bumps, bruises and pounding with a mallet,

One peg after another holding it together, just like Pellio's contraption.[51]

Erotium

Enough with the jokes. Come inside with me now.   405

Menaechmus II

I don't know what man you're looking for, lady, but it isn't me.

---

49 For the pun on Peniculus' name, see n. 20 above.

50 Some scholars take Erotium's consternation as evidence of sexual double entendre in the use of the
    word "ship" (*navis*: cf. Messenio's characterization of Erotium as "a pirate ship on the prowl" in 345)
    here and throughout the entire exchange at 391-405. According to this view, Erotium fears Menaechmus
    has been with another prostitute.

51 Titus Publilius Pellio was an actor-impresario in Roman theater with whom Plautus collaborated.
    The construction references here presumably are to the temporary theater where the play is being
    performed. For Plautine metatheater, see further Introduction pp. 8-9.

Erotium

    Oh, really? Am I not looking for Menaechmus, sired by Moschus,[52]

    Said to have been born at Syracuse in Sicily where

    King Agathocles reigned, and then King Phintia,   409-10

    And third in line was King Liparo, who at his death handed the reigns to Hiero,

    Who now is king?

Menaechmus II

             None of that's incorrect, lady.

Messenio

                           Holy Jupiter!

    You don't suppose she's from Syracuse? How does she know so much about you?

Menaechmus II

    Damn it all, I don't see how I can keep saying no to her!

Messenio

                        Don't do it!   414-15

    Enter that door and you're done for!

Menaechmus II (*aside to Messenio*)

                 Just quiet down now.

    Everything's cool. I'll agree with everything she says in exchange for a warm
      reception.

    Ma'am, I was contradicting you intentionally just now.

    I was afraid this guy here might report back to my wife   419-20

    About the full-length pashmina and the luncheon.

    Let's go inside whenever you'd like.

Erotium

              Are you going to wait for your parasite?

Menaechmus II

    No, I'm not, and I don't give a rat's ass about him. And if he does show up,

    Don't let him in.

Erotium

          Absolutely! That's just fine by me.

    But there is one thing I'd really love you to do for me.

Menaechmus II

                   Anything you like.   425

Erotium

Take the pashmina you gave me earlier to the embroiderer's.

I'd like to make some alterations and have a few things added to it too.

---

52 Erotium is comically pretentious and chronologically confused in her extended identification of
    Menaechmus here as being a Syracusan. Agathocles (d. 289 BCE) in fact ruled Syracuse and Hiero was
    tyrant there 269-215 BCE; Phintia was a tyrant at Agrigentum (Akragas) in Sicily *ca* 280 BCE; Liparo,
    however, is a fictitious name based on the Lipari Islands off the northern coast of Sicily. Syracuse was
    conquered by the Romans in 211 BCE after a prolonged siege, but none of this helps date the play with
    any precision.

Menaechmus II

Damn fine idea! It'll get a whole new look,

And my wife won't realize you're wearing it if she sees you on the street.

Erotium

Okay, then take it with you when you leave.

Menaechmus II

Absolutely.   430

Erotium

Let's go inside. (*exits*)

Menaechmus II

I'll be right in. I want to have a word with my man here first.

Hey, Messenio, come on over here.

Messenio

What's up?

Menaechmus II

An inquiry's what's up.   432-3

Messenio

Why do we need that?

Menaechmus II

Trust me, we need it.

Messenio

Oh, I get it, so you can get poorer. Fool!

Menaechmus II

The booty is all but in the bag! Take all these guys   435

And get to an inn as fast as you can.

And see that you meet me back right here just before sunset.

Messenio

Master, you really don't understand these hookers here—

Menaechmus II

Shut up!

If I do something stupid, I'm the one that pays for it, not you.

And the only person around here who's absolutely stupid is this woman.   440

The way I see it, the booty here is all ours. (*enters Erotium's house*)

Messenio

I'm a goner! Correction, you're gone,

And *we're* goners! A pirate ship's towing off a defenseless skiff.[53]

I'm the stupid one, to even try to steer my master to safety.

He purchased me: I'm the yeoman, he's the captain—not vice-versa.

Follow me (*to slaves*), so I can follow my orders to be back here on time.   445

---

53 For the ship imagery, see n. 50 above.

SCENE 8

Peniculus returns from the forum.

Peniculus

Over the course of the more than thirty years since I was born,
I have never done anything so odious and so atrocious as I did today
When I immersed my poor miserable self into the middle of that public meeting!
While I stood there like a mouthbreather,
Menaechmus must have given me the slip and gone back to his girlfriend.   450
I call upon all the gods to destroy the man who first devised public meetings[54]
To burden people already buried in too much business!
Shouldn't slackers be appointed to attend these meetings,
And slapped with the severest sanctions when they don't show up?

****
****

There's a glut of folks that eat just one meal per day with nothing to do,
And who don't attend dinner parties or extend invitations to them.
Shouldn't *they* be the ones forced to attend meetings and assemblies?
If only this were the rule! I can think of one less lunch I'd have lost!   460
As sure as I'm alive, that lunch wanted to be mine as much as I wanted it!
I'm going in: nothing cheers the soul like the prospect of leftovers.
But what's this? There's Menaechmus coming out wearing a garland.
That means the party's over[55] and I'm just in time … to take him home!
I'll observe from over here before I go up and talk to him.   465

SCENE 9

Menaechmus II enters from Erotium's house.

Menaechmus II (*to Erotium inside*)

Yes, yes, just take it easy! I'll bring this back to you today in due time,
Charmingly embroidered to absolute perfection!
In fact, it'll be in such an altered state, you'll no longer say it's yours!

Peniculus (*aside*)

So the feast's finished, the wine's been imbibed, and the parasite's been ostracized!
And now it's off to the embroiderer's with the pashmina!   470
By Hercules, I'm not the man that I am,
If I don't avenge this injustice with sweet, sweet revenge. Oh, just watch me, you!

Menaechmus II

By the immortal gods! What man ever expected less   473-4
And was granted more from you in a single day?   475
I've dined, wined, scored with a whore, snapped up this lovely pashmina

---

54 In accordance with a rhetorical formula common in ancient literature, Peniculus comically curses the (mythical) inventor (*primus inventor*) of such meetings. Cf. Terence, *Eunuchus* 247 and n. 24 there.

55 Garlands were worn at *symposia* ("drinking parties") that followed dinner.

From its rightful heir, a bequest to be put to rest for good—as cash for me.

Peniculus (*aside*)

I can't quite make out what he's saying from over here? He's full of himself all
    right,

And no doubt talking about how he made out and then made off with my share!

Menaechmus II

She says I stole it from my wife and then gave it to her.   480

I could see right away she was mistaken, so I agreed with her,

And pretended there was some kind of relationship between us.

Whatever the woman said, I nodded right back at her.

Hey, what else can I say?

I've never, ever spent so little to get so much as I did today!   485

Peniculus (*aside*)

That's it! I'm ready and rarin' to stir up a ruckus!

Menaechmus II

Who's that coming my way?

Peniculus

                    You irresponsible airhead!

You utterly foul and worthless person! You disgrace to the human race!

You disgusting cheater! Just what do you have to say for yourself?

What did I ever do to make you want to destroy me?   490

First you sneak away from me at the forum!

Then you devour lunch without me even there to give it a decent burial!

I was just as much its heir as you were! How could you?

Menaechmus II

Young man! We don't even know each other, and you're insulting me.

What possible business could there be between us?   495

Or were you hoping to get some rough treatment in exchange for your rough
    words?

Peniculus

Oh, I'm quite sure you've treated me to more than enough of that already!

Menaechmus II

Tell me, young man: what's your name?

Peniculus

Mocking me on top of everything else? As if you don't know my name!

Menaechmus II

I swear, as far as I can tell, I've never seen you before this very day   500

And I don't know you! This I do know for certain:

The proper thing for you to do, whoever you may be, is to stop bothering me!

Peniculus

Wake up, Menaechmus!

Menaechmus II

                  Damn it, as far as I can tell, I am awake!

Peniculus

Don't you know who I am?

Menaechmus
                    If I did, I wouldn't deny it.
Peniculus
    So you don't recognize your own parasite?
Menaechmus II
                            All I know, young man,   505
    Is that you're obviously not quite right in the head!
Peniculus
    Just answer me this: did you steal your wife's pashmina
    And give it to Erotium today?
Menaechmus II
    I didn't steal it or give it to Erotium! Damn it,
    I don't even have a wife!
Peniculus
                    You're quite insane.   510-11
    That's the end of that! But didn't I see you coming out of your house
    Wearing that full-length pashmina?
Menaechmus II
                    Screw you!
    Do you think everybody likes to be on the receiving end[56] just because you do?
    You swear you saw me wearing a pashmina?   515
Peniculus
    I sure as hell do!
Menaechmus II
                    Why don't you just go right where you belong?
    Or go get yourself cured, you hopeless nutcase!
Peniculus
    That's it! I swear, no one will ever talk me out of divulging
    Every last detail that's happened here to your wife,
    And every last insult of yours is coming right back at you!   520
    Oh, you'll pay, and pay dearly for eating that lunch—*my* lunch! (*exits*)
Menaechmus II
    Just what is going on here? No sooner do I glance at someone
    And they mock me! But wait! The door creaked.

SCENE 10

Erotium's maidservant enters with a bracelet.

Maid
    Menaechmus, Erotium would just love it if you took this bracelet to the jeweler's
    While you're having the pashmina worked on.   525
    Have him remodel the whole thing to look new again.

---

56 Transvestitism was commonly taken as an indication of a preference for passive homoerotic sex in the
    Roman world. Cf. n. 30 above.

Oh, and have him add an ounce of gold right here.

Menaechmus II

Tell her I'm glad to take care of it and anything else she'd like me to.
Really, anything she'd like to give me is fine.

Maid

You recognize it, don't you?

Menaechmus II

No, but I recognize it's gold.   530

Maid

It's the same one you said some time back
You stole right out of your wife's jewelry box.

Menaechmus II

Good god, I did no such thing!

Maid

Oh, please! You remember, don't you?
Well then, give it back if you really don't remember.

Menaechmus II

Wait, wait!
Oh, now I remember! Of course! That's the one I gave her all right.   535
And where are those amulets I gave her at the same time?

Maid

You never gave her any of those.

Menaechmus II

You're right. It was just this one item.

Maid

So you'll take care of it?

Menaechmus II

Yes, tell her I will. And I guarantee
The pashmina and the bracelet will be brought back to her at exactly the same
    time.[57]   539-40

Maid

And Menaechmus, do be a dear and get me some earrings—
Pendants, made of four drachmas[58] worth of gold.
I'd be *so happy* to see you the next time you came to visit our house.

Menaechmus II

No problem. Give me the gold and I'll pay for the labor.

Maid

Why don't you put up the gold yourself and I'll pay you back later.   545

Menaechmus II

No, I'd rather you did—and I'll return it to you doubled, so to speak.

---

57 I.e., never.

58 A substantial sum for earrings (cf. n. 38 above).

Maid

    I haven't got it.

Menaechmus II

            Well, when you do, be sure to hand it over.

Maid

    Anything else? (*starts to exit*)

Menaechmus II

            Just tell her I'm on top of it all …

If by that you mean my getting top market value for all this stuff!

She's gone inside, right? Okay, the door's closed.   550

The gods don't just love me—they're aiding and abetting me here!

But now's not the time for delay!

Here's my chance to blow right on out of this whore-haven.

Hop to it, Menaechmus! Forward march! Double time!

I'll just toss this garland off to the left,   555

So anyone following me will think I went that way.

I'm outta here, and off to see if I can find that slave of mine

To tell him all about these gifts the gods have bestowed on me.

SCENE 11

Peniculus and Menaechmus I's wife enter from her house.

Matrona[59]

So I'm supposed to put up with the kind of marriage

In which my husband steals everything there is in the house   560

And gives it to his girlfriend?

Peniculus

            Quiet down, now. I promise you,

Just follow me over this way and you'll catch him red-handed.

He was drunk, wearing a garland, and was carrying the pashmina

That he took from your house today. And he's on his way to the embroiderer's.

Hey, there's the garland! See, I'm telling the truth.   565

Now if you want to track him down, he must have gone this way.

But damn it all, there he is! Coming back right on cue.

Matrona

And he doesn't have the pashmina! How should I deal with him now?

Peniculus

Oh I vote for your usual treatment: give him absolute hell!

Let's slip on over here and draw a bead on our prey.   570

---

59 Menaechmus' wife is never named, but is just given the generic Latin name *matrona* ("married woman," "woman of the household").

SCENE 12

Menaechmus I returns from the forum.
(SONG through 603)

Menaechmus I

We have a terribly tedious tradition,
And the higher you're up in this singularly silly system of patronage,[60]
The harsher your service is to it!
We all want to have a pack of clients,
But does anyone care if they're decent or not?   575
No, it's net worth, not moral value
      That's the talk of the town!
An honest but poor man's considered worthless;
A rich and evil fellow's considered a fine catch.
And it's the clients who have no respect for justice and the law   580
      That create the most headaches:
They've never taken a loan they didn't later deny. They're litigious,
      Greedy, grasping frauds
Who owe absolutely everything they have to extortion and perjury.
      That's the mindset!   584a
When their day in court comes, it's just as trying for us patrons   585
Who must speak up for these felons and all their malfeasance,
Whether before a jury, a judge or a magistrate.[61]
Take my day. My colossal headache came in the form of a certain client
Who retained me and detained me from doing what I wanted to do.
I pled his case before the aediles, defending his flagrant and infinite offenses.   590
I offered twisted terms with impermeable provisions.
I said exactly what needed to be said,
      No less, no more, for there to be a settlement. And my client? Demands a trial!
And has the world ever seen anyone so guilty, so clearly caught in the act?
There were three top-notch witnesses for each of his crimes!   595
      May the gods damn that man
      Who's ruined my day of play!   596
      And they may as well damn me too
      For ever setting foot in the forum!   597
      Yes, my day of play's been wasted!
      A tasty luncheon made to order,   598
      A tastier mistress left in waiting ...

---

60 In his thoroughly Romanized song, Menaechmus refers to the fundamental patron-client relationship
    around which the Roman social hierarchy was constructed. In exchange for a few formal duties and
    their votes, patrons offered clients legal and financial assistance. For Romanization and its effects in
    Plautus, see Introduction pp. 3. 9.

61 A reference to thoroughly Roman (cf. n. 60 above) legal procedure, i.e., criminal cases held before the
    popular assembly, or civil cases heard before an arbitrator or magistrates such as the *aediles* (cf. line
    590), who also sponsored the religious festivals at which plays were performed.

The minute I was finished   599
I high-tailed it right on out of the forum.
She's angry, no doubt about that,   600
But I'll beat that rap with the pashmina—
Yes, the one that I stole from my wife and gave to Erotium today!   601

Peniculus (*to Matrona*)
Did you get that?

Matrona (*to Peniculus*)
         I got it all right—I'm married to a bum.

Peniculus (*to Matrona*)
                                        Heard enough?

Matrona (*to Peniculus*)
More than enough!

Menaechmus I
    If I had any brains, I'd go in and join the bash.

Peniculus
                   Stay here. We'll have a different sort of bash.

Matrona
    Damn it, you'll pay for that crime—with interest!

Peniculus
                                   That's it! Keep it coming!

Matrona
    Did you really think you could get away with this disgraceful behavior?   605

Menaechmus I
    What's the problem, dear?

Matrona
                   You're asking me?

Menaechmus I
                              Should I be asking *him*?

Matrona
    Get your sleazy hands off me!

Peniculus
                   Yes, keep it coming!

Menaechmus I
                              Why are you so grumpy?

Matrona
    I think you know why.

Peniculus
                   He knows why. The scumbag is just faking.

Menaechmus I
    What's the matter?

Matrona
             The pashmina—

Menaechmus I

Pashmina?

Matrona

—a certain someone—

Peniculus

Why so afraid?

Menaechmus I

I'm not afraid of anything!

Peniculus

There's one thing you seem all wrapped up in fear about.   610
And you really shouldn't have finished off that feast without me. Keep on him!

Menaechmus I

Quiet, you!

Peniculus

Damn it, I'm not going to be quiet! Look, he's giving me signals!

Menaechmus I

Damn it, I never blinked, winked or even nodded at you!

Peniculus

The audacity! To deny doing what we can obviously see you doing!

Menaechmus I

I swear by Jupiter and all the gods, wife—if that's good enough for you—   615
That I never nodded at him!

Peniculus

Right, right, I'm sure she believes you. Back to the matter, though.

Menaechmus I

Back to what matter?

Peniculus

The matter of the pashmina—bringing it back from the embroiderer's.

Menaechmus I

What pashmina is that?

Peniculus

I might as well quit, seeing as she's forgotten what she's here for.

Matrona

Oh my! I am a poor wretched woman!

Menaechmus I

Why so sad? Tell me why:
Is one of the slaves acting up? Some of the women or the men talking back
   to you?
                                                                      620
Just tell me. They won't get away with it!

Matrona

You're full of crap!

Menaechmus I

You're terribly grouchy, and I don't like that at all.

Matrona

You're full of crap!

Menaechmus I

You must be mad at someone of the slaves.

Matrona

You're full of crap!

Menaechmus I

Certainly you're not mad at me?

Matrona

Crap—free, at last!

Menaechmus I

But I haven't done anything wrong!

Matrona

You're full of crap again!   625

Menaechmus I

My dear wife! Why are you so upset?

Peniculus

So slick! Look at him stroke her.

Menaechmus I (*to Peniculus*)

Stop bothering me! Was I talking to you?

Matrona

Let go of me!

Peniculus

Keep it coming! Go right ahead and finish off a feast without me,

And then grab a garland, get drunk, and mock me right here in front of the house!

Menaechmus I

By god, I haven't had any lunch or even set foot inside here today!   630

Peniculus

You're denying it?

Menaechmus I

I sure as hell do deny it!

Peniculus

What audacity!

Didn't I just see you standing here in front of the house with a garland of flowers?

You denied knowing me, said I was off in the head

And that you had just arrived here.

Menaechmus I

I'm only returning home just now after we split up a while back.   635

Peniculus

I know what you're up to. Didn't think I'd have my revenge, did you?

Well, I sure as hell told your wife everything!

Menaechmus I

What'd you tell her?

Peniculus

Oh, I don't know—

Ask her yourself.

Menaechmus I

        Well, what was it? What exactly did he tell you?
C'mon! Why aren't you talking? Just tell me what he said.

Matrona

                          You're asking me
As if you didn't know!

Menaechmus I

        I wouldn't be asking if I knew.

Peniculus

                What a horrible human being!   640
The faker! You can't keep it hidden from her: she knows absolutely everything.
I damn well spelled out all the details!

Menaechmus I

           What details would that be?

Matrona

                    You are shameless!
Since you won't fess up on your own, stand over here and pay close attention.
Here's what he told me that made me so angry:
A pashmina was stolen from me at home.

Menaechmus I

          A pashmina was stolen from me at home?   645

Peniculus

See how this bag of crap is trying to trick you? Stolen from *her, not you*!
If it had actually been stolen from you, it wouldn't be safe and sound.

Menaechmus I (*to Peniculus*)

I've got nothing to do with you. But now what are you saying?

Matrona

                A pashmina has disappeared.

Menaechmus I

Who took it?

Matrona

      Certainly, the person who took it is the one to answer that!

Menaechmus I

What's his name?

Matrona

      He goes by Menaechmus.

Menaechmus I

          Damn! That's an awful thing to do!   650
Just who is this Menaechmus?

Matrona

      You.

Menaechmus I

      Me?

Matrona

Yes, you.

Menaechmus I

Who says so?

Matrona

I say so.

Peniculus

And so do I. And you brought it to your girlfriend Erotium here.

Menaechmus I

I did?

Matrona

That's exactly what you did—yes, you!

Peniculus

Should we get an owl

To say "YOU, YOU" over and over again to you? We're tired of it.

Menaechmus I

I swear by Jupiter and all the gods, wife (if that's good enough for you):   655

I did not give it to her!

Peniculus

No, damn it! Swear that we're not lying!

Menaechmus I

I didn't exactly give it to her … Er, I just loaned it to her.

Matrona

Good lord! I certainly don't loan out your cloak or your tunic to anyone!

It's proper for a woman to loan out women's clothing, a man men's.

Now how about bringing that pashmina right back home?   660

Menaechmus I

I'll see it gets back.

Matrona

You will if you know what's good for you:

You won't step foot in this house again unless you've got that pashmina.

I'm going home.

Peniculus

So what do I get for my efforts here?

Matrona

You'll get your payback when something's stolen form your home. (*goes inside*)

Peniculus

Damn, that means never, seeing as I've got nothing to steal.   665

May the gods curse you both, wife along with husband!

I'm off to the forum, seeing as I've obviously had a falling out with this family.

Menaechmus I (*left alone on stage*)

My wife may actually suppose that she's punishing me by shutting me out,

As if there wasn't a better place where I'll be let right in.

Don't like me now? I can handle that. Erotium here likes me just fine.   670

She won't close her door on me. She and her house will be all open arms.

I'll go beg her to return the pashmina I just gave her.

I'll buy her another better one. Hey, is anyone watching the door here?

Somebody open up and tell Erotium to come out here.

SCENE 13

Erotium comes out of her house.

Erotium

Who's looking for me?

Menaechmus I

Someone who loves you more than he loves himself.   675

Erotium

Menaechmus, dear! Don't stand out there in front of the house. Come in.

Menaechmus I

Wait.

Do you know why I'm here?

Erotium

Yes, to have a good time with me.

Menaechmus I

No, no! It's about that pashmina that I gave you a while ago!

Please give it back to me. My wife knows about everything, down to every last
  detail.

I'll buy you one twice as expensive, whatever one you want.   680

Erotium

But I just gave it to you to take to the embroiderer's,

Along with the bracelet to be taken to the jeweler's for remodeling.

Menaechmus I

You gave me a pashmina and a bracelet? I think you'll find that never happened!

I'm only returning for the first time now since I gave you the pashmina

And went off to the forum. I haven't seen you since then.

Erotium

Oh, I see what you're up to.   685

I handed over the item and now you're going to cheat me out of it.

Menaechmus I

No, no, not at all! I'm not trying to cheat you out of it! Really, it's like I told you:

My wife's found out.

Erotium

Well, I didn't even ask you for it in the first place.

You brought *it* to *me* on your own. You told me it was a present for me

And now you're asking for it back. Fine. Take it, keep it, wear it as you please,   690

Or let your wife wear it! You can lock it away in a vault for all I care.

And make no mistake about it: you'll never step foot into this house again!

After all I've done for you, you treat me with such contempt!

Unless you come with lots of cash, your days of having fun with me are over.

From now on, find somebody else to make fun of. 695
Menaechmus I
Damn, now she really is angry! Hey now, I'm talking to you!
Wait, come back! Stop, please! Won't you please come back—for me?
She's gone off and shut herself in. Could anyone possibly be left more left-out
than me?
So my word's as worthless at my whore's as it is at my house!
I'll go consult my friends about what I should do. 700

SCENE 14

Menaechmus II enters from the wing leading to the harbor with the pashmina.
Menaechmus II
How stupid was I when I handed over both my wallet
And my money to Messenio a while ago?
He must have sunk into a sleazy dive somewhere.
Matrona *(enters from her house)*
I'll go see if my husband's coming back anytime soon.
Oh, look, there he is! And he's got the pashmina. Oh, what a relief! 705
Menaechmus II
I wonder where Messenio's wandering about right now?
Matrona
I'll go up to him and give him just the welcome he deserves.
Aren't you even ashamed to show your face to me,
You shameless excuse of a human being? And wearing that pashmina?
Menaechmus II
                                                    Huh?
What's your problem, woman?
Matrona
                    You shameless pig! 710
How dare you so much as mumble one single word to me!
Menaechmus II
Why shouldn't I dare speak to you? What in the world have I done that's so heinous?
Matrona
You're shameless enough to ask? You're a disgrace to the human race!
Menaechmus II
Woman, do you happen to know why the Greeks of old
Called Hecuba[62] a bitch?
Matrona
                    I most certainly do not! 715
Menaechmus II
It's because she behaved exactly as you are now.

---

62 The wife of Priam, king of Troy. In the wake of the tragic fall of Troy, Hecuba is said to have become so
bitter that she was transformed into a dog.

She kept piling curse after curse on anyone she ran into.
Not surprisingly, she began to be known as "the bitch."

Matrona

I will not put up with your outrageous conduct anymore!
I'd sooner spend the rest of my life as a divorcee[63]   720
Than tolerate your disgusting and disgraceful deeds!

Menaechmus II

And why should I care whether or not you tolerate your marriage
Or if you're planning to divorce? Or is it the local custom here
To blather on about your personal business to every stranger who comes to town?

Matrona

Blather on? Why! I absolutely will not tolerate this anymore!   725
I won't stand for your behavior! I'd rather be a divorcee.

Menaechmus II

Oh hell, for all I care you can be a divorcee
Up until the very end of Jupiter's reign.[64]

Matrona

Have you no shame? Just a while ago you denied stealing the pashmina!
And now you're dangling it right before my eyes!   730

Menaechmus II

Good god, woman! You are a bitch *and* a witch!
You actually have the audacity to claim this was stolen from you
When another woman gave it to me to have some alterations done?

Matrona

My goodness, that just does it! Now I'm going to send for my father
So I can tell him about every despicable deed you've done to me.   735
Deceo! (*calling to the house*) Go find my father and have him come back here
To my house together with you. Tell him it's an emergency.
Soon he'll know all about your outrageous behavior!

Menaechmus II

                                        Are you nuts?
What outrageous behavior?

Matrona

                            Your stealing the pashmina and the jewelry
From the house—from your very own wife—and then giving it to your
        girlfriend!   740
Now how's that for blathering on truthfully?

Menaechmus II

Damn it, woman! If you know of a potion
Potent enough to neutralize your nastiness, please have it prescribed now!
I have no idea who you think I am!

---

63 Cf. n. 17 above.
64 I.e., forever.

I'm as familiar with you as I am with my old pal Porthaon.[65]   745

Matrona

Go ahead and mock me. You won't dare do the same to my father.
He's on his way here. Why don't you take a look?
Recognize him?

Menaechmus II

Yes, just as I'd recognize my old buddy Calchas.[66]
I must have met him on that same day I first set eyes on you.

Matrona

You deny knowing me? And knowing my father?   750

Menaechmus II

Hell, I'd say the same thing if you brought out your grandfather!

Matrona

Oh, the way you behave! Same old same old!

SCENE 15

Matrona's father enters from the wing leading to the forum.
(SONG through 774)

Senex[67]

As my old age allows and need be,
I'll plant a foot forward and plod forth as fast as I can.
It isn't easy for me—make no mistake about it.   755
I lost my nimbleness long, long ago.
Old age's buried me, I've got a burden for a body, my strength's a distant memory.
The rougher old age is, the rawer the deal for a sickly person:
It brings in its wake a mountain of miseries.
I could name every last one of them, but that'd take too long.   760
The thing that's weighing heaviest on my mind right now
  Is what trouble there could possibly be
  To make my daughter send for me so suddenly.
I've not a clue of what it is she wants   763a
    Or why she's summoned me.
Still, I can pretty well guess what's up: 764a
Some dispute with her husband's arisen.   765
That's the way it is with women who are armed with a dowry.[68]
They're out of control. Their goal? Enslaving their husbands!
Which is not to say the husbands are never at fault:
A wife's endurance has its rightful limits.

---

65 An obscure mythical king mentioned here by Menaechmus II precisely because of his obscurity.

66 The mythical soothsayer who accompanied the Greeks to Troy.

67 Menaechmus I's father-in-law is never named, and is simply given the generic name "Old Man" (*senex* in Latin).

68 For the dowered wife, see n. 17 above.

For sure, a daughter never summons her father   770
Unless there's grounds for a serious dispute.
Whatever it is, I'll soon find out. Ah, there she is—
In front of the house, and her husband too. He looks grim!
    It's just as I thought.
I'll go meet her and have a word with her.

Matrona

                                     Good afternoon, father.   775

Senex

Yes, that's my hope. Now that I'm here, how are you? Everything okay?
But why so glum? And why's he looking so mad over there?
The two of you have had some sort of scrap, haven't you?
Just tell me who's to blame. And keep it brief—no long stories!

Matrona

You'll be relieved to know I've done absolutely nothing wrong, father.   780
But I cannot live here, there's no way I can put up with it anymore!
So take me away from here!

Senex

                      What's the problem?

Matrona

                               I'm being mocked, father.

Senex

By who?

Matrona

          By my husband. The man you had me married to!

Senex

So you're quarreling again! Now how many times have I told the both of you
NOT to come to me with your bitching?   785

Matrona

But how can I not come to you about this, father?

Senex

                          You're asking me that?

Matrona

Yes, if you don't mind?

Senex

                  How many times have I told you to pamper your husband, 787-8
And not monitor what he's doing, where's he going, and what he's up to?

Matrona

But he's having sex with the hooker living right next door!

Senex

Makes sense to me.[69]   790

And thanks to your surveillance, I guarantee you he'll be having even more of it.

Matrona

And he drinks there!

Senex

Do you think he'll stop drinking there

Or anywhere else he wants to because of you? Damn it, now you're way out of line!

You might as well order him to refuse dinner invitations,

Or not invite a guest into his own home! What do you want your husband to be? 795

Your slave? Oh, and while you're at it, sit him down among the maids,

And give him all the tools he needs to card wool.[70]

Matrona

Well, it seems I only brought you here to plead my husband's case, not mine!

You're supposed to be on my side, but here you are taking his!

Senex

If he's done wrong,

I'll chew him out all right—and even more so than I did you.   800

But as it is, you're very well stocked with jewelry and clothes, maids,

And household supplies. How about taking a healthier attitude about things?[71]

Matrona

But he swipes my jewelry and my pashminas right out of the house,

Robs me blind, and carries the loot to his prostitutes on the sly!

Senex

Hmm, bad stuff, if that's what he's doing. If not, it's your bad   805

For accusing an innocent man.

Matrona

Father, at this very moment he's got a pashmina of mine,

And he's bringing back a bracelet that I found out he'd taken to her.

Senex

I'll find out what happened from him myself. I'll go over and speak with him.

Tell me now, Menaechmus: what's your side of the story here? I'm all ears.

Why so glum? And why's she looking so mad over there?   810

Menaechmus II

Whoever you are, whatever your name is, old man,

As mighty Jupiter and all the gods are my witnesses—

Senex

Witnesses of what possible thing?

---

69 The old man's tolerance of his son-in-law's extramarital dalliance with a prostitute is in keeping with
    traditional Roman mores (cf. Introduction p. 20). Note how Senex only takes an interest in Menaechmus
    I's behavior when Matrona reveals (805ff.) that he has given expensive household property to Erotium.

70 Woolworking is the most traditional form of women's work in the ancient world.

71 The old man's attitude closely mirrors that of Menaechmus I (cf. 120-22).

Menaechmus II

That I've done nothing wrong to that woman
Who's accused me of stealing this pashmina from her house!

Matrona

Perjurer!

Menaechmus II

If I ever have so much as stepped foot within her house once,   815-6
May I become the most forsaken of all the godforsaken men in the world!

Senex

Are you nuts? You'd deny you ever set foot in the very house
In which you live? Are you completely insane?

Menaechmus II

You think I live in that house there, old man?   820

Senex

You claim otherwise?

Menaechmus II

I do in fact, damn it!

Senex

Then, damn it, you do so untruly,
Unless you moved away from there last night. Come over here, daughter.
Answer me now: have you moved away from here?

Matrona

Where to? Why?

Senex

Don't ask me!

Matrona

Don't you get it? He's just fooling around with you.

Senex

Enough fooling around, Menaechmus. Now concentrate on the matter at hand.   825

Menaechmus II

What business do the two of us have? I don't know who you are or where you're
    from.
I've nothing to do with you or that woman who's been a complete nuisance to me!

Matrona

Just look at the color of his eyes! He's so pale
About his forehead and temples! And his eyes are flashing!   829-30

Menaechmus II (*aside*)

That gives me an idea. Since they've already declared me insane,
Why not just go with the flow and scare them away?

Matrona

His face is all twisted and his mouth's hanging open! What should I do, father?

Senex

Come over here, daughter, as far away from him as you can get!

Menaechmus II

Yowweee, Bacchus![72] To what wood are you calling me to the hunt? 835
I'm hearin' you, Bromius,[73] but I can't leave this place right now,
Seeing as I'm guarded by a rabid bitch on the left,
And in back of me there's a perjurious Monkeyman[74]
That has ruined the life of an innocent citizen many times.

Senex

Damn you!

Menaechmus II

Look! Apollo's oracle[75] commands me 840
To cauterize her eyes with blazing flambeaus.

Matrona

I'm done for, father! He's threatening to cauterize my eyes!

Menaechmus II *(aside)*

Well, I'll be! Do these crazy people really think I'm nuts?

Senex

Oh, daughter!

Matrona

Yes? What should we do?

Senex

How's about I go fetch some slaves?
I'll bring them here to carry him off and tie him down at home 845
Before he causes any more trouble.

Menaechmus II *(aside)*

Now I'm stuck.
If I don't come up with some plan, they're sure to carry me off to their house.
Apollo, you forbid my fists to flee in any direction away from her face,
Unless she leaves my sight and goes straight to the center of hell!
Your will is my command.

Senex

Run home, as fast as you can 850
Before he pummels you!

---

72 For the god Bacchus, see Appendix I p. 335. Menaechmus here feigns the inspired madness of Bacchus' cult followers. The Roman authorities were highly suspicious of the cult, and eventually banned it as a threat to the general public order in 186 BCE. Cf. Introduction p. 2.

73 Bromius = "The Thunderer," one of the cult titles of Bacchus (cf. n. 72 above).

74 The "Monkeymen" (*Cercopes*) were a race of mischievous dwarves who tried to trick Zeus/Jupiter and were turned into monkeys and banished to "Monkey Island" (Cercopia or Pithecusae), i.e, modern Ischia in the Bay of Naples.

75 For the god Apollo, see Appendix I p. 335. In paratragic fashion, Menaechmus II pretends to have been enjoined by the oracle of Apollo to kill Matrona and Senex (cf., e.g., Apollo's command to Orestes to kill his mother Clytemnestra and her lover Aegisthus, best known from the 5th century BCE Greek tragedian Aeschylus' *Oresteia* trilogy).

Matrona
>   I'm running! Please watch him, father!

Don't let him get away! For a woman to have to hear such things! (*exits*)

Menaechmus II (*aside*)

  Nice work in disposing of that piece of work! And now for this human garbage,

  This whiskery, toddling Tithonus,[76] the famous Bitchfather—

  Apollo, thou sayest: "pulverize his bones, limbs and joints   855

  With the stick he carries."[77]

Senex
>   Come any closer to me

Or touch me and you will be very, very sorry!

Menaechmus II

  I do thy bidding, Apollo. I'll grab a double-edged axe and slice off

  This old man's guts right down to the bone.

Senex

  This calls for some caution.   860

  The way he's threatening me, I'd better look out for my safety!

Menaechmus II

  More commands, Apollo? "Take a span of horses, untamed, vicious.

  Mount your chariot and pave the path beneath you

  With this elderly, toothless, and smelly lion."

  Now I mount my chariot. I've got the reins. The whip is in my hand.   865

  Stir now, my steeds! Let the din of your hoof-beats be known by swift surge!

  Let the swerve of your feet be mighty fleet![78]

Senex

  You're coming after me with yoked horses?

Menaechmus II
>   Ah, once again, Apollo?

  "Attack him and slaughter him right in his tracks!"

  But who is this who takes hold of my hair and hurls me from my chariot?   870

  How dare he alter Apollo's edict and command!

Senex

  Holy Hercules, such a severe and acute attack!

  Almighty gods! Struck by madness so swiftly!

  And just a short time ago he was perfectly sound.

  I'll go get a doctor as fast as I can!   875

---

76 Aurora (= Greek Eos), the goddess of dawn, became the lover of Tithonus, a young Trojan prince. She ensured his immortality, but forgot to obtain eternal youth for him and he consequently shriveled up with age.

77 Old men in Roman comedy by convention have a walking stick; cf. Introduction p. 6-7.

78 Mock-tragic language. Cf. n. 75 above.

SCENE 16

Menaechmus II, left alone on stage, addresses the audience.

Menaechmus II

Tell me, are those two who forced a perfectly sane person like me
To go nuts finally out of sight?
And shouldn't I go straight to the ship while it's safe?
I've one favor to ask you all: if the old man returns   879-80
Don't point out my getaway route to him!

SCENE 17

Matrona's father returns with a doctor in tow.

Senex

My poor aching ass and sore eyes!
Sitting, watching, waiting for that damn doctor to finish his rounds!
Finally, the big bore just barely got away from his patients.
He said he had to set a broken leg for Asclepius, [79]   885
And then an arm for Apollo. So I'm starting to wonder
Whether I've brought back a doctor or a statue-repairman.
Look at how he walks! Can you get it out of ant-gear?

SCENE 18

Doctor enters.

Doctor

Now, what's that you say he has? Out with it, old man!
Case of Goblinitis? Ceresmania? [80] Give me the scoop.   890
Does he have a history of narcolepsy? Angioedema?

Senex

That's why *you*'re here—to make a diagnosis
And then cure him.

Doctor

            And that I shall do. Cured as ham.
Simple enough, you've got my absolute word on that.

Senex

Now my main concern is that he gets the best possible care.   895

Doctor

No need to worry: I'll sigh deeply at his bedside six-hundred times a day.
That's proof that I'm concerned he gets the best possible care.

Senex

Oh, there he is right now. Let's observe his behavior.

---

79 Asclepius, as Apollo, is a god of medicine and healing.

80 The goddess Ceres (see Appendix I p. 335) is associated with the onset of madness.

SCENE 19

Menaechmus I enters from the wing leading to the forum.

Menaechmus I

Damn it all, what a screwed-up and just plain screwy day this has been for me!

Thanks to that parasite, everything I thought I had privatized has been publicized!

My own personal Ulysses[81] has painted me in disgrace and I'm afraid!   901

The trouble he's stirred up for his patron!

So long as I'm still breathing, I swear I'll send his life into a tailspin!

Did I say *his* life? Silly me, I meant to say *my* life,

Seeing as he subsists on my food at my expense! But I can cut off his support
    system.   905

And my girlfriend here! No real surprise she subscribes to the Hooker's Code of
    Ethics!

I ask her for the pashmina so I can give it back to my wife,

And she says she's already handed it over to me. Damn! My life really is a pain!

Senex (*to Doctor*)

Hear what he said?

Doctor (*to Senex*)

Yes, he says he's in pain.

Senex (*to Doctor*)

Go on up to him.

Doctor

Hello, Menaechmus. Oh my, you shouldn't expose your arm like that.[82]   910

Don't you know how deleterious that is for someone in your condition?

Menaechmus I

Screw you!

Doctor

Feel anything?

Menaechmus I

Yes, of course I feel something!

Doctor

His case couldn't be cured with a whole acre of Hellebore![83]

Tell me now, Menaechmus.

Menaechmus I

Tell you what?

---

81 I.e., Peniculus. Homer's Odysseus (= Ulysses) is an admirable warrior and hero, but he is also
    a trickster, and in post-Homeric literature he experiences a general devaluation of character. In
    Greek drama, his capacity for deception and intrigue is often portrayed negatively (as in Sophocles'
    Philoktetes), and it is in this pejorative light that Menaechmus I here labels Peniculus his "Ulysses."
    Elsewhere in Plautus, the figure of Odysseus more positively embodies the clever slave's comic heroism
    (cf. *Pseudolus* 1063-64 and *Bacchides* 925-78).

82 He presumably rolls up his sleeve to make a threatening gesture here.

83 A poisonous plant (*elleborum*) commonly used for medicinal purposes in the ancient world (esp. to cure
    insanity).

Doctor

I'll ask the questions here.

Do you drink white or red wine?

Menaechmus I

Oh, go to hell!   915

Doctor

Oh, heavens, now he's starting to rave!

Menaechmus I

Why not interrogate me

About the color of bread I'm in the habit of eating? Crimson? Purple? Yellow?
Do I eat birds with scales? Fish with wings?

Senex

Oh, my!

Listen to his crazy talk! Get him a dose of something!   919-20
Hurry, before the madness seizes control of him!

Doctor

Hold on, I have some more questions for him.

Senex

Your blather's what's killing him.

Doctor

Tell me, do your eyes ever become crustaceous?

Menaechmus I

You scumbag! What do you think I am, a lobster?

Doctor

Tell me this: have you ever noticed your intestines rumbling?   925

Menaechmus I

When I'm full, there's no rumbling. There's lots of rumbling when I'm empty.

Doctor

Geeze, that doesn't sound like crazy talk to me!
Do you sleep straight through the night? Do you fall asleep right away?

Menaechmus I

I sleep perfectly, if all my bills are paid.   929-30
May Jupiter and all the gods blast you, Mr. Inquisitor!   931-3

Doctor

Now he's starting to rave. Judging by what he says, you'd better watch out.

Senex

Compared with the way he was talking before he sounds like Nestor[84] now.   935
A little while ago he was calling his wife a rabid bitch.

Menaechmus I

I was?

---

84 Legendary Mycenean king of Pylos on the Peloponnesus of Greece, known (from Homer) for his
    extreme old age and, despite his garrulousness, wisdom gained through experience.

Senex

        Yes, you raved like a nut.

Menaechmus I

                I did?

Senex

                        You certainly did,

And you said you'd flatten me with a four-horse chariot.

I witnessed it all myself and can prove you did it.   939-40

Menaechmus I

And I can prove you stole the sacred crown from Jupiter's head,[85]

And that you were locked up in prison for this,

And after they released you, you were put in stocks and beaten with birch rods.

Then you killed your father and sold your mother into slavery.

There, my abuse is a match for yours—still doubt that I'm sane?   945

Senex

Good god, Doctor! Please hurry up and do whatever you're going to do!

Can't you see he's insane?

Doctor

                I think the best thing to do

Is to have him transferred to my house.

Senex

                    You really think so?

Doctor

                            Absolutely!

That way I can treat him just the way I want to.

Senex

                      As you wish.

Doctor

I'll have you on liquid hellebore for twenty days or so.   950

Menaechmus I

I'll hang you up and poke you with spikes for thirty days.

Doctor

Go get some men to take him to my house.

Senex

                  How many do you need?

To be a match for his madness? Four, at least.

Senex

They'll be here soon. Watch him, won't you Doctor?

Doctor

                    No, I'm going home

To make all the necessary preparations. You have your slaves   955

Bring him to my house.

---

85 I.e., from a statue in the god's temple, an extremely heinous crime.

Senex

I'll see he's there soon.

Doctor

I'm off.

Senex

Goodbye.

Menaechmus I

My father-in-law's gone, the doctor's gone, and I'm alone.
By Jupiter, what's making these men declare that I'm insane?
I've never been sick for a single day in my entire life,
I'm not insane, and I don't pick fights or even start quarrels!   960
I'm sane, and I know and talk with other people who are sane.
Or maybe the ones claiming I'm insane are really the insane ones themselves?
So what do I do now? I'd like to go home, but my wife won't let me in.
And no one will let me in over there. What a mess! I never should have left the house.
Guess I'll stay here. I'll be let in home by nighttime … I think.   965

SCENE 20

Messenio enters from the wing leading to the harbor.
(SONG through 988)

Messenio

This is the trademark of a good slave: his eyes are fixed
On his master's affairs (watching, gauging, arranging them
So that when Master's away, his orders still hold sway)
  And then some, just as if he were there.
A slave with horse-sense respects his back more than his craw,   970
  His shanks more than his belly.
    And he must always be mindful of what masters
Mete out to wicked and worthless slaves:
    Whips, chains
  Millstones,⁸⁶ fatigue, famine, piercing frost—   975
    These are the wages of slacking!
This is just the sort of trouble I take pains to escape: ergo, I'll be good, not bad this time.
I can stand a tongue-lashing, but my back just can't hack that type of treatment.
I like my bread ground, but I'd rather not be part of that grind!
  That's why I follow Master's orders calmly and carefully,   980
    That's what works best for me.
Others can do as they think is best for them; I'll be as I ought to be.
That's my rule: to be blameless and always at Master's beck and call.
The best slaves are afraid of their masters even when they've nothing to fear.   983a
Those who don't fear them, become afraid too late—after a well-deserved beating!   983b

---

86 Disobedient slaves might be consigned to mills, where they were forced to perform tedious and
    debilitating labor as a form of punishment.

Since their masters mete out punishment, that kind of fear doesn't really work for them.
My service is dedicated to the principle of doing what's best for my back.   985
I checked the luggage and the slaves into the inn, just as Master ordered,
And I've come here to meet him. I'll knock on the door to tell him I'm present,
And guide my Master out safely from this forest of evil.
But I'm afraid I've come too late—and the battle's over.

SCENE 21

Senex returns with slaves.
(SONG, 995 through 1009)

Senex

By heaven and earth, you need to follow all my orders, to the letter,   990
Both the ones I've given you and the ones I'm giving you now.
Now pick that man up and carry him off to the doctor's house,
Unless you don't give a rat's ass for your shanks and flanks!
And don't pay the least bit of attention to any of his threats.
Don't stand there! You should have already picked him up.   995
I'm off to the Doctor's. I'll meet you there when you arrive. (exits)

Menaechmus I

Now I'm dead!

What's going on? Why in the world are these men rushing at me?
What is it you want from me? Why are you all surrounding me?
What's the big rush? Hey, where are you taking me? I'm done for!
Help, citizens of Epidamnus, help me! Hey, let go of me!   1000

Messenio *(aside)*

By the almighty gods! I can hardly believe my own eyes!
Some strangers are carrying off Master as if he's a criminal!

Menaechmus I

Doesn't anyone have the backbone to help?

Messenio

I'm all backbone, Master!

People of Epidamnus, what a disgraceful and wrongful act!
In a civilized city, on a street in broad daylight, my master,   1005
A freeborn tourist, openly mugged!
Let go of him!

Menaechmus I

Whoever you are, please help me!
Don't let them commit this heinous crime against me!

Messenio

No, I won't! You can count on me to assist and rescue you!
I'll die first myself before I allow you to die!   1010
Rip out the eye of that guy who has you by the shoulder, Master!
I'll plow down these guys and plant my fists all over their faces!
By Hercules, you'll be so sorry you carried him off! Let go!

Menaechmus I

I've got this one's eye.

Messenio

      Keep a hold on to it 'til the socket shows!

You delinquents, marauders, and thieves!

Slave

      We're dead!   1015

Please help!

Messenio

    Let go then!

Menaechmus I

     How dare you put your hands on me!

(*to Messenio*) Give 'em a makover with your fists!

Messenio

        Get lost—and go to hell!

And here's one for you—you win the prize for last one to leave!

Well, I really worked over their faces and had my way with them!

Damn, I sure did come to the rescue just in time, Master!   1020

Menaechmus I

May the gods always bless you, young man, whoever you may be!

If it hadn't been for you, I wouldn't have lived to see another sunset.

Messenio

Then certainly the right thing to do, Master, would be to free me.

Menaechmus I

Me? Free you?

Messenio

    Yes, because I saved your life, Master!

Menaechmus I

        What?

I'm afraid you're mistaken, young man.

Messenio

     How so?

Menaechmus I

       By almighty Jupiter,   1025

I'm not your master!

Messenio

    Oh, be quiet!

Menaechmus I

      I'm telling you the truth:

No slave of mine has ever done what you just did for me!

Messenio

All right then, if I'm not your property, you can just let me go free.

Menaechmus I

By god, as far as I'm concerned, you can go wherever you like and be free.[87]

Messenio

That's on your authority?

Menaechmus I

      Damn straight. Yes, on whatever authority I have over you. 1030

Messenio

Hail, my patron and protector! "I rejoice that you are free now, Messenio!"[88]
Holy Hercules, I trust in you! But, my patron, I do have one request:
Please continue to give me orders just as when I was your slave.
I'd like to live at your house, and when you leave for home I'll go with you.[89]

Menaechmus I (*aside*)

That's not gonna happen.

Messenio

      I'm going to the inn to get our luggage and cash.   1035
Your wallet and our travel funds are all sealed in the trunk.
I'll get those and bring them back to you here.

Menaechmus I

      Yes, bring them—and fast!

Messenio

I'll have every last penny of it back for you. Wait right here.

Menaechmus I

Miracle of miracles! The dumb luck I've stumbled onto today!
I've got some folks saying I'm not who I am and then shutting me outside.   1040
And then there's this guy who said he's my slave and saved my life.
I emancipated him and now he went off to get me some money,
Which he says he'll bring back to me in a wallet!
If he actually brings it, I'll tell him to go off and be free wherever he wants,
So he doesn't try to get it back when he comes to his senses again.   1045
It's so strange that my father-in-law and that doctor said I'm insane.
This all seems to me to be exactly like a dream.
I know my girlfriend's mad at me, but I'm going into her house
To see if I can get that pashmina back from her and take it home.

---

87 Menaechmus I here flippantly utters the formula for manumission (*liber esto*), which was accomplished by this mere speech act.

88 Messenio acts as a witness to his own manumission (cf. n. 87 above) and exclaims accordingly.

89 Emancipated Roman slaves not uncommonly remained with their former masters and continued to provide them with some services. Messenio here aspires to serve Menaechmus I in a patron-client relationship (cf. n. 60 above) after his liberation.

SCENE 22

Menaechmus II and Messenio enter from the harbor wing.

Menaechmus II

You have the brazen audacity to claim you met up with me today 1050
Since the time I told you to come back here and meet me?

Messenio

But I just
Grabbed you away from those four men who had picked you up
And were carrying you away in front of this house here! You were calling on
The whole universe for help, and in spite of them all, I ran up and rescued you by
    force!
And then you emancipated me because I'd saved your life. 1055
After I told you I'd go get the luggage and the money,
You must have run on ahead to meet me and deny everything you'd done.

Menaechmus II

I told you that you could go free?

Messenio

Definitely!

Menaechmus II

Yeah? Well I most definitely
Would sooner become a slave myself than emancipate you!

SCENE 23

Menaechmus I enters from Erotium's house.

Menaechmus I (*shouting back toward the house*)

Damn! You can swear by your own eyeballs for all I care! 1060
I never took the pashmina and the bracelet away today! Bitches!

Messenio (*to Menaechmus II*)

By the immortal gods! I can't believe my eyes!

Menaechmus II (*to Messenio*)

What do you see?

Messenio (*to Menaechmus II*)

Your mirror image!

Menaechmus II (*to Messenio*)

How's that?

Messenio (*to Menaechmus II*)

Your very image! You couldn't be more like you!

Menaechmus II (*to Messenio*)

Damn right! There's quite a likeness when I carefully examine my own appearance.

Menaechmus I

Young man! Hey you, yes you, my rescuer there, whoever you are! 1065

Messenio

Yes, young man. I don't mean to bother you, but could you please tell me your name?

Menaechmus I

No bother at all. I owe you for all you did for me, that's for sure!
My name is Menaechmus.

Menaechmus II

But that's my name!

Menaechmus I

I'm from Sicily-Syracuse.

Menaechmus II

That's my city and country too!

Menaechmus I

No! What are you saying?

Menaechmus II

The simple truth.

Messenio

Of course I know him—he's my master, 1070
And I'm his slave, though I thought I was *his* slave.
When I thought he was you, I'm afraid I made some trouble for him.
Please forgive me, if I accidentally said anything stupid to you.

Menaechmus II

Now you're babbling nonsense. Don't you remember
Coming ashore here with me today?

Messenio

Yes, you're absolutely right.   1075
You are my master. *You* need to find another slave. Goodbye to you,
And HELLO, Menaechmus!

Menaechmus I

But I'm Menaechmus!

Menaechmus II

What sort of blather is this?
You're Menaechmus?

Menaechmus I

But um, um, I'm the son of Moschus!

Menaechmus II

You're the son of my father?

Menaechmus I

Ah, beg your pardon—that's son of *my own* father!
I've no interest in hijacking yours or claiming squatter's rights on him! 1080

Messenio (*aside*)

Immortal gods! Am I looking at what I've looked forward to for so long?
Unless I'm mistaken, these two are identical twins! And according to their stories,
They were fathered by the same father and hail from the same country!
I'll call my master aside. Menaechmus!

Menaechmus I & II

What do you need?

Messenio
                                        Not both of you,
    Just the one who came here with me onboard the ship.

Menaechmus I
                                        That's not me.   1085

Menaechmus II
    No, it's me.

Messenio
        I want you to come over here then.

Menaechmus II
                                        Okay—what's up?

Messenio
    That guy's either an imposter or he's your twin brother.
    I've never seen two men that looked more alike!
    A drop of water or milk couldn't look
    More like another drop of water or milk than you two do!   1090
    And then there's the identical father and country. We'd better go up and question him.

Menaechmus II
    By Hercules, thanks so much for the good advice!
    Please keep on it! You'll be a free man
    If you prove he's my brother.

Messenio
        That's my hope!

Menaechmus I
        And mine too!

Messenio
    Tell me: I believe you said that your name is Menaechmus?   1095

Menaechmus I
    I sure did.

Messenio
      This man's also named Menaechmus.
    You said that you were born in Sicily. He was born there too.
    You said that your father was Moschus. That's his father too.
    Now help me out here—and help yourselves out as well.

Menaechmus I
    You deserve to be granted whatever you want from me.   1100
    Though I'm a free man, I'll serve you as if you owned me.

Messenio
    I hope to prove that you two are identical twin brothers,
    Born at the very same time to the very same mother and father.

Menaechmus I
    Absolutely astounding! If only what you hope to prove proves to be true!

Messenio
    Back to the proof: I need each of you to carefully answer my questions.   1105

Menaechmus I
Ask away—I'm all answers, and won't hide anything I know.
Messenio
Is your name Menaechmus?
Menaechmus I
                                Yes.
Messenio
                                        And it's yours too?
Menaechmus II
Yes.
Messenio
    And you say your father's Moschus?
Menaechmus I
                                            Absolutely!
Menaechmus II
                                                    He's mine too.
Messenio
Are you from Syracuse?
Menaechmus I
                        I sure am.
Messenio
                                And you?
Menaechmus II
                                        Yes, of course.
Messenio
Great! Everything squares so far. Let's keep at it now.   1110
What's the earliest memory you have of Sicily?
Menaechmus I
I remember going with my father to Tarentum on a business trip,
And then wandering off from him into the crowd and being grabbed—
Menaechmus II
Almighty Jupiter! Save me now!
Messenio
                        No need to shout. Quiet down now!
How old were you when your father took you to Tarentum?   1115
Menaechmus I
Seven. My baby teeth were just starting to fall out.
And I haven't seen my father again since then.
Messenio
                                        Tell me this now:
How many sons did your father have?
Menaechmus I
                                Two, to the best of my recollection.

Messenio
Which of you was older?
Menaechmus II
                        We were exactly the same age.
Messenio
How that possible?
Menaechmus I
              The two of us were twins.
Menaechmus II
                              The gods do love me!   1120
Messenio
Keep interrupting me and we won't get anywhere.
Menaechmus II
                              My lips are sealed.
Messenio
                                        Tell me:
Did you both have the same name?
Menaechmus I
                        No, no! I was called Menaechmus then,
Just as I am now. He was called Sosicles back then.
Menaechmus II
That's proof enough for me! I've got to give you a hug!
My twin brother, hello! I'm Sosicles!   1125
Menaechmus I
How did you come to get the name Menaechmus?
Menaechmus II
After we got news that you and father were dead,
Our grandfather changed my name to yours—Menaechmus!
Menaechmus I
Yes, that's probably just what happened. But tell me this.
Menaechmus II
                                        Yes?   1129-30
Menaechmus I
What was our mother's name?
Menaechmus II
                        Teuximarcha.
Menaechmus I
                              That's right.
To see you, to greet you after so many years!
Menaechmus II
And you too, brother! After so many toils and travails,
And endless searching, to have found you at last—pure joy!
Messenio
So this is why that hooker knew your name!   1135

She invited you to lunch because she thought you were him.

Menaechmus I

Yes, I had actually requested a luncheon to be prepared here for me today,
Without my wife's knowledge. I stole her pashmina a while back
And gave it to Erotium.

Menaechmus II

Is this the pashmina in question, brother?

Menaechmus I

That's it!

How'd you come by it?

Menaechmus II

The hooker dragged me off to lunch   1140
And said that I had given it to her. The luncheon was lavish!
Lots of wine, sex with the whore for dessert, and I left with the pashmina and a
    gold bracelet!

Menaechmus I

I'm so glad for any fun you had on my account!
She obviously thought it was me when she invited you in.   1144-5

Messenio

You don't have a problem with my being freed, do you? You did order it.

Menaechmus I

His request is quite fair and reasonable, brother. Do it for my sake.

Menaechmus II

You hereby are a free man.[90]

Menaechmus I

I'm so happy that you're free, Messenio.

Messenio

I sure could use some sort of send-off, so my freedom lasts this time.   1149-50

Menaechmus II

Seeing that things have turned out the way we wanted them to,
Let's return to our native land.

Menaechmus I

Yes, brother, let's do that.

I'm going to hold an auction and sell off everything I have. In the meantime,
Let's go inside my house, brother.

Menaechmus II

Sure.

Messenio

I have a favor to ask.

Menaechmus I

What's that?

---

90 Cf. n. 87 above.

Messenio

> I'd like to be the auctioneer.[91]

Menaechmus I

> > Job's yours.   1155

Messenio

So should I announce the auction now?

Menaechmus I

> > Sure, for a week from today.

Messenio

Announcing an auction at Menaechmus' a week from today!
Everything must go: slaves, furniture, house, country estate.
Each and every thing goes to the highest bidder, all sales cash only!
Even his wife's on the block, if any blockhead wants her!   1160
I doubt she'll account for more than a penny's worth of the proceeds.
As for right now, spectators: give us a loud round of applause. And good luck to
   you all!

---

91 A potentially profitable, but low-status occupation commonly assumed by Roman freedmen.

Rudens

("The Rope")

CHARACTERS WITH SPEAKING PARTS

ARCTURUS, *the bright star who delivers the prologue*
SCEPARNIO, *a slave of Daemones*
PLESIDIPPUS, *a young citizen of Athens currently living in, or visiting Cyrene*
DAEMONES, *an old Athenian citizen currently exiled in Cyrene*
PALAESTRA, *Daemones' lost daughter, currently enslaved by Labrax*
AMPELISCA, *Palaestra's fellow slave*
PTOLEMOCRATIA, *a priestess of Venus' temple near Cyrene*
PISCATORES, *unnamed group of fishermen of Cyrene*
TRACHALIO, *a slave of Plesidippus*
LABRAX, *a pimp of Cyrene*
CHARMIDES, *a Sicilian guest-friend of Labrax*
SPARAX & TURBALIO, *slave-enforcers of Daemones*
GRIPUS, *a fisherman and slave of Daemones*

SCENE

North Africa near Cyrene: the action takes place on the seashore near the farm and cottage of Daemones; there is also a temple of Venus nearby. One side wing of the stage leads to the city and harbor of Cyrene, while the other leads to the seashore.

PROLOGUE

Arcturus[1]
In the great state of the gods I'm a fellow citizen[2] of the One[3]

---

1 Arcturus ("Warder of the Bear" in Greek) is the brightest star in the constellation Boötes (Arcturus may also refer to the constellation itself), and the third brightest star in the night sky. An ancient audience was much more in tune with the sky than we generally are, and would have been familiar with Arcturus' celestial movements. Arcturus is especially important to sailors, and figured prominently in ancient nautical cults.

2 Several plays of Plautus feature, as here, prologues delivered by omniscient deities, a practice found already in Greek New Comedy.

3 For the god Jupiter, see Appendix I p. 335. Jupiter was the most powerful of the Olympian gods, and his status thus sometimes lends an air of monotheism to ancient polytheistic religion.

Who controls all the peoples, lands, and seas of the world.
I am what you see: a bright and brilliant light,
A star who makes his entrance right on cue,
Both here *and* in the sky.[4] Acturus is my name.   5
At night I shine bright on high among the gods,
But by day I promenade in the company of men,
Not unlike the other stars that slide down toward Earth.
Jupiter, the commanding officer of both men and gods,
Assigns each of us a post somewhere across the world,   10
To study the acts of men, their character and conviction,
Their honesty, and how they handle the wealth they're granted.
We take down the names of those who suborn perjury,
File frivolous lawsuits or deny their debts before a judge,
And we report them directly to Jupiter.   15
Thus, he knows who's up to no good here each and every day.
When the wicked aspire to perjure their way to victory here,
Or win false claims in a court of law,
He retries the case that's already been tried,[5]
And his punishment's far more costly than their ill-gotten gains!   20
He keeps a separate list of the names of the good,
Though this doesn't keep the scumbags from supposing
That they can win Jupiter over with gifts and sacrifices.
They're just wasting both their energy and expense,
Seeing that he accepts no offerings from perjurers.   25
A righteous person who prays to the gods
Is more likely to be liked by them than a scumbag.
My advice for all of you fine folks
Who lead your lives with conviction and honor
Is to continue on that course—you'll be glad for it later.   30
Now as to why I've come here: let me divulge the plot.
First of all, it was Diphilus'[6] preference to name this city here Cyrene.[7]
On that farm over there Daemones lives in a cottage right along the seashore.
He's an old man who came here in exile from Athens,
But not because he's wicked in any way.   35
No, he wasn't exiled because of any wrongdoing on his part:
He tripped himself up while trying to help others,

---

4   The prologist plays on his dual identity as a (celestial) star and actor. For his "entrances" and "exits,"
    see 70-71 and n. 12 below.

5   There was no regular right of appeal in Roman republican law, and so the retrial of the malefactors here
    fantastically reflects Jupiter's absolute power and omniscience.

6   Popular Greek New Comedy playwright (cf. Introduction pp. 3-4), who provided the source play for this
    and a few other surviving Roman comedies.

7   A Greek colony on the North African coast famous for the export of products derived from the silphium
    plant (cf. 630 and n. 55 below).

And owing to his generosity lost his honestly earned fortune.
And his sweet little baby daughter was also lost,
Seized by pirates and sold to the worst sort of man—a pimp!   40
The pimp has brought her here to Cyrene now that she's grown up.
A certain young man, the old man's fellow Athenian,
Saw her coming home from music-school[8]
And fell in love with her. He goes straight to the pimp
And draws up a contract to buy her for thirty minae,[9]   45
Gives him a down-payment and makes him swear an oath.
The pimp, true to his kind, doesn't give a rat's ass for the pledge
That he solemnly swore to the young man.
The pimp had a houseguest, an old man from Sicily (Agrigentum,[10] to be precise),
Just as sleazy as himself, the type of guy who'd sell out his own country.   50
He bends the pimp's ear about how beautiful the young girl is,
And how fine all his other little ladies are too.
Gradually he starts to talk the pimp into accompanying him back to Sicily,
Seeing as how the place is full of hedonists
And a pimp like him could get very rich there,   55
Fetch the highest possible price for his hookers, etc., etc.
It works. The pimp secretly charters a ship
And loads his entire household into it at night.
He tells the young man who had purchased the girl from him
That he wants to pay a vow to Venus[11]—   60
That's her temple right over there—
And then invites him to lunch back here.
But instead, he immediately boards the ship and sails off with his cargo of hookers.
The young man finds out what happened,
And how the pimp left town. The young man goes to the harbor,   65
But by then their ship had made it far out to sea.
Now when I notice that the young girl is being taken away,
I decide to wreck the pimp and rescue the girl in one fell swoop.
I raised up a storm and stirred up the sea:
I'm Arcturus after all, the most savage of all the stars,   70
Fierce when I rise, fiercer when I fall![12]

---

8   She most likely has been trained to play a small, lyre-like instrument. Prostitutes typically provided
    musical entertainment at both Greek and Roman parties, in addition to sexual services. The fact that
    Palaestra is still in training suggests that she has not yet been prostituted. Cf. n. 38 below.

9   For the value of thirty minae see Appendix II p. 337.

10 Also known as Akragas, a Greek colony on the southern coast of Sicily.

11 For the goddess Venus, see Appendix I p. 335. For her thematic importance in the play, see Introduction
    pp. 17-18.

12 Arcturus rises in September (pre-dawn) and falls in November (after sunset), and so was associated
    with the onset of seasonal storms in the Mediterranean region. Arcturus here describes himself as
    "fiercer when I fall" because November is marked by the most severe tempests.

Right now the pimp and his guest are perched on a rock,
Two castaways, their ship smashed to bits.
The young girl and a similarly young fellow slave-girl,
Terrified as they were, managed to leap down into the ship's lifeboat.   75
The waves are now carrying them away from the rock and toward the shore,
And they're headed for the cottage of the exiled old man.
The storm-winds have blown off the tiles from his roof.
There's one of his slaves coming out from the cottage right now.
You'll also see the young man soon   80
Who bought the girl from the pimp arriving here too.
Farewell and good luck to you all—and the opposite to your enemies![13]

SCENE 1

Sceparnio enters from the cottage of Daemones carrying a shovel.
Sceparnio[14]
Immortal gods! What a storm
Neptune[15] let loose upon us this past night!
The wind unroofed the cottage. Did I say "wind?"   85
Hardly a wind, but it must have been an *Alkmene* of Euripides[16]
That blew every last tile off the roof
And created all new light and windows for us!

SCENE 2

*Plesidippus enters from the wing leading to the city and harbor of Cyrene
with three friends.*
Plesidippus[17] (*to friends*)
I took you away from your own business,

---

13 Plautus' prologues usually end with a flattering valediction such as this to the audience, whose goodwill
is being sought on behalf of the play and the troupe. But as the Romans were often at war during
Plautus' career (see Introduction pp. 1-3), the reference to enemies here does not help to date the play.

14 His name means "carpenter's axe" in Greek, which alludes to one of his typical duties as a rural slave,
i.e., woodcutting.

15 For the god Neptune, see Appendix I p. 335.

16 This suggests that a version of the Athenian tragedian Euripides' (d. 406 BCE) *Alkmene* that featured
a dramatic storm scene had been performed on the Roman stage within recent memory. The surviving
fragments of Euripides' play show that Amphitryon, convinced that his wife Alcmene has committed
adultery (she has in fact been duped into having sex with Zeus (= Roman Jupiter: cf. n. 3 above)
disguised as Amphitryon), chases her to an altar, where he builds a pyre and is about to ignite it when a
violent rainstorm suddenly arises and Zeus appears to reconcile the couple. Plautus presented a comic
version of the Alkmene-Amphitryon myth (i.e., *Amphitryon*) ca 190-185 BCE. For the possible date of
the *Rudens*, see Introduction p. 16. For Plautine metatheater, see pp. 8-9.

17 The *-ippus* suffix of his name (= Greek *hippos*, "horse") indicates that he is an aristocrat. We learn
later (1197-99) that he is an Athenian and a relative of Daemones, but his presence in Cyrene is never
explained.

And it turns out this was all in vain, 90
Since the pimp has slipped away from me at the harbor.
But I didn't want to just hopelessly scrap this project,
And so, my friends, that's why I've kept you even longer.
Now I'd like to take a look around this temple of Venus
Where he said he was going to make a sacrifice. 95

Sceparnio

If I had any sense at all, I'd get right to work on this clay.

Plesidippus

Someone's talking close by here.

Daemones (*entering from his cottage*)

Hey, Sceparnio!

Sceparnio

Who's calling my name?

Daemones

The person who paid for you.

Sceparnio

Why not just come right out and call me your slave, Daemones?

Daemones

We need a lot of clay, so that means lots of digging for you. 100
It's as clear as day I've got to cover up this whole cottage.
As it is, it's got more holes in the roof than a colander.

Plesidippus

Hello, father (*respectfully*)—hello to both of you!

Daemones

Hello.

Sceparnio

Are you a man or a woman—seeing as you call him father?

Plesidippus

I most certainly am a man!

Sceparnio

Then seek your father elsewhere. 105

Daemones

The one little daughter I once had I lost.
I never had a son.

Plesidippus

Surely the gods will give you one!

Sceparnio

And surely they'll give you—whoever you are—one giant load of trouble,
Seeing as you like to bother busy people with your blather.

Plesidippus

Do you live over there?

Sceparnio

Why do you want to know? 110

Casing the place so that you can come back and rob us?
Plesidippus
   It takes a very prosperous[18] and righteous slave
   To spout off like that when his master's present,
   And to be so rude to a free man!
Sceparnio
   It takes a very brash and rash man   115
   To march right up to someone else's house
   To pester folks who don't owe him anything.
Daemones
                              Pipe down, Sceparnio!
   What can I do for you, young man?
Plesidippus
                         You can beat him to a pulp,
   For daring to speak out first when his master's present.
   If it isn't too much trouble, I'd like to ask you   120
   A few questions.
Daemones
                   All right—though I'm quite busy.
Sceparnio
   Why don't you run down to the swamp and cut some reeds
   So we can cover the cottage while the weather's still good?
Daemones
                                        Pipe down!
   Tell me what I can do for you.
Plesidippus
                      Answer me this one thing:
   Have you seen a graying, curly-haired guy around here?   125
   Nasty temperament, dishonest, slick-talking—
Daemones
   Oh, lots of them! My life's been ruined by just that sort of person.
Plesidippus
   I mean here though, at Venus' temple,
   A guy with two young ladies,
   And all prepared to do a sacrifice, either yesterday or today?   130
Daemones
   No, by Hercules,[19] young man! I haven't seen anyone sacrificing over there
   For the past several days, and it's impossible for anyone
   To do so without my knowing it. They always come here
   To ask for water or a light for a fire or containers or a knife or a spit or a pot

18 Roman slaves in fact were allowed to accumulate their own property and money (*peculium*), and were
    in large part motivated to work by the prospect of purchasing their freedom from their masters.
19 For the god Hercules, see Appendix I p. 335.

To boil organs or something else.[20] What can I say?   135
My utensils and my well are more Venus' than my own!
But I've had a reprieve from that for several days now.

Plesidippus
What you've said amounts to a death sentence for me!

Daemones
Heavens! For my part, I'd rather see you safe and sound!

Sceparnio
Hey you! You'd be better off ordering up lunch at home   140
Than hanging around temples for your belly's sake.

Daemones
So am I to assume that you were invited here for lunch
And your host was a no-show?

Plesidippus
                                        Yup.

Sceparnio
It won't do you any harm to go home from here without lunch.
And you'd be better off hunting down Ceres[21] rather than Venus: 145
She's in charge of love, Ceres is in charge of lunch.

Plesidippus
The shameful way this guy mocks me!

Daemones
By the immortal gods, Sceparnio! What do you make
Of those men alongside the shore over there?

Sceparnio
                                        If I had to make a guess,
I'd say they've been invited to a bon-voyage feast.   150

Daemones
Why's that?

Sceparnio
                    Because they took quite a bath last night,[22] it seems.

Daemones
Their ship's been shattered at sea.

Sceparnio
                                        That's for sure!
And the same damn thing happened to our cottage and tiles here on land!

Daemones
                                                                   Ah,
Poor little fellows! Look at those castaways swim!   154-5

---

20 These are items needed to sacrifice (and cook) an animal at the temple.

21 For the goddess Ceres, see Appendix I p. 335.

22 Sceparnio plays on two different senses of "bath," i.e.: (1) a ritual cleansing made as a preliminary
    to a trip, and (2) a disaster—here a literal soaking at sea due to shipwreck. For the motif of water (in
    association with rebirth), see Introduction, pp. 16-17.

Plesidippus
Tell me now—where are these men?
Daemones
Over here to the right.
See them alongside the shore?
Plesidippus
Yes. Follow me (*to friends*).
I can only hope it's that god-forsaken jerk I'm after.
Take care of yourselves. (*exits*)
Sceparnio
We don't need you to tell us to do that.
But Holy Palaemon,[23] comrade of Neptune   160
And close companion of Hercules!
What do I see here?
Daemones
What is it?
Sceparnio
Two young ladies
Sitting together alone in a lifeboat,
Being beaten by the waves. Poor things! Oh, wait a second ... great!
Their boat has been turned away from the rock by a sudden surge!   165
Could a helmsman possibly have done it better?
I don't think I've ever seen such powerful waves as these!
If they can just escape those breakers, they're home free.
Watch out now! Oh, one of them's been cast overboard by a wave!
But it's shallow and she'll make her way out. Excellent!   170
She's got herself up and is coming this way. Safe so far ...   172
Now the other one's jumped ship and is headed toward land.
She's so scared, she's fallen down onto her knees in the water!
Oh, now she's safe, and out of the water and onto the shore!   175
Damn it! She's headed off to the right.
Shoot! She's sure to get lost today.
Daemones
What's that matter to you?
Sceparnio
If she falls off that cliff she's headed for,
She'll make very quick work of her wandering.   179-80
Daemones
If you're planning to dine at their table tonight, Sceparnio,

---

23 An obscure, though apropos mythical reference: driven mad by the goddess Hera (= Roman Juno:
see Appendix I p. 335), Ino threw her son Melicertes into the sea. A dolphin took him safely ashore,
where he was "reborn" and renamed Palaemon. Subsequently, the Isthmian Games at the sanctuary of
Poseidon (= Roman Neptune: see Appendix I p. 335) near Corinth in Greece were established in his
honor. No extant myth connects Palaemon with Hercules.

Do by all means devote your full attention to them.
But if you want to eat at my house, get to work for me now!
Sceparnio
Fair enough.
Daemones
        Follow me this way then.
Sceparnio
              Right behind you.

SCENE 3

Palaestra enters from the wing leading to the sea.
(SONG through 219)

Palaestra[24]
The stories told of human misery pale in comparison   185
  With the bitterness of our actual experience.
Was it really the god's[25] plan to have me cast out
  Onto unknown lands, all afraid and costumed as I am?
  Was it for this life of misery I was born?
  Is this my reward for my personal piety?   190
  If I'd dishonored a parent or the gods,
  Enduring this hardship would be no hardship.
  But since I've struggled and striven to avoid this,
  Your treatment of me is unfair and unwarranted,
Oh, you gods! What lesson will the wicked learn for the future   195
If they see you meting out this sort of reward to the innocent?
  If I knew for sure that I—or my parents—had offended
    You, I'd let go of this self-pity.   197a
But I'm sure my master's wicked crimes are the cause of my torment.
  His ship and everything he owns are lost at sea.
  You're looking at the remains of his fortune: even the girl   200
Who shared the lifeboat with me is lost. Now I'm all alone.
  If only she were safe and sound with me!
  Her presence would lighten my load.
Where can I look now for some hope or some help,
All alone as I am, the landlord of a lonely place?   205
  There's nothing here but rocks and the roar of the sea,
  Not a single person to cross my path,   206a
  Everything I own I'm wearing,

---

24 The *palaestra* is the Greek wrestling school. Sex is often portrayed as a vigorous form of exercise in Latin (a prostitute in Plautus' *Cistellaria* is named Gymnasium), hence the appropriateness of the name for a girl destined for prostitution.

25 When Latin and Greek authors refer simply to (a/the) "god," the most powerful of the gods Jupiter/Zeus is often meant (as here: cf. pp. 18-19 and n. 3 above).

I've no notion of how to find food or shelter.
What hope do I have, what reason to live?
I don't know this place, I've never been here before.   210
If only someone would appear to show me
A road or a path to escape from this place!
But minus a guide, should I go this way or that?
Everywhere I look it's wild, and the land's untilled.
I'm cold and roaming in fear—I'm so overwhelmed by it all!   215
My poor parents! You know nothing of this,
      Nothing of how truly wretched I am!   216a
   There's no doubt I was born a free person, but I was born free in vain.
   How now am I any less a slave than if I had been born one?
I've been of absolutely no good to the parents who brought me into the world.

SCENE 4

Ampelisca enters from the wing leading to the sea.
(SONG through 258)

Ampelisca[26]
What's better, what's more timely for me than severing my body from life?   220
My life's so terrible as it is, and my heart is heavy with deadly fears.
The way things are, I no longer care for life, and all hope for the future is lost.
I've traversed the entire shore and crept through every last cranny,
Using my voice, eyes, and ears to track down my fellow-slave.
There's no trace of her and I can't figure out where to go from here.   225
Nor is there a trace of anyone anywhere to answer my questions:
No desert could be more deserted than this region all about me,
But I'll never stop searching for her as long as she and I are alive!
Palaestra
      Whose voice is that?
      Who's that nearby?   229
Ampelisca
      Who's that speaking nearby? I'm so afraid!   230
Palaestra
      Great goddess Hope,[27]
      Please come to my aid!   231a

---

26 Her name is related to Greek *ampelis*, "young vine-plant," probably to suggest her sexual "ripeness." To a Roman audience, it may also call to mind the Latin verb *amplector* ("to embrace") and the corresponding noun *amplexus*, which are used as euphemisms for sexual intercourse; Ampelisca is treated exclusively as a sexual object by Scepenario in Scene 9. For prostitutes' names in Plautus, cf. n. 24 above and *Truculentus* n. 28.

27 One of many abstractions that were personified in Roman religion; there was a temple dedicated to Hope (*Spes*) in Rome by the 5th century BCE and others followed.

Ampelisca
 Are you here to rescue me from my fears?
Palaestra (*aside*)
 I'm quite certain a woman's voice has grazed my ears.
Ampelisca (*aside*)
 It's a woman! That's a woman's voice I hear!
Palaestra (*aside*)
 Could it possibly be Ampelisca?
Ampelisca (*aside*)
       Is that you, Palaestra? 235
Palaestra (*aside*)
 I'd better call her name so she hears me.
 Ampelisca!
Ampelisca
    Oh who is it?
Palaestra
      It's me—Palaestra!
Ampelisca
 Tell me where you are.
Palaestra
     Well, I'm in a pile of trouble right now.
Ampelisca
 I'm right there beside you, your partner in misery.
 I'd really love to see you!
Palaestra
     Same here! 240
Ampelisca
 Let's follow the sound of our voices. Where are you?
Palaestra
          Right here!
 Keep coming toward me this way.
Ampelisca
      Yes, I'm trying to.
Palaestra
 Give me your hand.
Ampelisca
    Here it is.
Palaestra
     So you really are alive!
Ampelisca
 Yes, and now that it's possible for me to touch you,
 I'm glad to be alive! I can hardly believe 245
 I'm holding you! Please hug me,
 My only hope! How you take me far away from all my troubles!

Palaestra

   You took the words right out of my mouth!
   Now we should get away from here.

Ampelisca

                            But where to?

Palaestra

   Let's follow the shoreline here.

Ampelisca

                            I'll follow wherever you want.   250
   But should we roam about like this in our wet clothing?

Palaestra

   We have to deal with things as they are.
   Oh my, what's this?

Ampelisca

                  What's what?

Palaestra

                            Can't you see it?
   This temple here.

Ampelisca

                  Where?

Palaestra

                  To the right.

Ampelisca

   I do see a place that seems worthy of the gods.   255

Palaestra

   This place is so delightful! There must be people nearby!
   I call upon this god, whoever it may be, to bring some help
   To two wretched and resourceless women in terrible, terrible trouble!

SCENE 5

                  Ptolemocratia enters from the temple.
                     (SONG through 289)

Ptolemocratia

   Who seeks the favor of my patroness?
   The sound of their supplications has roused me from within.   260
   She's a goodly goddess that they seek, forever gracious,
   And always a favorable and kind patronness.

Palaestra

   Good morning, mother. (respectfully)

Ptolemocratia

                       Good morning to you,
      Girls. But where have you come from?
      And why the wet clothes,   265
         And dreary appearance?   265a

Palaestra

>   *We came from over there, not too far from here.*
>   *But we were carried off from a place far, far away.*

Ptolemocratia

>   *Over greenish-blue paths on a wooden steed,*
>   *I presume?[28]*

Palaestra

>   　　　　　*Precisely.*

Ptolemocratia

>   　　　　　　*Then it would have been proper to show up*
>   *Dressed in white and with sacrificial animals.* 270
>   *Pilgrims don't appear at this temple looking like that.*

Palaestra

>   *And just where did you expect two shipwrecked castaways*
>   *To have found sacrificial victims to bring here?*
>   *Helpless and in need, unaware of where we are,*
>   *We fall helplessly at your knees, and beg you* 275
>   *To rescue us and take us in under your roof—*
>   *Please pity two utterly wretched girls*
>   *Without any place to call our own or hope for the future,*
>   *And owning nothing except what you see!*

Ptolemocratia

>   *Get up off your knees and give me your hands.* 280
>   *There's no woman more compassionate than I am.*
>   *But resources are scanty here and our life is simple, girls.*
>   *I can scarcely keep myself alive, and I serve Venus at my own expense.*

Ampelisca

>   　　　*Oh, this is Venus' temple then?*

Ptolemocratia

>   　　　*Yes, and I'm known as the temple's priestess.* 285
>   *But I'll graciously share whatever I have with you*
>   *To the extent that I can.*
>   *Come this way with me.*

Palaestra

>   　　　*Your concern for us, mother,*
>   *Is warm and kind.*

Ptolemacratia

>   　　　*As it should be.* (they go inside the temple)

---

28 I.e., by ship (a parody of the language of early Roman tragedy). Cf. Introduction pp. 8-9.

SCENE 6

A group of fishermen enter from the wing leading to the city and harbor.
Piscatores[29]

    Life is miserable in every conceivable way for poor folks,   290
    Especially those of us without a steady income or any skills:
    Whatever we happen to have at home must always suffice.
    You all can pretty much tell how well to do we are by our get-up:
    Our income and expense money rest solely on these hooks and rods.
    Each day we march from city to seashore to forage for seafood.   295
    Instead of training our bodies in the gym and palaestra,[30]
    We search for sea-urchins, limpets, oysters, shell-fish,
    Mollusks, sea-nettles, mussels, and fluted scallops.
    And then on some nook on the shore we advance on fish armed with just a hook!
    We seek our sustenance from the sea. If no issue issues,   300
    And the catch of the day is nada, we're the ones that slink back home
    Neatly cleaned and salted, and we go straight to bed without dinner.
    The way the sea is surging right now, our situation is hopeless.
    Unless we stumble on to some shell-fish, it's another dinnerless night.
    Let's pay worship to venerable Venus here in the hope she'll grace us today.   305

SCENE 7

Trachalio enters from the city/harbor wing.
Trachalio

    I've taken great pains not to miss my master anywhere.
    When he left the house just now, he said he was off to the harbor,
    And told me to meet him here at the temple of Venus.
    Ah, how lucky! Some men I can question! I'll walk over to them.
    Greetings, ye highwaymen of the sea, Shellfishians, Hookemites, and
        Hungrarians![31]   310
    How's life treating you? How's death beating you?
Piscatores
    In the usual way for the fisherman—via thirst, hunger, and hopelessness.
Trachalio
    Tell me now: while you've been standing here,
    Have you seen a vigorous young man—strapping fellow with a ruddy complexion?
    Had three guys with him, wearing military cloaks and carrying swords?   315

---

29 The men are generically named "Fisherman" (cf. Latin *piscis*, "fish").

30 The *gymnasion* (literally, "the naked place") was not only the training ground for Greek (nude) athletics, but also the primary educational and social center of Greek male culture. The *palaestra*, properly a "wrestling school" (cf. n. 24 above), shared many architectural features with the gymnasium, and the two structures were often conjoined and virtually indistinguishable.

31 Mock-tragic language. See note 28, above.

Piscatores
No one looking like that's come here, as far as we know.
Trachalio
How about
A Silenus-like[32] fellow, bald, pot-bellied guy on the largish side,
With slanty eyebrows and a permanent scowl, a con-man,
The bane of both gods and men, pure evil, a mass of depravity and criminality?
And he would have had two rather charming young ladies with him.   320
Piscatores
Anyone blessed with qualities and a resume like that
Belongs in the executioner's line, not at the shrine of Venus!
Trachalio
But have you seen him?
Piscatores
Absolutely no one's come this way.
Goodbye.
Trachalio
Goodbye. Just as I thought! He's done exactly what I suspected.
That depraved pimp fed Master a line and then skipped town.   325
He's taken the ladies and boarded a ship. I must be a clairvoyant!
That demon-seed even had the audacity to invite Master here to lunch.
What else can I do except wait for Master here?
Meanwhile, if I see that priestess of Venus, I'll ask her if
She knows anything more about this. She'll tell me.   330

SCENE 8

Ampelisca enters carrying a pitcher from the temple of Venus.
Ampelisca (*to the priestess inside*)
Yes, I get it. You want me to go knock on the door of the cottage
Next to Venus' temple and ask for some water.
Trachalio
Whose voice
Hath winged its way to my ears?[33]
Ampelisca
Oh, my! Who's talking? Who's there?
Trachalio
Is that Ampelisca coming out of the temple there?
Ampelisca
Is that Trachalio,
Plesidippus' sidekick that I see?   335

---

32 Sileni—indistinguishable from satyrs in myth—are wild and unrestrained male figures who usually
appear nude (with permanent erections) and are always in search of sex, food, or drink.

33 Paratragic language. See note 28, above.

Trachalio
    It's her!
Ampelisca
            It's him! Hello, Trachalio!
Trachalio
                        Hello, Ampelisca!
    How are you?
Ampelisca
            I'm not bad. My life is horrible, though.
Trachalio
                            Shush! Saying that's bad luck!
Ampelisca
    Any person with sense should speak out the truth.
    But, please tell me: where's your master Plesidippus?
Trachalio
                        Now, really!
    As if he weren't inside there!
Ampelisca
                    No, he's not there, and hasn't been here at all.   340
Trachalio
    He hasn't been?
Ampelisca
            That's the honest truth you're speaking.
Trachalio
                            How unusual for me.
    But when will lunch be ready?
Ampelisca
                Lunch? What lunch?
Trachalio
    You're conducting a sacrifice here, aren't you?
Ampelisca
                        In your dreams maybe.
Trachalio
    Your master Labrax did in fact invite my master Plesidippus
    To lunch here today?
Ampelisca
                Oh, now you're starting to make sense.   345
    Cheating gods and men? Straight out of the Pimps' Manual of Conduct, of course.
Trachalio
    So neither you nor your master is sacrificing here?
Ampelisca
                        You are a clairvoyant!
Trachalio
    Why are you here then?

Ampelisca
>   When we were in the midst of many miseries,
> And overwhelmed by dread and the most dire dangers, deprived of all aid and
>   assistance,
> Venus' priestess here took us in—Palaestra and me, that is.   350

Trachalio
> So Palaestra's here? My master's girlfriend?

Ampelisca
>   She most certainly is.

Trachalio
> That is absolutely delightful news, my dear Ampelisca!
> But I'd really like to know about that danger you were in.

Ampelisca
> Last night our ship was shattered, my dear Trachalio.

Trachalio
> What ship is that? What are you saying?

Ampelisca
>   You haven't heard?   355
> The pimp was planning to secretly take us away from here.
> He put everything he had in his household onto a ship headed for Sicily.
> And all that is lost now.

Trachalio
>   Bless you, Neptune, there's no one smarter than you
> When it comes to throwing the dice!
> Your latest toss was right on target: you pummeled a perjurer!   360
> But where is Labrax the pimp now?

Ampelisca
>   I'm thinking he died of drink—
> Neptune served him up some mighty big mugs last night.

Trachalio
> By Hercules, my guess is every round was bottoms-up!
> I love you Ampelisca! You're so sweet, and all your words drip with honey!
> How is it you and Palaestra were rescued?

Ampelisca
>   I'd be glad to tell you.   365
> We saw that our ship was being driven toward the rocks,
> So the two of us cast aside our fears and leapt down into the lifeboat.
> I quickly untied the rope while the others were paralyzed by fright.
> The storm carried us off to the right and away from them, and so for the whole night
> We were tossed about by the waves and the winds in the most miserable way!   370
> The wind brought us to shore this morning virtually drained of life.

Trachalio

That's just the way Neptune is: always the fussiest inspector![34]
Any shoddy wares he finds are immediately tossed out.

Ampelisca

Damn you! You can just die!

Trachalio

　　　　　　　　　　　Same to you.　　　　　　　　　　　374-5
Didn't I predict the pimp would do exactly what he's done?
I should grow out my hair and become a professional clairvoyant.

Ampelisca

Seeing that you knew this, shouldn't you and your master have stopped him?

Trachalio

What could he have done?

Ampelisca

　　　　　　　　　You're asking what a lover could have done?
He would have watched her day and night and been on constant guard!　　　380
His "concern" for her in this shows just how much he cares for her.

Trachalio

How can you say that?

Ampelisca

　　　　　　　　Isn't it obvious?

Trachalio

　　　　　　　　　　Look, even if a person who goes
To the public baths[35] watches his clothes with the utmost care,
They still get stolen, since he doesn't know which person to watch.
The thief can easily eye his victim, but the victim doesn't know the thief.　　　385
But take me to her.

Ampelisca

　　　　　　　All you have to do is enter Venus' temple here.
She's sitting in there crying.

Trachalio

　　　　　　　I don't like the sound of that.
Why's she crying?

Ampelisca

　　　　　　Let me explain. The real reason she's so upset
Is that the pimp took a small box away from her in which she kept some items
That would allow her to identify her parents.[36]　　　　　　　390

34　The Roman magistrates called *aediles*, in addition to sponsoring public festivals (cf. Introduction p. 5), were in charge of the public markets, where they did in fact have the power to reject shoddy wares. For Romanization in general, see Introduction p. 3.

35　Public baths played a central role in Roman social life, and the theft of clothes there was a perennial problem, as it was also in the Greek gymnasium (cf. n. 24 above). Cf. 527-28 and Introduction p. 17.

36　These are items preserved from Palaestra's childhood that will secure her identity, i.e., the so-called "tokens of identification" stereotypical in recognition scenes of New Comedy.

She's afraid it's lost.
Trachalio
                         Just where was the little box?
Ampelisca
                                        On board the ship.
The pimp kept it locked in his trunk, so she wouldn't have any chance
Of discovering who her parents were.
Trachalio
                         What a sleazy trick!
Willfully keeping someone who should be free enslaved!
Ampelisca
It no doubt went straight down to the bottom of the sea with the ship.   395
And the same is true for all the pimp's gold and silver as well.
Trachalio
I bet someone's already dived in and retrieved it.
Ampelisca
                                        That's why she's so sad.
She assumes these things are lost.
Trachalio
                         All the more reason
For me to go in and console her, and try to relieve her anguish.
Good fortune sometimes happens when it's least expected.   400
Ampelisca
And bad fortune also happens when people most expect it not to.
Trachalio
That's why the best seasoning for sorrow is a level head.
I'm going in. You don't need anything else, do you?
Ampelisca
                         No, go on in.
I still need to go next door and ask for water.
The priestess said they'd hand it right over if I said it was meant for her.   405
I don't think I've ever met such a worthy old lady.
She deserves to be showered with goods by both gods and men.
We were afraid, needy, drenched and nearly-dead castaways;
She took us in with such decency and warmth, generosity and grace,
Just as she would have if we were her very own daughters!   410
And then she tucked up her robe and heated water for our baths.
I mustn't keep her waiting, so I'll get the water she wants.
Anyone here? Is someone going to come out and open the door?

SCENE 9

Sceparnio responds to the knock on the door of Daemones' cottage.

Sceparnio

Who's violating our door like that? Why so pushy?

Ampelisca

It's me.

Sceparnio

       Wow! Here's a nice piece of luck! *Meow*! What a fine-lookin' woman.   415

Ampelisca

Good morning, young man.

Sceparnio

       And a very good morning to you, young lady!

Ampelisca

I'm here to—

Sceparnio

       If you come back this evening, I'll welcome you warmly,

And tend to you like a sick person in bed, but right now the love-doctor is out.

How about it, my glistening little sweetheart?

Ampelisca

       No, no! Way too familiar with

The touching there![37]

Sceparnio

       By the immortal gods! She's like a statue of Venus!   420

What a gleam in her eyes! Oh, and her erotic—

No, no, I meant to say exotically dark skin!

And what tits … not to mention her naturally talented mouth!

Ampelisca

Mind keeping your hands off me? I'm not a dish at a potluck!

Sceparnio

How about being a nice little girl and giving me a nice little feel?   425

Ampelisca

There'll be a time and a place for fooling around later.[38] As for right now,

There's a reason I came and I need a yes or no answer. Now please!

Sceparnio

What do you want?

Ampelisca

       Doesn't what I'm holding here make that quite obvious?

Sceparnio

And doesn't what *I'm* holding here make it quite obvious what *I* want?

---

37 Ampelisca is made all the more vulnerable to Sceparnio's advances here by the fact that she carries the water-urn on her head with both hands.

38 Ampelisca's skill in fending off Sceparnio's advances (cf. 436) suggests that she has some experience as a prostitute. Cf. n. 78 below.

(*obscenely gesturing*)

Ampelisca

Venus' priestess over there told me to ask you for some water.   430

Sceparnio

But I'm Jupiter here.[39] You don't have a prayer of getting a drop unless you beg me.

That well was built with our blood, sweat, and tools.

You'll have to pour it on smooth and thick if you hope for so much as a drop.

Ampelisca

Oh, please! You'd begrudge me what perfect strangers give each other?

Sceparnio

You'd begrudge me what next-door neighbors give each other?   435

Ampelisca

No, no, darling—I'll do everything you want me to.

Sceparnio

Woohoo! Now she's calling me "darling!"

That's the kind of attitude I'll make worth your while: hand me the urn.

Ampelisca

                                                                        Here.

Please hurry back with it.

Sceparnio

                          Wait right here, darlin'. I'll be right back.

Ampelisca

How do I explain my lingering here so long to the priestess?   440

I still shudder miserably when I look upon the sea!

But what's that miserable sight I see down at the shore there?   442-450

It's my master the pimp and his Sicilian guest!

I'd assumed the two of them had suffered a miserable death at sea.

This means there's more trouble brewing for us than we thought.

I'd better run into the temple and tell Palaestra everything,

So that we can take refuge at the altar   455

Before the pimp shows up and grabs us here.

Given what's happening, I don't know what else to do! (*exits*)

SCENE 10

Sceparnio returns with the water.

Sceparnio

I swear by the immortal gods! I never imagined I'd find so much pleasure in water!

What a delight it was to draw this up!

The well seemed to be so much more shallow than it used to—   460

Hardly what you would even call work (knock on wood!).

I am one bad dude to have started up this little romance today!

---

39   There is a pun on ancient gambling terms here: a "Venus" was a good toss of the dice, and the best of
     all throws was "The King" (*basilicus*), here translated by "Jupiter."

Here's your water, my little sweety-cheeks.
Look, here's the proper way to carry it: do it just like me and I'll be a happy man!
Where are you, my little pretty? Please take the water! Where are you?   465
She must really like me—the naughty little girl's playing hide-and-seek!
Hey, where are you? Aren't you going to take the pitcher?
Okay, you're a pretty good player, but seriously now:
Aren't you going to take the pitcher? Where in the hell are you?
Damn! She's nowhere in sight! Making fun of me, are you?   470
Well then, damn it, I'll just leave this pitcher right here in the middle of the road.
But what if someone steals it?
It's the sacred property of Venus, and I'd be in a heap of trouble!
Damn it all! I think this woman's laid a trap for me!
She wants me to get caught with the sacred pitcher.   475
No question about it—if anybody saw me with it,
A judge would be perfectly justified in ordering my execution.
And it's a pitcher of letters, and so it can chant its owner's name![40]
I sure as hell am going to call the priestess out from the temple here
And have her take it. Here goes.   480
Hey, Ptolemocratia! Come out and get your pitcher here!
Some young lady I don't know brought it over to me.
So I've got to carry it in? Some job!
On top of everything else, I've got to make a personal delivery!
   (*goes into the temple*)

SCENE 11

Labrax and (some distance behind him) Charmides enter from the
seashore wing.

Labrax[41]

If you've got a preference for misery and poverty,   485
Just trust your entire being over to Neptune!
Enter into any kind of transaction with him
And you'll be sent home looking like this.
To be sure, Lady Liberty[42] was quite clever
To never consent to set foot on a ship with Hercules.   490
But where's that guest of mine who's ruined my life?
Oh look, there he is.

Charmides

          Damn it, Labrax, what's the rush?

---

40 I.e., its owner's name is inscribed on it.

41 Indicative of his stereotypically pimpish greed and the play's aquatic themes, his name means "ravenous bass" in Greek.

42 "Freedom" (*Libertas*) was one of many personified abstractions worshipped in Roman religion. No account of the story involving her and Hercules alluded to here survives.

There's no way I can keep up with you at that pace.

Labrax

I wish you had been slowly tortured to death in Sicily
Before I ever had a chance to meet you! 495
You are the cause of all this misery of mine!

Charmides

And I wish I'd found a bed in prison to sleep in the day
I let you drag me into your house!
I pray to the immortal gods that all your guests
Be just like you so long as you're alive, pimp! 500

Labrax

Taking you into my house was like inviting Bad Luck[43] herself in.
Whatever possessed me to listen to a scumbag like you,
Or to board a ship and go away from here?
That's where I lost everything I had and then some!

Charmides

Big surprise that your ship was shattered, 505
Seeing as it carried scuzzy cargo and a scuzzbag like you!

Labrax

It's all your slick talk that's sunk me for good!

Charmides

The dinner you served me was more disgusting
Than anything either Thyestes or Tereus ever ate.[44]

Labrax

Oh, no—I'm going to be sick! Please hold my head. 510

Charmides

I sincerely hope you puke up a lung.

Labrax

Oh me oh my! Where are you, Palaestra and Ampelisca?

Charmides

I believe they're providing piscine provisions in the deep.[45]

Labrax

Listening to all your pompous prevarications
Has made me a pauper! It's all your fault! 515

---

43 "Luck" (*Fortuna* or *Fors*) was a personified deity widely worshipped in Rome and throughout Italy,
   though not, as here (comically), in her capacity to bring misfortune as "Bad Luck" (*Mala Fortuna*). The
   personification and deification of abstractions is more a feature of Roman than Greek religion.

44 In Greek myth, Thyestes was fed his sons by his brother Atreus, with whose wife Aerope he had
   committed adultery. Tereus raped Philomela and cut out her tongue to conceal his crime. Philomela
   conveyed the story of her rape to her sister Procne in a narrative tapestry, and the sisters exacted their
   revenge on Tereus by serving him his son Itys for dinner.

45 I.e., they're "fish-food." Charmides waxes poetically here, by mocking the language of tragedy.

Charmides

You really ought to be offering me hearty thanks.

You used to be bland and dry: now you're downright salty.

Labrax

Why don't you just go find a cross and die there?[46]

Charmides

That's precisely what I had in mind for you.

Labrax

Oh poor, poor, pitiful me! Am I not the most wretched man alive?   520

Charmides

No, Labrax, I am—much so by far.

Labrax

How's that?

Charmides

Because I don't deserve any of this. You do—and more.

Labrax

Oh sedge-grass, oh sedge-grass, how glorious is your fate,

To forever sustain the splendor of your aridity.[47]

Charmides

I must be training myself for a skirmish: 525

I'm trembling so much that my own words are flashing before me.[48]

Labrax

Good lord, Neptune, you do operate one cold bathhouse!

I'm still c-c-c-cold after leaving your establishment *with* my clothes.[49]

Charmides

And there isn't even an adjoining café that serves warm drinks.

No, nothing but cold and salty draughts served up there.   530

Labrax

Oh, blessed are the blacksmiths!

See how they sit around the coals, forever toasty.

Charmides

If only I were a d-d-d-duck right now:

No ac-quack-quatic fowl's life is fairer or drier.

Labrax

I should go get a job as Chomper-Man at a festival.[50]   535

---

46 Crucifixion was such an old and established punishment for capitol crimes in Rome that the phrase (*in malam crucem*) translated literally here meant little more than "screw you" or "go to hell" do today.

47 Paratragic language.

48 An obscure joke, owing to the fact that we know little about the training of "skirmishers" (*velites*), i.e., light-armed foot-soldiers in the Roman army.

49 For the (common) joke about the theft of clothes at public baths, see n. 35 above.

50 "Chomper" (*Manducus*) was a stock character of Italian farce (see Introduction p. 4) whose mask featured large, moveable jaws.

Charmides

Why?

Labrax

Because of the cl-cl-click and cl-cl-clatter of my teeth of course!

Charmides

Guess I deserved to get cleaned out like this.

Labrax

Why?

Charmides

Because I was reckless enough to board a ship with you.

Your presence was enough to agitate all the sea depths against me.

Labrax

It was all your idea. You kept telling me   540

That my prostitutes would fetch the highest price there

And that I'd be raking in the riches, blah, blah, blah ...

Charmides

You filthy pig! Did you really expect

To consume the island of Sicily whole hog?

Labrax

Speaking of which: what whale do you think wolfed down my suitcase   545

With all my gold and silver packed into it?

Charmides

No doubt the same one that got my bag

And the wallet full of silver inside it.

Labrax

Oh geeze! All I've got left is this one tunic

And this wretched little cloak! I'm completely done for!   550

Charmides

How about if you and I make a joint venture?

We'd be equal shareholders in nothing.

Labrax

                                        If only

My ladies were salvaged! Then I'd have some hope.

As it is, if I run into that young Plesidippus

Who gave me the down payment for Palaestra,   555

I'll be in all sorts of trouble!

Charmides

Stop whining, dumbass! As long as that tongue of yours

Wiggles in your mouth, you can wangle your way out of anything.

SCENE 12

Sceparnio enters from the temple of Venus.

Sceparnio

What's going on? There are two young ladies here

In Venus' temple crying and clinging to her statue,   560

And terrified of god knows what!

They claim they were shipwrecked last night and cast out from the sea today.

Labrax

Good lord, young man! Tell me where these women are.

Sceparnio

Right here in Venus' temple.

Labrax

                              How many are there?

Sceparnio

                                        Same total as you and I.

Labrax

Surely they're mine?

Sceparnio

                    I surely can't tell you.

Labrax

                              How do they look?

Sceparnio

                                        Pretty sweet.   565

I'd do either one of them if I were pretty drunk.

Labrax

Surely they're just girls?

Sceparnio

                    You sure are a pest! Go look for yourself!

Labrax

Those have to be my ladies in there, Charmides my friend!

Charmides

Whether they are or they aren't, I just want Jupiter to blast you.

Labrax

I'm breaking into the temple right now! (*exits*)

Charmides

                              And how about into hell too while you're at it?   570

Kind stranger, how about giving me a place to sleep?

Sceparnio

Sleep wherever you like. No one's stopping you. It's public land.

Charmides

But look at how wet my clothes are.

Can't you take me inside and give me some dry clothes to wear while mine dry out?

I'll pay you back for the favor somehow.   575

Sceparnio

    See that mat made out of sedge-grass? It's the only dry thing I've got

    And it's yours if you want it. I use it for a raincoat.

    Just give me your clothes and I'll see they're dried out.[51]

Charmides

                                                          I don't think so.

    Will you only be satisfied after I've been cleaned out on land as well as on sea?

Sceparnio

    Cleaned out or out-slickered? I couldn't care less.   580

    I wouldn't trust you an ounce without some collateral.

    Sweat away or die of a chill, get sick or get well—

    I don't care to entertain foreigners in my home. End of conversation.

Charmides

    So you're leaving me here? What a slave-driver, whoever he is!

    No compassion whatsoever! But why stand here all pitiful and wet?   585

    I'm going into that temple of Venus over there to sleep off my hangover.

    I drank a whole lot more than I'd planned or even wanted to last night.

    Neptune kept pouring sea-water into us as if we were cheap Greek wines[52]

    And he wanted to turn our guts inside out with a salty laxative.

    Bottom line: if he kept toasting us like that just a little longer,   590

    We'd have passed out for good right there. We made it home—half-dead.

    Now I'll go see what my drinking buddy the pimp is up to inside.

SCENE 13

Daemones enters from his cottage.

Daemones

    The gods sure do put on a strange show for us mortals![53]   593-4

    They don't even let us rest when we're sleeping.   595

    Just last night, for instance, I had a dream

    That was so astounding, so very strange!

    A monkey appeared to me to be struggling

    To climb up to a nest of swallows,

    But was unable to snatch them.   600

    So then the monkey comes to me

    To ask me if I'd loan him a ladder.

    I respond to the monkey as follows:

---

51 Minus mass production and the equivalent of modern sweatshops, everyday clothes had relatively much higher value in antiquity than they do today, and thus were a common target of thieves. Cf. n. 35 above.

52 Cheap Greek wine was mixed with salt-water in antiquity to preserve it (cf. the use of resin in *retsina* in Greece still today). The reference to poor quality Greek wine here is obviously from a Roman perspective of cultural superiority.

53 The description of the dream that follows here obviously reflects Labrax's pursuit of (esp.) Palaestra (cf. 771-73) and Ampelisca.

****   603a

That swallows are descended from Philomela and Procne,[54]
And so I plead with it not to harm my compatriots.   605
At that point the monkey got nasty and aggressive,
And threatened to do me some serious harm:
It was planning to sue me. In the dream I get really angry
And somehow manage to take hold of the monkey's midsection,
And then I chain up the utterly disgusting beast.   610
Though I've pondered it all day,
I haven't reached a conclusion about what all this dream means.
But what's that racket coming from
Venus' temple next door? How strange!

SCENE 14

Trachalio enters from the temple of Venus.

Trachalio
Fellow citizens of Cyrene, I call upon you and your sense of justice!   615
Farmers and neighbors who inhabit these rustic regions,
Bring aid where it's needed and extreme vengeance where villainy invites it!
Protect the innocent from the all-too-potent power of the unrighteous,
And don't allow them to become known and notorious for being victims!
Make an example of brazenness and requite decency!   620
Show that we live by the rule of law, not oppression by force!
If you are nearby and hear my call,
I again call upon your sense of justice! Run straight here to Venus' temple!
Bring aid to those who seek sanctuary in the ancient way,
And have entrusted their lives to Venus and the priestess of Venus!   625
Wring the neck of injustice before it wrings yours!

Daemones
What's the problem?

Trachalio
        I beg you, old man, whoever you are,
By your knees—

Daemones
        How about letting go of my knees
And telling me what all this commotion's about?

Trachalio
        Please, I beg you: if you want to see

---

54 Tereus pursued Philomela and Procne for feeding him Itys (see n. 44 above), but was turned into
  a hoopoe before he could exact his revenge. Philomela and Procne are usually said to have been
  transformed into a swallow and a nightingale, respectively. Daemones refers to the sisters as
  "compatriots" (605) because they were the daughters of a legendary Athenian king named Pandion.

A bumper crop of silphium[55] and asafoetida this year,   630
And its safe and sound export to Capua,[56]
And so that you may be free of inflamed and runny eyes—
Daemones
Are you insane?
Trachalio
                    —and enjoy plenty of silphium juice,
I ask that you not be irked by my request for help, old man!
Daemones
Well, I beseech you by your shins, ankles and back: 635
If you'd rather not see a bumper crop of elm rods[57]
And reap a colorful harvest of whippings this year,
I demand that you tell me what all the commotion is about!
Trachalio
Why all the abuse? I simply wished the best for you.
Daemones
That's the opposite of abuse. I simply wished you get what you deserve.   640
Trachalio
Please listen up then.
Daemones
                    What's the trouble?
Trachalio
                                        There are
Two innocent women inside here who really need your help.
In violation of all justice and law, a most remarkable injustice
Has been committed against them right here in Venus' temple!
Even worse, the temple's priestess is being dishonored.
Daemones
                                        What human being's   645
Brash enough to disrespect a priestess' sanctity?
And who are these women? How have they been mistreated?
Trachalio
                                        Let me explain:
They have taken sanctuary at the statue of Venus in there,
And now a reckless man is trying to drag them off. Both are actually free persons!
Daemones
Who is it that could be so blasphemous before the gods? Out with it now!   650

---

55 The cash crop of Cyrene (cf. n. 7 above), a now extinct form of fennel (the stalk is depicted on ancient
    coins from Cyrene) that was used as a cure-all in ancient medicine (thus the reference to eye disease in
    632), as well as in cooking. Its resin (*laserpicium*), identified with asafoetida, was especially sought after.

56 A prosperous and powerful Italian city in the region of Campania, just to the northeast of Naples.

57 Commonly used to beat slaves.

Trachalio

The worst imaginable fraud and felon, a murderer and perjurer,
A scofflaw, degenerate, human garbage, a shameless dog!
To sum it all up in a word: HE'S A PIMP. Need I say more?

Daemones

My lord! You're describing someone who should be strung up for a beating!

Trachalio

Absolutely, seeing that the scumbag choked a priestess.   655

Daemones

Well, damn it, he'll be very sorry for that. Turbalio, Sparax![58]
Come on out here, now! Hey, where are you?

Trachalio

                             Please go and help them!

Daemones

I'm not going to repeat myself: follow me this way!

Trachalio

                              Come on now!
Have them pound his eyes out, just as cooks do to cuttlefish!

Daemones

And drag him out here by his heels like a pig for slaughter! (*exits*)   660

Trachalio

Hear that commotion? The pimp's getting a comb-over with their fists!
I really hope they've defanged that snake of a man!
But look! Here come the women, and do they ever look frightened!

SCENE 15

Palaestra and Ampelisca enter from the temple.
(SONG through 681a)

Palaestra

This is it! We've absolutely no support or assistance,
No chance of safety or security here at hand,   665
Not the slightest ray of hope on the horizon!
    Both of us are so scared, we have no idea
    Which way to turn, which way to run!
The way our master treated us so violently,
So unjustly just now inside here!   670
The reckless scumbag even pushed around the aged priestess
With unbelievable disrespect!
And then he dragged us away from the cult-statue by brute force!
When I see how things are going and the state we're in,
    Death is the most reasonable course. In the midst of a mountain of misery,   675

---

58 Turbalio ("Trouble-maker;" cf. Greek *turbe* and Latin *turba*) and Sparax ("Attacker," from Greek *sparassein*) are enforcers (*lorarii*), who are called upon in Roman comedy to chain and beat characters.

It's better just to die.
Trachalio
                    Huh? What kind of talk is that?
I've got to console them. Hey, Palaestra!
Palaestra
                                        Who's that?
Trachalio
   Ampelisca?
Ampelisca
                Hey, who's that calling there?
Palaestra
Who's that saying my name?
Trachalio
                        Turn around and see.
Palaestra
Oh my hope and salvation!
Trachalio
                        Shhh! Take it easy now!   680
Just trust me.
Palaestra
                I would if I knew I was free from his violence—   680a
That's what's compelling me to do violence to myself.
Trachalio
                Stop that, you're being silly!   681a
Palaestra
   Mere words won't console me in my present misery.
   Unless you provide some real protection, we're done for, Trachalio.
Ampelisca
   I'll die before I let that pimp commit violence against me.
   But I do have the courage of a woman after all: when I think of death,   685
   My miserable body is gripped with fear. Oh, what a bitter day!
Trachalio
   Be strong, girls.
Palaestra
                And just where am I supposed to find that strength?
Trachalio
   Don't be afraid now! Sit here by the altar.
Ampelisca
                            Just how is this altar
   Going to protect us any better than the cult statue of Venus inside here did?
   We were clinging to it just now and he still tore us away by force.   690
Trachalio
   Just sit here now and I'll protect you from right here.
   Consider this altar your camp. These are your fortifications. I'll defend you from
      here.

I'll march against that menace of a pimp with Venus providing me cover.

Palaestra

As we cling to your altar on our knees and in tears, blessed Venus,

We remain obedient to you and beseech you   695

To take us under your wing and keep us safe.

Exact vengeance from that wicked man who scorned your sacred temple so,

And allow us to occupy this altar with your blessing.

We both were given a thorough soaking by Neptune last night,

So don't despise us or hold it against us if in any way   700

We seem less well-scrubbed than ritual requires.

Trachalio

A fair request, Venus, and one you should grant.

You should forgive them—fear has driven them to these extremes.

They say you were born from a shell, so please don't turn your back on these
   two tacos. [59]

Look, there's the old man who's protected both you and me.   705

SCENE 16

Daemones and slave-enforcers enter, dragging Labrax from the temple.

Daemones

(*to Labrax*) Out of the temple, you! You are the all-time most brazen blasphemer!

(*to the girls*) You two go sit at the altar! Hey, where'd they go?

Trachalio

                                                                    Right over here.

Daemones

Great, just as I wanted. Just let him come close to them now.

Thought you could get away with violating the gods' laws here?

Punch him in the face!

Labrax

                                   You'll pay for this mistreatment!   710

Daemones

You still have the nerve to make threats?

Labrax

                                        You've already deprived me of my rights,

And now you're taking away my slave girls?

Trachalio

                                        Choose an arbiter

From the senate of Cyrene, anyone who's very wealthy,

---

59 For the birth of Venus from a seashell/the sea and its thermatic relevance in the play, see Introduction p.
    17. Trachalio literally says, "You were born from a shell, so please don't turn your back on the shells of
    these girls." The latter use of "shells" (*conchae*) is obviously obscene (the online *Urban Dictionary s.v.*
    "taco" has "used to describe a woman's vagina" as its first definition, hence my translation), though a
    precise parallel in Latin for Trachalio's expression is lacking.

To decide whether these girls should be yours or should be declared free,
And whether or not you should be tossed into prison for life—   715
Or at least until you wear the floor out there by pacing!

Labrax

I didn't plan my day around conversing with a dirtbag like you.
(*to Daemones*) It's you I want to speak with.

Daemones

Deal with him first. He knows you.

Labrax

I'm dealing with you.

Trachalio

You'll have to deal with me first: are these your slaves?

Labrax

Yes.

Trachalio

Go on, then: touch either one with just the tip of your finger.   720

Labrax

What if I do?

Trachalio

As Hercules is my witness, you'll instantly become my punching bag,
And I'll hammer you as you hang there, you perjurer!

Labrax

So I can't take my own slave girls away from Venus' altar?

Daemones

No. According to our law—

Labrax

Your laws don't relate to me,
And I'm going to take the two of them right away from here.   725
If you're so hot for them, old man, hand over some cold cash.
But if Venus has taken a shining to them, they're hers—and she owes me.

Daemones

She owes *you*? Now listen up closely to my position on all this:
If you so much as commit the slightest violence against them, or even joke about it,
I'll give you such a complete makeover that you won't recognize yourself!   730
As for you guys (*to enforcers*): if you don't un-socket his eyeballs on my signal,
My whips will be wound around you as tightly as string on a ball!

Labrax

That's violence!

Trachalio

You're complaining about violence, you flaming disgrace!

Labrax

How dare you be so rude to me, you three-time felon!

Trachalio

Let's suppose I'm a three-time felon and you're a pillar of the community: 735

Does that make these girls any less free?
Labrax

What do you mean—free?
Trachalio

They actually should be *your* master: they're real Greeks.[60]
This one here is descended from free-born Athenians.[61]
Daemones

What'd you say?
Trachalio

This one was born a free-person in Athens.
Daemones

So she's my compatriot?
Trachalio

I thought you were from Cyrene.   740
Daemones

No! I was born, bred, and raised in Attica[62]-Athens that is.
Trachalio

Then I call upon you to defend your countrymen, old man!
Daemones

Oh my daughter,
The sight of this girl here reminds me of you and all my miseries!
I lost her when she was three. She'd be about your size now if she's alive.
Labrax

I paid their owner good money for the both of them.   745
Why should I care if they're Athenian or Theban,[63]
As long as they do a proper job of serving me?
Trachalio

Is that so, you shameless pig?
You prowl about like a cat and steal free virgins from their parents
So you can wear them down and out in your disgraceful profession.
I really don't know what country the other girl's from,   750
But I do know she's more respectable than you, you heap of garbage!
Labrax

Right back at you.
Trachalio

Let's see whose back makes a better witness:
If yours doesn't have more scars than a warship has nails,
Then I'm the biggest liar on the earth.

---

60 They are from Greece proper (i.e., the mainland), not a Greek colony such as Cyrene.

61 He indicates Palaestra. We never learn the details of Ampelisca's lineage.

62 Attica is the region that surrounds and includes Athens.

63 Thebes is an important Greek city in Boeotia, here randomly selected by Labrax to express his total disdain for her origins.

I'll examine your back first and then you'll look at mine: 755
If my hide isn't so perfectly smooth
That a maker of leather flasks would declare it "Grade A,"
Is there any reason I shouldn't lash yours until I'm bored?
Why are you staring at them? So much as touch them and I'll rip out your eyes!

Labrax
I've a plan to take them both away with me—just to spite you.   760

Daemones
And what's that?

Labrax
        I'm bringing in Vulcan.[64] He and Venus are at war.

Trachalio
Where's he going?

Labrax
        Hey, anyone there?

Trachalio
           So much as touch that door
And I sure as hell will thrash your face with pitchforks made out of fists.

Sparax & Turbalio
We don't keep any fire. We subsist on dried figs.

Daemones
I'll provide fire—to convert your head into a blazing torch.   765

Labrax
Then, by god, I'll go find fire elsewhere.

Daemones
        And once you find it?

Labrax
I'll set one big bonfire.

Daemones
        To burn out your inhumanity?

Labrax
No, no! My plan is to burn these two woman alive at the altar.

Daemones
By god, my plan's to take hold of you by your beard and toss you into that fire;
And when you're a little crisp around the edges, I'll feed you to some large birds.   770
Now that I think of it, this is the monkey
That tried to take these swallows from the nest against my will,
Just like in my dream.[65]

Trachalio
        I have a favor to ask, old man.
Can you watch the girls and defend them while I go get my master?

---

64 For the god Vulcan (= fire, by metonymy), see Appendix I p. 335.

65 Cf. nn. 53 and 54 above.

Daemones

Find him and bring him back.

Trachalio

Don't let him—

Daemones

If he touches them,   775

Or even tries to touch them, he'll be very, very sorry.

Trachalio

Take care!

Daemones

Everything's taken care of.

Trachalio

Watch him carefully: we've made a promise to the executioner
To either hand him over today or a talent in gold.[66]

Daemones

Just go. I'll take care of everything here just fine.

Trachalio

I'll be right back.

SCENE 17

*Daemones and his enforcers, Labrax, Palaestra and Ampelisca remain
on stage.*

Daemones

Your call, pimp: is it your pleasure   780
To settle yourself down with or without the aid of a beating?

Labrax

I don't give a rat's ass about what you say, old man.
They're mine and I'm going to drag them away from the altar by their hair,
Even if you, Venus, and mighty Jove don't like it!

Daemones

Go ahead—touch them.

Labrax

Damn right I'll touch them.

Daemones

Okay, then. Come right this way.   785

Labrax

Then tell those two to step back a ways.

Daemones

No, they're coming your way.

Labrax

I don't think so.

---

66 For the value of a talent, see Appendix II p. 337.

Daemones

What's your plan if they do come closer?

Labrax

I'll be, er ... slipping off.

But if I ever meet up with you in the city, old man,

May no one, damn it, ever call me a pimp again   790

If I don't turn you and your life into a miserable farce!

Daemones

Good luck with that threat. But in the meantime now,

If you touch them, you'll earn yourself a rough beating.

Labrax

Really? How rough?

Daemones

Just the right roughness for a pimp.

Labrax

I don't give a rat's ass about your threats,   795

And I'm definitely dragging them off in spite of you!

Daemones

Go ahead and touch them.

Labrax

Damn right I'll touch them!

Daemones

Go right ahead—at your own risk.

Turbalio! Run inside the house

And get two clubs.

Labrax

Clubs?

Daemones

Nice, stout ones. Hurry it up!

I'll see you get just the reception you deserve today.   800

Labrax

Damn! My helmet went down with the ship!

If it had survived, it sure would come in handy right now.

May I at least speak to the girls?

Daemones

No.

Oh, look! Excellent! My clubman is back.   804-5

Labrax

Just the sight of that makes my ears ring.

Daemones

Take one of those clubs, Sparax! Come on, now.

One of you stand on this side, one of you on the other.

Yes, both of you just like that. Listen up now:

If he so much as lays a finger on those two against their will 810

And you don't give him a clubby welcome
To the point that he can't even find his way home,
You're both dead men. If he speaks to either one,
Answer for them from right there.
But if he tries to run away from here,   815
Have those clubs give his legs a nice firm hug, and pronto!
Labrax
They're not going to let me leave?
Daemones
                                        Enough talk.
When that slave who went off to get his master returns with him,
Come home immediately.
See to all this with the utmost care now. (*exits into his cottage*)   820
Labrax
Damn, temples do change owners fast around here!
What was Venus' temple here a while ago now is Hercules',
To judge by these two statues with clubs[67] at least!
By Hercules, I don't know where in the world to run to!
It seems like both land and sea are now conspiring against me.   825
Palaestra!
Turbalio
                        What do you want?
Labrax
                                        Yikes! That's not right!
That doesn't sound like my Palaestra's voice.
Hey, Ampelisca!
Sparax
                        You'd best watch out for trouble!
Labrax (*aside*)
These statues give as good advice as real human beings.
But listen up, you two: is there any problem   830
With my going up closer to them?
Turbalio & Sparax
                                Not for us.
Labrax
How about for me?
Turbalio
                        No problem—if you're careful.
Labrax
Careful of what?
Turbalio
                        Oh, of being dealt a very heavy misfortune.

---

67 Hercules' club and his lionskin are the two standard elements of his iconography.

Labrax

Oh please! Just let me go away.

Sparax

Go on, if you want.

Labrax

That's the spirit! Thanks so much! 835

On second thought, maybe I'll just go over here—

Turbalio & Sparax

Stop right there!

Labrax

Damn! Everywhere I turn turns out badly!

I'm resolved to taking the girls by a siege.

SCENE 18

Trachalio returns with Plesidippus.

Plesidippus

That pimp got violent and tried to forcibly snatch

My girlfriend away from Venus' altar?

Trachalio

Exactly. 840

Plesidippus

Why didn't you just kill him on the spot?

Trachalio

I didn't have a sword.

Plesidippus

You could have grabbed a club or a rock.

Trachalio

You mean hunted him down with rocks like a dog?

He's utterly depraved—but human nonetheless.

Labrax (*aside*)

Damn it, now I'm finished! Plesidippus is here.

He'll make a clean sweep of me—pulverize me, actually! 845

Plesidippus

Were the ladies still sitting by the altar

When you left?

Trachalio

Yes, and they're still there now.

Plesidippus

Who's watching over them there?

Trachalio

Some old man

Who lives next door to Venus. He's been extremely helpful.

He and his slaves are guarding them, just as I told them to. 850

Plesidippus

Take me straight to the pimp. Where is he?

Labrax (*suddenly steps up*)

Good morning.

Plesidippus

Forget the "good morning." You have a choice but make it snappy:

Once you're wearing a noose, do you want to be carried off or dragged away?

Take your pick while you still have one.

Labrax

I'll go with neither.

Plesidippus

Run on down to the shore, Trachalio, and tell the friends   855

I brought with me there to return to the city

And meet me at the harbor, so we can deliver this guy to the executioner.

Then come back here and stand guard over the ladies.

I'm taking this vile convict to court.

Come on, off to court with you. (*Trachalio exits*)

Labrax

What did I do?

Plesidippus

You dare ask?   860

Didn't you take my down-payment for the young lady

And then take her away from here?

Labrax

I didn't actually take her away.

Plesidippus

You're denying it?

Labrax

Yes, because, unlucky as I am, I was only able to take her a little ways from shore.

Now I did in fact say that I'd meet you here at Venus' temple.

That was the plan, wasn't it? Well, here I am.   865

Plesidippus

Save it for court. I've had more than enough of your jabbering.

Follow me.

Labrax (*calling toward the temple*)

Charmides! Please come help me.

I'm being dragged off in a noose.

Charmides (*enters from the temple*)

Who's that calling me?

Labrax

Look at what's happening to me!

Charmides

Yes, it's quite a pleasing spectacle!

Labrax

You're not going to help me?

Charmides
　　　　　　　　　　Who's got hold of you there?　　　　　　　870
Labrax
　　That young guy, Plesidippus.
Charmides
　　　　　　　　　What goes around comes around.
　　You might just as well crawl calmly into custody:
　　You've got what most folks just pray for.
Labrax
　　What's that?
Charmides
　　　　　　　　To actually get what they're looking for.
Labrax
　　Please come with me!
Charmides
　　　　　　　　Just the sort of invitation I'd expect from someone like you!　875
　　You're being hauled off to jail and want me to accompany you there?
　　Still holding on to me?
Labrax
　　　　　　　　I'm ruined.
Plesidippus
　　　　　　　　　I wish!
　　My darling Palaestra—and you too, Ampelisca—wait right here
　　Until I come back.
Turbalio
　　　　　　　　I'd really recommend
　　That they stay at our house instead until you come back.
Plesidippus
　　　　　　　　　　　　　　　　Sure,　　　　　　　880
　　Good idea.
Labrax
　　　　　　Thieves!
Turbalio
　　　　　　　　Us, thieves? Drag him away!
Labrax
　　Please, Palaestra, help me!
Plesidippus
　　　　　　　　Come along, scum!
Labrax
　　My guest and friend—
Charmides
　　　　　　　　I'm neither. I repudiate any prior association with you.
Labrax
　　You're dumping me, just like that?

Charmides

                                   Yes. One drink with you was enough.

Labrax

   May the gods curse you!

Charmides

                                   Right back at you.   885
   I do believe that men are morphing into beasts.
   Take the pimp: he's becoming a bird—a jailbird that is.
   His neck will soon be cooped up in a pillory
   And he'll be nesting in his own pigeon cell.
   I'll tag along nonetheless as his advocate.   890
   Maybe I'll find a way to get him convicted sooner.

SCENE 19

Daemones enters from his cottage.

Daemones

   My helping out these little ladies today
   Has turned out to be a mighty sweet deal.
   I've picked up some fans, both of them pretty fine and in their prime.
   If only my damn wife weren't eyeballing me all the time,   895
   So I could give the little ladies some sort of sign …
   Hey, I wonder what my slave Gripus is up to?
   He went off deep-sea fishing in the middle of the night.
   Would have been smarter to have just gone to bed,
   The way it's been storming since last night.   900
   He's just making a mockery of his nets and his efforts.
   The way I see it, the sea is so rough today,
   I bet I could cook his entire catch on the tips of my fingers.
   Oh, the wife is calling me to lunch.
   Home it is—and now for an earful of her chatter.   905

SCENE 20

Gripus enters from the seashore wing.
(SONG through 937a)

Gripus[68]

   Hearty thanks to my patron of the sea, Neptune,
   Who haunts the briny and fishy domain!
   He has sent me forth from his hallowed foam
   Laden down with a load of loot!
   He even saved the skiff that's yielded me   910
   This strange and fertile harvest of the stormy sea.

---

68 His name means "fisherman" in Greek.

This lovely haul leapt forth for me in a most miraculous manner!
    I may not have landed an ounce of fish, but what a catch in my net!
    And what initiative, my leaping out of bed at midnight,   914-5
    Putting profit ahead of rest and slumber!
    Despite the raging storm,
    I spared no effort to soften
        The blow of Master's poverty and my slavery.
Who's more worthless than a lazy man? There's nothing I despise more.   920
A man who's always on call is a man who does his duty on time;
He doesn't even wait for his master's command to commit to a task!
    The lover of sleep lies in a bed of poverty and pain.
        Thanks to my initiative, I made quite a find,
        And now find I can truly sleep peacefully if I please.   925
        Whatever this holds sure is heavy!   925a
    It's gold, solid gold I'm guessing,
        And no one knows about it but me!   926a
The time is ripe, Gripus, for you to be the freest man on the face of the earth!
Here's the plan: I march up to Master all confident and smart.
I'll offer him more cash for my freedom[69] *(upping the offer as needed).*
Once I'm free, I'll buy a farm, a house, and some slaves.   930
I'll become a shipping magnate, and be proclaimed king of kings!
I'll build a pleasure-boat and live like Stratonicus,[70]
    Yachting my way around the world!
    Once I'm the ultimate celebrity,   933a
    I'll found my own city—
    Gripopolis by name,   934a
    As a monument to my glorious deeds!   935
    And this will be the seat of my mighty empire.   935a
    Oh, my mind is mulling over such greatness now—
    But I'd better hide this trunk.   936a
    For now, My Majesty will lunch on sour wine and salt—
    Sans the fancy hors d'oeuvres.   937a

---

69 Slaves could in fact have their own money and property (*peculium*), with which they could purchase their freedom from their masters.

70 A celebrated touring musician of Diphilus' time (cf. Introduction p. 4), and so this is a clear case where Plautus has not updated a topical reference in his Greek source for the benefit of his contemporary audience.

SCENE 21

Trachalio enters from the seashore wing.
(SONG through 962b)

Trachalio
   Hey, wait!

Gripus
          What for?

Trachalio
              Until I coil up this rope you're dragging.

Gripus
   Let go!

Trachalio
            I'm just trying to be helpful: what you do comes back to you.

Gripus
   There was a wild storm yesterday,   940
Young man, and I've got no fish. So don't bother asking.
Look at my wet net here: completely devoid of the scaly flock.[71]

Trachalio
Well, damn it, I'm in need of a conversation with you, not fish.

Gripus
Whoever you are, you're boring me to death.

Trachalio
                      You can't leave. Wait!

Gripus
You're cruisin' for a bruisin'. Why are you delaying me, damn it?

Trachalio
                                    Listen—   945

Gripus
No thanks.

Trachalio
          I'm sure you'll listen later.

Gripus
                    Go ahead and say whatever you want.

Trachalio
   What I have to say is well worth your while.

Gripus
   Out with it then.

Trachalio
               See anyone shadowing us?

Gripus
             Does it have anything to do with me?

---

71 Paratragic language.

Trachalio

Absolutely.

But tell me: are you discrete?   950

Gripus

Just tell me what's up.

Trachalio

I'll do that

If you pledge to maintain absolute confidentiality about this.   952-3

Gripus

Yes, yes, I will, whoever you are.

Trachalio

Listen up: 954-5

I saw someone commit a robbery.

I knew the owner of the stolen goods,   956a

And so I went up to the thief

And presented him with this proposition: 957a

"I know the victim of this robbery.

If you go halvsies with me,   958a

I'll have no reason to inform him."

Not a word in response to my offer!   959a

What's a fair share for me, then?   960

I'm thinking you'll say "half."

Gripus

Why even more than half, damn it,

And if he doesn't hand it over, by all means   961a

Notify the owner!

Trachalio

I like your way of thinking.

Pay attention now,   962a

As this all pertains to you.

Gripus

How so?   962b

Trachalio

I've known that trunk's owner for some time now.

Gripus

Huh?

Trachalio

And I know how it was lost.

Gripus

And I know how it was found,

And I know who found it and who its owner is now.   965

And all of this is no more your business than mine.

You see, I know the current owner. You know the former owner.

No one's taking it from me, so don't get your hopes up.

Trachalio

    Not even if the owner shows up?

Gripus

                          Its only owner is me,

    The person who caught it while fishing.   970

Trachalio

    Is that so?

Gripus

                Is a fish mine when it's still in the sea?

    It's only after I catch them—if I'm lucky—that they become mine.

    And then they're all mine. No one lays a claim to them or seeks a share.

    I sell them as my personal property in the pubic market.

    The sea, as we know, is the common property of all.

Trachalio

                          Agreed on that.   975

    So how is my share in this trunk less than anyone else's?

    It was found in the sea which we all share.

Gripus

                      You utterly shameless swine!

    If the law were interpreted that way, that'd be the end of fishermen.

    The instant fish were delivered to market, there'd be no buyers,

    But everyone would stake a claim to his share   980

    Of all the fish caught in the sea that is common to all.

Trachalio

                      You utterly shameless swine!

    You're brazen enough to equate trunks with fish?

    Are they really the same?

Gripus

               The minute I cast my net and hooks,

    It's out of my hands. Whatever takes the bait, I appropriate.

    And whatever my net and hooks take hold of is all mine.   985

Trachalio

    Not so, by Hercules! Not when you pull up a piece of equipment.

Gripus

                         You Einstein!

Trachalio

    Listen you, you bum! Surely you've never seen

    A fisherman catch a trunkfish or sell one at the market?

    Trying to become a jackass-of-all trades in these parts?

    Scum! You can't be both a fisherman and a trunk-maker!   990

    You need to show me how a trunk can be a fish,

    Or you can't have what wasn't born in the sea and doesn't have scales.

Gripus

    You've really never heard of a trunkfish before?

Trachalio
$\qquad$ There is
No such thing, you convict!

Gripus
$\qquad$ There is too! I'm a fisherman and I should know!
It's just that they're rarely caught and, ah, landed. $\qquad$ 995

Trachalio
Nonsense, you felon! Think you can bamboozle me?

Gripus
The tiny ones that are caught are the color of mine here.
The bigger ones are crimson-backed. There are black ones too.

Trachalio
You should sure as hell be careful or you'll morph into a two-toned trunk yourself!
Your hide will turn crimson first and then black later on.[72] $\qquad$ 1000

Gripus
What a damn mess this is I've stumbled into!

Trachalio
$\qquad$ Let's cut the chatter—we're wasting time.
How about choosing an arbiter to decide for us?

Gripus
$\qquad$ How about the trunk?
Yes, the trunk will decide.

Trachalio
$\qquad$ You're a moron!

Gripus
$\qquad$ Hail, Professor Thales![73]

Trachalio
You won't pull that off today: you need to choose a trustee or a mediator
To decide this.

Gripus
$\qquad$ Tell me: are you insane? $\qquad$ 1005

Trachalio
I'm on medication for it.

Gripus
$\qquad$ I'm just plain nuts, but there's no way I'm letting go of it.

Trachalio
One more word out of you and I'll plant my fists inside your brain.
If you don't let go of this, I'll wring every last drop of liquid out of you,
Just like people do with brand new sponges.

---

72 Such jokes about beatings (especially by whipping) are commonplace in Roman comedy.

73 6th century BCE Greek philosopher, geometer, and astronomer, and one of the Seven Sages of the ancient world. His name became a proverbial way to describe genius (cf. the similar use of "Einstein").

Gripus

Just touch me and I'll smash you against the ground like I would an octopus.   1010
Want to duke it out?

Trachalio

Do we have to? Why not just divide the loot in half instead?

Gripus

Resign yourself to taking nothing away from this but a fistful of trouble.
I'm outta here.

Trachalio

I think I'll just reorient the ship here, so that's impossible. Hold on.

Gripus

If you're the look-out man for that ship, I'm the skipper.
Let go of the rope, scumbag.

Trachalio

You let go of the trunk and I'll drop the rope.   1015

Gripus

Damn it, you will never become a penny richer today from this!

Trachalio

And you'll never win just by saying "no" over and over again.
Give me a cut or take it to a trustee or mediator.

Gripus

The trunk I pulled out of the sea—

Trachalio

Yes, the one I spotted from the shore.

Gripus

—with my labor, my net, and my boat?

Trachalio

If the owner shows up,   1020
How am I any less a thief than you, seeing as I watched you take it
From a ways off here?

Gripus

You're not.

Trachalio

Hold on now, you human punching bag:
How can I be your accomplice and not get a share of the loot? Explain that, please.

Gripus

I can't. I'm just plain ignorant of those fancy city-laws of yours.
All I know is that *it's mine.*

Trachalio

Well, I say *it's* mine.   1025

Gripus

Hey, I've figured out how for you not to be an accomplice *and* not get a share.

Trachalio

How?

Gripus

       Let me go away from here and then just quietly move on your way.

Don't tell anyone at all about this, and I won't give you anything at all.

You shut up, I'll keep quiet. How fair and square is that?

Trachalio

So you're not offering me a deal?

Gripus

                     I have been for some time now: 1030

Drop the rope, stop bothering me, and get lost!

Trachalio

Hold on! I've got a counter-offer.

Gripus

                  I'm counting on your leaving asap.

Trachalio

Do you know anyone around here?

Gripus

                My neighbors, as I should.

Trachalio

Where do you live?

Gripus

          Quite a ways off there at the far edge of that field.

Trachalio

How about letting the guy who lives in this cottage be our mediator?   1035

Gripus

Let go of the rope for a second while I think that over by myself.

Trachalio

Okay.

Gripus (*aside*)

       Excellent! That should just about seal it, and make the trunk mine for good!

He wants my master to mediate! Talk about home-field advantage!

He wouldn't award so much as a half-drachma[74] away from a family member!

This guy has no idea what a deal he's offering me. Arbitration it is.   1040

Trachalio

Well?

Gripus

       Though I'm totally sure this is legally mine,

I'll agree to that rather than duke it out with you.

Trachalio

                        That's the attitude!

Gripus

I don't know this mediator you're pushing on me, but if he proves to be fair,

Even if I don't know him, I'll recognize him. If not, he's absolutely no one to me.

---

74 For the value of a half-drachma (a very small amount), see Appendix II p. 337.

SCENE 22

Daemones, the enforcers, Palaestra and Ampelisca enter from his cottage.

Daemones

Ladies, I really am sympathetic and want to help you,   1045
But I'm afraid of my wife. She'd say I held my mistresses right under her nose,
And then kick me right out of the house.
Better for you to take refuge at the altar than with me.

Palaestra & Ampelisca

We're totally done for!

Daemones

Don't worry, I'll see you're safe. But why are you two (*to enforcers*) following us out?
As long as I'm here, they won't be harmed.   1050
Back inside now, both of you! Off guard, guards!

Gripus

Good morning, Master!

Daemones

Morning, Gripus. How's it going?

Trachalio

This guy's your slave?

Gripus

Yup, and proud of it.

Trachalio

I'm not interested in you.

Gripus

Then get lost.

Trachalio

Tell me, old man:

Is he your slave?

Daemones

Yes.

Trachalio

Well, isn't that just special—he's yours!

Good morning again.

Daemones

Same to you. Aren't you the guy who went away   1055
To get your master a little while ago?

Trachalio

That's me.

Daemones

What do you need now?

Trachalio

He really is yours?

Daemones

Yes.

Trachalio

That's just special—he's yours.

Daemones

So what's the matter?

Trachalio

The guy is a total scumbag.

Daemones

What did this total scumbag do to you?

Trachalio

I'd like to see his ankles shattered.

Daemones

Why? What are you two arguing about now?

Trachalio

Let me explain.   1060

Gripus

No, I'd better do the explaining.

Trachalio

I have the right to go first.

Gripus

If you had

Any decency, you'd go right away from here.

Daemones

Shut up and pay attention, Gripus.

Gripus

So he can speak first?

Daemones

Yes, listen up. You, speak.

Gripus

You'd really give

Someone else's slave the first word?

Trachalio

It's all but impossible to shut him up!

As I was saying: this slave of yours has the trunk   1065
Of that pimp you booted out of the temple a while ago.

Gripus

No I don't.

Trachalio

I'm not looking at it with my own eyes?

Gripus

You can just poke those out for all I care.

Maybe I have it, maybe I don't. Why are you so concerned with my business?

Trachalio

What matters is whether you have the trunk legally or illegally.

Gripus

You can escort me straight to my crucifixion[75] if I didn't actually catch it.   1070

But if I removed it from the sea in my net, how is it yours rather than mine?

Trachalio

He's conning you. The matter stands just as I told you.

Gripus

Which is how?

Trachalio

Let me be the first to tell you—if you would kindly see that his pie-hole is shut!

Gripus

Oh? You want him to do to me what your master's in the habit of doing to you?

It may be your master's custom to plug up his slave's holes, but it's not ours'.   1075

Daemones

Round one goes to Gripus. Tell me what it is you want.

Trachalio

I'm not actually asking for a cut of what's in that trunk there,

And I never claimed it was mine today.

But inside it there's a small chest that belongs to the woman I told you was freeborn.

Daemones

You mean the woman you said was my compatriot?   1080

Trachalio

Exactly. And the rattle she played with in her childhood

Is inside that chest that's inside of the trunk.

It's of no use to him, and if he hands it over to her,

It'll help the poor woman find her parents.

Daemones

I'll see he does. Quiet you!

Gripus

Damn it, I won't give him a thing.

Trachalio

I'm only asking for the chest   1085

And the rattle.

Gripus

What if they're made of solid gold?

Trachalio

Not to worry:

You'd get the equivalent in gold for the gold, or silver for the silver.

Gripus

Show me your gold first and then I'll show you the chest.

Daemones

Watch it now, and shut up! Keep on with your story.

---

75   For crucifixion in the Roman world, see n. 46 above.

Trachalio

> The only thing I ask is that you show compassion for the girl—   1090
> Assuming, that is, it's the pimp's trunk.
> At this point I'm only speculating, and not entirely sure about that.

Gripus

> See! The bum is just setting us up.

Trachalio

> If I may continue?
> If it really is this scummy pimp's trunk,
> The women will recognize it. Just show it to them.

Gripus

> What? Show it to them?   1095

Daemones

> It's not an unfair request to show them the trunk, Gripus.

Gripus

> It damn well most certainly is unfair!

Daemones

> How so?

Gripus

> The minute
> They see it, they'll of course *say* they recognize it.

Trachalio

> You human crime wave!
> Do you assume everyone's just like you, you fountain of fraud?

Gripus

> I can put up with all that, as long as my master is on my side here.   1100

Trachalio

> He's on your side now but he'll take evidence from here.

Daemones

> Pay attention, Gripus. And you: keep it very brief!

Trachalio

> I thought I'd told you, but if you need clarification, I'll say it again.
> To repeat: both of these women should be free.
> This one was taken away from Athens when she was very small.

Gripus

> Tell me: 1105
> What's their being slaves or freeborn have to do with the trunk?

Trachalio

> Want it all repeated, scumbag? Trying to kill time?

Daemones

> Enough of the insults! Just clarify what I've asked you to.

Trachalio

> There should be a little wicker chest in that trunk
> Where there are keepsakes she can use to find the parents   1110

She lost when she was kidnapped from Athens back then.
Gripus
To hell with you! Listen up, you degenerate:
Can't those women speak for themselves? They aren't mute, are they?
Trachalio
They're quiet because a woman's at her best when she's not speaking.[76]
Gripus
So then I assume you're neither a man nor a woman, properly speaking?   1115
Trachalio
How's that?
Gripus
                    Because you're utterly useless when you're silent or speaking.
Please! Will I ever get a chance to speak today?
Daemones
                                        Just one more word
Out of you now today and I'll shatter your skull to bits!
Trachalio
As I started to say, old man, I'm asking that you tell him to give the chest back to
    them.
He can have a reward if he wants one for returning it.   1120
And he can keep whatever else is in the trunk.
Gripus
Finally! So you do recognize my right to it!
A little while back you were demanding a cut.
Trachalio
                                        And I still do now.
Gripus
I've noticed hawks stay on the prowl too, even when there's no prey.
Daemones
Can you just shut your pie-hole? Do I have to beat you?
Gripus
                                        If he shuts up,   1125
So will I. If he keeps talking, I deserve my say as well.
Daemones
Hand over the trunk to me now, Gripus.
Gripus
                              Here it is,
But if those things aren't in it, I get it back, right?
Daemones
                                        Yes, fine.

---

76 A misogynistic stereotype commonly found among Greek and Roman writers. There is metatheatrical
    play here as well in that Palaestra and Ampelisca—played by male actors—have been mute since 1048,
    but are visible to the audience. Trachacio's assertion serves mainly as a set-up to the gender joke that
    follows at 1115ff.

Gripus

Take it.

Daemones

Listen up closely now, Palaestra and Ampelisca:
Is this the trunk you said the little wicker chest was in?

Palaestra

It is. 1130

Gripus

Damn! That's it for poor little me! She hardly even glanced at it before declaring it
hers.

Palaestra

I know this seems complicated, but let me simplify.
There should be a little wicker chest in that trunk.
I can give you a precise inventory of everything in there.
Don't show me any item; if I make a mistake, my claim is void, 1135
And you can have whatever's in there for keeps.
If I'm right, then I ask that you return my things to me.

Daemones

Agreed.

That seems perfectly fair to me.

Gripus

And completely unfair to me!
What if she's a witch or a clairvoyant and can name everything that's in there?
Does the clairvoyant get it all then? 1140

Daemones

She'll only get what she lists correctly. Clairvoyance won't help.
Unlock the trunk so I can discover the truth here immediately.

Trachalio (*aside*)

Now he's had it!

Gripus

It's unlocked.

Daemones

Open it up. I see a small chest. Is that it?

Palaestra

That's it! My dear parents! Here I've kept you hidden,
Here lie buried all means and hope of knowing you! 1145

Gripus

Damn, the gods must be angry at you, whoever you are!
The idea of locking your parents up in such a tight space!

Daemones

Gripus, come here: this concerns you now. From right where you are, young lady,
Name and describe every last item that's in there.
If, by Hercules, you make the slightest error 1150
And hope to correct it after the fact, you'll be completely out of luck.

Gripus
    A fair request.
Trachalio
            Yes, since he's not asking you! You don't know what fair is.
Daemones
    Speak up now, young lady. Pay attention, Gripus!
Palaestra
    There are some toys.
Daemones
            Oh yes, they're here.
Gripus
                Down and out in the first round!
    Hey, don't show them to her now.
Daemones
            Describe them in detail.   1155
Palaestra
    First, there's a little gold sword with an inscription.
Daemones
               Tell me:
    What's the inscription say?
Palaestra
            The name of my father.
    Next, there's a little two-headed axe, also gold,
    And also inscribed. My mother's name is on that.
Daemones
               Hold on.
    What's the name of your father on the little sword?
Palaestra
              Daemones.   1160
Daemones
    Immortal gods! Do I dare get my hopes up?
Gripus
            What about *my* hopes?
Trachalio
    Please do continue.
Gripus
         Take it easy there—or just take yourself to hell!
Daemones
    Tell us the name of your mother on the double-axe here.
Palaestra
    Daedalis.
Daemones
      The gods do love me!

Gripus

And despise me!

Daemones

This must be my daughter, Gripus!

Gripus

She might just as well be for all I care.   1165

I wish the gods would damn you for setting your eyes upon me today!

And what a damn fool I was for not looking around a hundred times

To see if anybody was watching when I dragged my net out of the sea!

Palaestra

And there's a little silver sickle and two tiny joined hands

And a little piglet.

Gripus

Why don't you, your piglets, and pork cutlets go straight to hell! 1170

Palaestra

And there's a gold locket that my father gave me on my birthday.

Daemones

It's really her! I've got to hug you right this instant!

Hello, my own daughter! I'm the father that raised you!

I'm Daemones and right inside here is your mother Daedalis!

Palaestra

Oh, hello, father! I had lost all hope of finding you!

Daemones

What a pleasure to hug you!   1175

Trachalio

It's a pleasure to see things turn out so well for good people.

Daemones

Take hold of this trunk, Trachalio, and take it inside if you can.

Trachalio

Look at Gripus the scumbag! Seeing how badly this has turned out for you, Gripus,

Makes me want to … celebrate!

Daemones

Come on, let's go in and see your mother, my daughter!

She'll be able to piece all these things together better,   1180

Seeing as she took care of you more than me and knows these keepsakes better.

Palaestra

Let's all go inside, since we all have a stake in this.

Come with me, Ampelisca.

Ampelisca

I'm so happy to see the gods have blessed you!

Gripus

What a damn piece of bad luck it was to pull up that trunk today!

Or why didn't I at least hide it in some out-of-the-way place after I did?   1185

I really thought this would turn out to be one rip-roaring fortune for me,

Seeing as I ripped this trunk out of one roaring sea!
And I'm just sure there's a pile of sliver and gold in there.
What else can I do but skulk my way inside and hang myself—
At least until I no longer have this sickening feeling?   1190

SCENE 23

Daemones enters from his cottage.

Daemones

By the immortal gods! Who could ever be luckier than me!
To have found my daughter is beyond my wildest dreams!
If the gods want something good to happen to a man,
And he's dutiful, they will find a way to grant his wishes!
Take my case: what I never expected or believed could happen has!   1195
Completely out of the blue, I've found my daughter!
And I'm going to give her in marriage to a young man
Of the Athenian nobility who's a relative of mine!
I'll have him called here as quickly as possible.
I've already called that slave of his out here to send him off to the forum.   1200
But I wonder why he hasn't come out yet?
I think I'll go up to the door. Now what's that I see?
My wife has grabbed our daughter and is hanging off her neck;
That sort of affection is a bit silly and almost annoying.

SCENE 24

Daemones shouts to his wife inside as Trachalio enters.

Daemones

Isn't it about time to put an end to all that kissing, wife?   1205
You need to prepare for the sacrifice to our household gods,[77]
Seeing that they've blessed our household so.
We've got sacrificial lambs and pigs here.
But why are you holding up Trachalio? Oh look, here he comes out now.

Trachalio

I'll track down Plesidippus, wherever he is, and bring him back here   1210
With me.

Daemones

                    Tell him all the news about my daughter
And ask him to drop whatever he's doing and come here pronto!

Trachalio

                                                                        Okay.

Daemones

Tell him I'll give my daughter to him in marriage.

---

77 *Lares* were Roman household gods worshipped (in the form of imposing, omnipresent statues) by
    members of the family.

Trachalio

Okay.

Daemones

And that I know his father, and we're related.

Trachalio

Okay.

Daemones

And hurry!

Trachalio

Okay.

Daemones

Do that and we'll take care of dinner here.

Trachalio

Okay.   1215

Daemones

So everything's okay?

Trachalio

Yes, okay. But do you know what I want the most?
I want you to keep your promise that I'll be made free today.

Daemones

Okay.

Trachalio

So you've got to convince Plesidippus to free me today.

Daemones

Okay.

Trachalio

And have your daughter plea my case, too: she'll win him over for sure.

Daemones

Okay.

Trachalio

And arrange for me to marry Ampelisca once I'm freed.[78]

Daemones

Okay.   1220

Trachalio

And see that I get what I deserve for all I've done?

Daemones

Okay.

Trachalio

So everything's okay?

---

78 While Palaestra must be a virgin to marry an Athenian aristocrat such as Plesidippus (cf. n. 8 above), the same is not true for Ampelisca (cf. n. 38 above), who will marry Trachalio once he is manumitted and assumes the lowly status of a freedman.

Daemones

              Yes, and I'm paying you back in kind, okay?
But hightail it to the city and then come right back here.

Trachalio

                        Okay.
I'll be back soon. In the meantime, prepare everything we'll need. (*exits*)

Daemones

                              Okay.
And may Hercules curse him and all his okay-itude!   1225
My ears are still ringing with his "Okay's" to whatever I said!

SCENE 25

Gripus enters from Daemones' cottage.

Gripus

Is it okay for me to speak with you now, Daemones?

Daemones

What's the problem, Gripus?

Gripus

                    It's about that trunk:
If you were smart, really smart, you'd keep what the gods have given you.

Daemones

So you think it's right to claim what belongs to someone else   1230
As my own?

Gripus

              But it's something I found in the sea!

Daemones

All the better for the owner who lost it.
The fact that you found it doesn't make it any more yours.

Gripus

You are so damned righteous! No wonder you're so poor.

Daemones

O Gripus, Gripus! The human condition is fraught   1235
With so many traps to fool and out-fox us,
And more often than not these traps are baited.
If we greedily grasp at that bait,
We're grabbed, trapped, and ensnared by our very own greed.
But if a person's careful and cautious, cagey and wary,   1240
He harvests long-lasting gain from what he's honestly obtained.
To my way of thinking, lucre such as yours is never lucrative:
It leaves a marriage with a larger dowry than it brought.
You really think I'd knowingly accept and conceal plunder taken from another?
That's absolutely not the way of this Daemones!   1245
Masters who are smart are wise to take the utmost caution
Against becoming willful accomplices to the crimes of their slaves.

I don't care for any lucre landed in unlawful collusion.

Gripus

I've seen comic actors speak words of wisdom like that
And win all sorts of applause for   1250
Enlightening the folks in the crowd.
But when the show was over and people made their way home,
To judge by their behavior anyway, they all forgot those lines.[79]

Daemones

Stop bothering me and go inside! And watch your tongue!
And just so you know: you're not getting anything from me.   1255

Gripus

Then I ask all the gods: whatever's in that trunk,
Whether silver or gold—please see that it's reduced to ashes! (*exits*)

Daemones

That's exactly why we have such worthless slaves.
If he had met up somewhere with a fellow slave,
He would have implicated him in his crime too.   1260
He'd assume the spoils were his,
But at some point would himself become the plunder,
And it'd be a case of spoiled spoils. I'm going inside to sacrifice now,
And then I'll see that dinner's prepared immediately.

SCENE 26

Trachalio returns with Plesidippus.

Plesidippus

Oh my dearest Trachalio! You are my freedman, no, how about my patron ... 1265
No, my very own father![80] Repeat it all one more time!
Palaestra has found her father and mother?

Trachalio

                                        Yes.

Plesidippus

And she's Athenian?

Trachalio

                        I think so.

Plesidippus

                                And she's going to marry me?

Trachalio

                                                        I suspect so.

Plesidippus

So it's your belief that he'll promise her hand in marriage to me?

---

79 For Plautine metatheater, see Introduction pp. 8-9.

80 The Roman social hierarchy was built around a rigidly stratified system of patrons and their dependent
    clients. The *patronus* took on many of the prerogatives of the all-powerful Roman father; the lovesick
    Plesidippus is struggling to find a metaphor powerful enough to express his indebtedness to his slave here.

Trachalio

I do believe so.

Plesidippus

And do you believe I should congratulate her father?

Trachalio

I do believe so.   1270

Plesidippus

And her mother?

Trachalio

I do believe so.

Plesidippus

What exactly do you believe?

Trachalio

I believe

Whatever you ask me I believe.

Plesidippus

How much do you believe?

Trachalio

Me? I just believe, period.

Plesidippus

So you'd question your belief that I'm here If I asked you to?

Trachalio

I do believe so.

Plesidippus

Do you believe I should run?

Trachalio

I do believe so.

Plesidippus

Or go slow like so?

Trachalio

I do believe so.

Plesidippus

Should I greet her too when I get there?

Trachalio

I do believe so.

Plesidippus

And her father too?   1275

Trachalio

I do believe so.

Plesidippus

Then her mother?

Trachalio

I do believe so.

Plesidippus

And then what?

Should I also hug her father when I get there?

Trachalio

Er, I don't believe so.

Plesidippus

What about her mother?

Trachalio

I don't believe so.

Plesidippus

And her?

Trachalio

I don't believe so.

Plesidippus

Oh, damn it! He's lost all his beliefs, and just when I need them most!

Trachalio

You're nuts! Follow me.

Plesidippus

Take me wherever you'd like, my patron![81]   1280

SCENE 27

Labrax enters from the wing leading to the city/harbor.

Labrax

Is there anyone alive in the whole world more unlucky than me?
Plesidippus got me convicted by the Commission of Disputed Property,
And now I've lost Palaestra! I'm utterly screwed!
You'd think we pimps we're all descended from the Goddess de Light,
Seeing as how the whole world takes so much de-light in our downfall!   1285
I'll go look for that other girl of mine here in the temple of Venus.
At least I can abscond with what remains of my property.

SCENE 28

Gripus enters from Daemones' cottage.

Gripus

By god, you'll never see Gripus alive again this evening
Unless I get that trunk back!

Labrax (*aside*)

I cringe every time I hear
That word "trunk." It's like having a stake driven into my heart.   1290

Gripus

That scumbag is free! Here I am, the guy who caught the trunk in my net
And pulled it out of the sea—and you give me absolutely nothing for it!

---

81 Cf. n. 80 above.

Labrax (*aside*)

By the immortal gods! This guy's remarks have pricked up my ears.

Gripus

I'll put up signs everywhere with letters two feet high saying

That anyone who's lost a trunk full of gold and silver should contact Gripus.   1295

(*to audience*) You at least won't be getting it!

Labrax (*aside*)

I think this guy knows who has my trunk!

I'll have to go talk to him. Please, gods, be on my side!

Gripus (*to Daemones inside*)

What are you calling me in for? I'm cleaning this spit up outside the door here.

It seems it's made more out of rust than iron!   1300

Every time I scrub it, it just gets redder and thinner.

The way it wastes away like an old man, it must be bewitched!

Labrax

Hello, young man.

Gripus

May the gods bless you and your unshaven head.

Labrax

What's happening?

Gripus

Spit-washing.

Labrax

What ails you today?

Gripus

Why do you ask? You some kind of faith-healer?

Labrax

Not exactly … close, though. Play with it.

Gripus

Okay, so you're   1305

A heel and a faker?

Labrax

You hit the nail right on the head!

Gripus

You certainly look the part.

What happened to you?

Labrax

I was cleaned out by the sea last night.

Poor me! My ship was shattered and I lost everything I had there.

Gripus

What'd you lose?

Labrax

A trunk full of silver and gold.

Gripus
Do you remember exactly what was in the trunk you lost?   1310
Labrax
What's it matter, now that it's gone?
Gripus
                  Still—
Labrax
                      Let's just change the subject.
Gripus
What if I know who found it? Prove to me it's yours.
Labrax
There were eight-hundred gold coins in a wallet there,
Along with one-hundred minae worth of Philips[82] in a separate leather purse.
Gripus (*aside*)
Holy Hercules what a haul! I'm in for a big fat reward!   1315
The gods do pay heed to human beings! I'll walk away loaded with loot!
It's his all right! Continue with the inventory.
Labrax
There was one solid standard talent[83] of silver in a bag,
Along with a wine bowl, a goblet, a pitcher, a water urn, and a ladle.[84]
Gripus
My! You certainly had quite a load of lucre in there!   1320
Labrax
"Had?" Could any word be sadder to hear than that when you have nothing?
Gripus
What would you give to someone as a finder's fee for all your stuff?
I'd appreciate a quick answer.
Labrax
                Thirty nummi.[85]
Gripus
                      Ridiculous!
Labrax
Forty.
Gripus
       Filthy cobwebs!
Labrax
             Fifty.

---

82 For the value of a Philip, see Appendix II p. 337.

83 For the value of a talent, see Appendix II p. 337.

84 All these items were used at parties where wine was served. In Greco-Roman antiquity, it generally was considered uncivilized to drink wine (which was high in alcohol content) without first diluting it with water—hence the items for mixing here.

85 For the value of thirty nummi, see Appendix II p. 337.

Gripus

Rotten acorns!

Labrax

Sixty.

Gripus

Now you're talking tiny beetle bugs!   1325

Labrax

I'll make it seventy then.

Gripus

You're just blowing smoke!

Labrax

I'll make it a thousand.

Gripus

You're dreaming!

Labrax

Not a penny more.

Gripus

Get lost!

Labrax

Listen:

Damn it, if I go away … then I'll be gone. How about eleven-hundred?

Gripus

Still dreaming!

Labrax

Then tell me what you want.

Gripus

A solid talent,

Not a penny more (unless you want to add something), not a penny less!   1330
Just say yes or no.

Labrax

What choice do I have? I hereby yield to necessity:

A talent it is.

Gripus

Come this way: I want Venus here to swear you in.

Labrax

Yes, I'll do whatever you want.

Gripus

Touch Venus' altar here.

Labrax

All right.

Gripus

Now you must swear an oath by Venus.

Labrax

What do I swear?

Gripus

What I tell you to.

Labrax

Dictate as you like. I'm no stranger to swearing oaths.   1335

Gripus

Hold on to the altar here.

Labrax

I've got it.

Gripus

Swear you'll pay me the money

As soon as you take possession of the trunk.

Labrax

Agreed.

Gripus

"Venus of Cyrene, I call you to be my witness

That if I find that trunk that I lost at sea in the shipwreck,

With all my gold and silver intact,   1340

And I take possession of it,

Then to this fellow Gripus here I ..." Touch me and say it.

Labrax

"... then to this fellow Gripus here I—and I pray you hear me now, Venus—

Will pay a solid talent of silver at once."

Gripus

"If you cheat me in any way, Venus will destroy you,   1345

Your filthy profession, and your entire life.

And may that last part hold regardless, once you've sworn."

Labrax

"If in any way I violate these conditions, Venus,

As you are my witness, I ask that all pimps suffer horribly."

Gripus

That'll happen anyway, even if you keep your pledge.   1350

Wait here while I go get the old man.

The minute he's here, demand the trunk back. (*exits*)

Labrax

Even if he does return the trunk to me,

I won't feel obligated to pay him a single penny.

I'm the one who decides what my tongue swears to.   1355

I'd better be quiet. Here he comes back with the old man.

SCENE 29

Gripus returns with Daemones.

Gripus
Follow me this way.

Daemones
                    So where is that pimp?

Gripus
                                        Hey you! Here's the man with your trunk.

Daemones
I acknowledge I have it, and if it's yours, I'll return it.
You'll get everything back intact just as it was.
Take it if it's yours.

Labrax
                    Oh, immortal gods! It's mine! Hail, trunk!   1360

Daemones
It's yours?

Labrax
            You have to ask? It'd still be mine if it had Jupiter's initials on it!

Daemones
Everything's intact, with the exception of the little chest
With the toys that allowed me to find my daughter today.

Labrax
What daughter?

Daemones
                Turns out your former property Palaestra is *actually* my daughter.

Labrax
Wow, that's just great! I'm so happy everything in this matter   1365
Has turned out just the way you wanted.

Daemones
                                That's a bit hard to believe.

Labrax
No, damn it, to prove just how happy I am,
I won't ask you to pay me a penny for her.

Daemones
                            Oh how generous of you!

Labrax
No, you're the only one being generous.

Gripus
                            Hey, you! You have the trunk now.

Labrax
I do.

Gripus
So hurry up!

Labrax

Hurry up what?

Gripus

With paying me the money. 1370

Labrax

I'm sure as hell not paying you, and I don't owe you a thing!

Gripus

How's that?

You don't owe me anything?

Labrax

Damn straight I don't!

Gripus

You deny swearing to me?

Labrax

I did swear and I'll swear now if I feel like it:
Oaths are for preserving assets, not losing them.

Gripus

Give me a solid talent of silver now, you oath-perverter! 1375

Daemones

Gripus, why are you asking for that talent?

Gripus

He swore he'd give it to me.

Labrax

I'm fond of swearing oaths. Are you the State Priest of Perjury?[86]

Daemones

What'd he promise you the money for?

Gripus

He swore that if I
Returned the trunk to him, he'd give
Me a talent of silver.

Labrax

Name your representative for an arbitration: 1380
I'll show you entered into an agreement with fraudulent intent,
And that I'm under the age of twenty-five.[87]

Gripus

Let's stick with him.

Labrax

It should be someone else.

---

86 A playful twist on the powerful Roman office of "High Priest" (*pontifex maximus*); for Romanization, see Introduction p. 3.

87 A Roman law (*lex Plaetoria*) prevented young men under twenty-five from entering into contracts on their own. As Labrax is clearly older than twenty-five (cf. 125), his assertion here illustrates the fraudulent extreme to which he would resort to win his case. For the very precise type of Romanization here, cf. n. 86 above.

If I won my case, I'd still hesitate to collect anything from him.
Daemones
Did you promise him the silver?
Labrax
                            Yes.
Daemones
                                    Anything you promised my slave
You also promised me. Don't even imagine, *pimp*,   1385
That you can pimp your way out of that!
Gripus
                            Thought you'd found
Someone you could hoodwink? The cold hard cash is mine!
And then I'll give it straight over to Master, so he'll free me.
Daemones
In light of my kindness toward you and my efforts in saving
All this for you—
Gripus
                    Your efforts? I don't think so, damn it!   1390
Daemones
—the smart thing for you to do would be to shut up. As for you,
The appropriate thing is to return a favor with a favor in kind.
Labrax
                                            You are of course
Considering my rights here?
Daemones
                    It's amazing I don't just consider ripping those away from you!
Gripus
I'm good: the pimp's going limp! Freedom's right around the corner for me!
Daemones
This fellow who found the trunk is my property.   1395
What's more, I saved the trunk and its valuable contents for you.
Labrax
I'm grateful, and there's no reason you shouldn't have that talent
I swore to give him.
Gripus
                    Hey you! The smart thing would be to give it to me.
Daemones
How about putting a lid on it?
Gripus
                            You pretend to support me while you fill your own coffers!
You may have cheated me out of the rest, but the reward's mine!   1400
Daemones
One more word and you'll be beaten.

Gripus
You can go ahead and kill me, damn it!
But I won't shut up unless you plug my pie-hole up with that talent!

Labrax
Your master's looking out for you. Shut up!

Daemones
Come on over here, pimp.

Labrax
Okay.

Gripus
Out in the open with it, please. No chummy whispering!

Daemones
All right, pimp: how much did you pay for the other girl?   1405
I mean Ampelisca.

Labrax
A thousand nummi.

Daemones
Interested in making
A fantastic deal?

Labrax
I sure am.

Daemones
I'll split the talent with you.

Labrax
Okay, that's fair.

Daemones
Take half
A talent for yourself to free Ampelisca, and give me the other half.

Labrax
That's fine.

Daemones
With my half I'll free Gripus,   1410
Seeing as you found a trunk and I found a daughter because of him.

Labrax
That's fair
And I'm immensely grateful.

Gripus
So when do I get my money?

Daemones
Everything's settled, Gripus—I have it.

Gripus
Damn it! I should have it!

Daemones
There's not a damn thing for you here, so stop hoping.

And you should let him off his oath.

Gripus

                                    Damn, that's the death of me!   1415

Death if I don't hang myself first! At least that way you'll damn well never cheat
    me again!

Daemones

Have dinner with us today, pimp.

Labrax

                             Sure, that's an offer I can stomach.

Daemones

Come on in, you two. Spectators, I'd also invite you to dinner too,
If I didn't have absolutely nothing to serve you—
And if I didn't know that you all had dinner invitations already.   1420
But if you want to give this play some thundering applause,
You can all come to party at my house—in sixteen years or so.
You two will dine here today.[88]

Labrax & Gripus

                    All right!

All

                      Applause please!

---

88   The invitation to Gripus to join them at dinner indicates that the slave will indeed be freed.

Truculentus

("The Fierce One")

CHARACTERS WITH SPEAKING PARTS

DINIARCHUS, *a young Athenian citizen*
ASTAPHIUM, *a slave (i.e., "maidservant") of Phronesium*
TRUCULENTUS, *a country slave of Strabax's family*
PHRONESIUM, *a prostitute/brothel owner living next door to Strabax's family*
STRATOPHANES, *a Babylonian mercenary soldier*
CYAMUS, *a cook and slave of Diniarchus*
STRABAX, *a young Athenian man who has grown up in the countryside*
CALLICLES, *an elderly citizen of Athens whose daughter has been raped by Diniarchus*
MAID, *an unnamed slave (i.e., "maidservant") of Callicles*
SYRA, *a slave of Phronesium*

SCENE

Athens: the action takes place in front of the houses of Phronesium and Strabax's father. One stage wing leads to the forum/city-center, the other to the harbor and country.

PROLOGUE[1]

Plautus seeks a small slice of your city,
Just a section of your enormous and glorious edifices,
Where he can construct Athens without a construction crew.[2]
What'll it be? Giving it to him or not? They say *"Yea!"*
Then it'd be best for me to take it from you this instant.   5
What if I asked for some of your private property? They say *"Nay!"*

---

1   The Roman comic playwrights introduced the use of an impersonal prologist (perhaps the head of the acting troupe) to ancient comedy to speak on behalf of the play and playwright. There are doubts as to whether this prologue is genuinely Plautine or arose from a later revival performance or manuscript editing (some Plautine plays do not have a formal prologue). The incomplete information about the plot this prologue divulges is repeated in Diniarchus' more informative opening monologue (see esp. 77-94).

2   For the self-conscious artifice of Plautine theater in general, see Introduction pp. 7-9, and for the arbitrariness of the theatrical space, cf. *Menaechmi* 72-76.

Hurray by Hercules,[3] then! What pillars of our good old-fashioned values you are,
And how ready your tongues are to refuse!
But let's get down to the business we're here for.
This stage you see is set up to be Athens,   10
At least for as long as we're putting on this comedy.
A woman by the name of Phronesium[4] lives here.
Now she truly embodies the morality of our time:
She takes no interest in what her lover has already given,
But dedicates herself to taking what's not yet taken.   15
Her method? Asking and absconding,
As all women do when they sense someone's hot for them.[5]
She's pretending she's given birth to a baby for a soldier's sake,
So she can swiftly abscond with every last morsel of his money.
What more can I say ...[6]   20

****

SCENE 1

Diniarchus enters.

Diniarchus

A lover could spend an entire lifetime trying to count
All the ways there are to die for love—and he'd fail.
Not even Venus[7] herself, the consummate accountant
Of all things amorous, could ever render an accurate account   25
Of all the ways to make a spectacle out of a lover,
All the ways to ruin him, all the ways to con and cajole him,
Or how much soft-soap, or how many hard feelings to expect,
Or how many desperate pleas must be made to the gods, by god!
On top of a mountain of gifts, there's a pile of lies to be dished out.   30
First, there's her annual fee, or I should say, her first haul:
Worth, maybe, three nights in all!
In the meantime, she tries to determine if you're lavish or stingy
By asking for cash, wine, oil or just some grain.
It's just like when a fisherman casts his net into a pond.   35
When the net has made it all the way to the bottom, he tugs on the line.
Once he's cast it just right, he takes care to keep the fish from scaring,
And shifting the net this way and that he blocks its escape,
Until net and fish pop right out of the water!

---

3   For the god Hercules, see Appendix I p. 335.
4   For the significance of her name, see n. 28 below.
5   For the (undercutting of?) traditional misogyny in the play, see Introduction pp. 24-25.
6   The text is mutilated here.
7   For the goddess Venus, see Appendix I p. 335. For her ironic role in the background of this play, see n. 73 below.

It's exactly the same for the lover who's lavish, not stingy,   40
And gives all that he's asked for:
Add a few nights and he swallows the hook whole.
Give him just one straight shot of love
And watch it course through his veins and wend its way to his heart—
That spells the end for him, his finances, and all his credibility.   45
When a whore gets mad at her lover, it's a double homicide:
It means the end of both his spirit and his money.
And if she takes another lover? That's the end of him yet again.
If his nights with her are few and far between? The end of his spirit.
If he becomes a regular customer? He's happy, but it's the end for his money.   50
Before you give her one thing, she's asked for a hundred:
"I'm completely out of cash;" "This dress is falling apart;"
"I had to buy a new maid;" "There's this silver bowl ..."
Or it's a bronze bowl, or an inlaid couch,
Or a Greek[8] jewel box, or there's always something   55
That a lover has to give to his whore!
We voluntarily destroy all our finances, our credibility and ourselves,
And on top of that, we must expend every ounce of our energy
On keeping our parents and relatives in the dark about it all.
But if instead of conning them we made them cognizant of it all,   60
They'd dampen our youthful indiscretion just in the nick of time,
And we'd hand down a decent legacy to our heirs!
I guarantee there'd be far fewer pimps and whores,   62a
And a lot fewer bankruptcies than there are now!
But as things are, we've got just about as many pimps and whores
As there are flies on a wickedly hot summer afternoon.   65
On any given day, the highest concentration of them both
Can be found around the bankers' booths.[9]
In fact, you couldn't count them all—I can personally assure you[10]
That there are more whores at those booths than there are scale-weights!
I have no idea what business they have around the bankers,   70
Unless they're there to monitor the transactions
Of current borrowers and future customers—
I of course refer to accounts outstanding, not accounts received.
Bottom line: in this great nation of ours,
Made up of so many men living in leisure following the defeat of our foes,   75
It behooves all who have the wherewithal to buy themselves some lovin'.

---

8   Note Diniarchus' Roman perspective here; cf. Introduction pp. 3, 9.

9   A Roman audience would think of the bankers' stalls along the Sacred Way in the forum, which had
    probably recently been rebuilt (i.e., in 193 BCE) after being destroyed several years earlier by fire. For
    the possible date of the play, see Introduction pp. 19-20.

10 Ancient narrators are usually careful to distinguish between events they have only heard about from
    others and those they have personally observed (i.e., by "autopsy").

In my case, the prostitute who lives in this house here, Phronesium,
Has entirely excised her name from my heart.
I used to be on the closest possible terms with her—
Which are the worst possible terms for a lover's finances. 80
Once she discovered an even bigger sucker than myself,
Someone who'd give her more than I could, he took my place,
Even though the little sneak says she finds him annoying and repulsive.
He's a Babylonian soldier.[11] He's supposed to be arriving from abroad soon,
And that's why she's worked up a plot. 85
She's pretending that she's just had a baby
And that the baby is the soldier's, so she can boot me out of her house,
And the two of them can party down there like Greeks.[12]
So that's why the slut needs a faux-baby. 88a
Does she really think she's pulling the wool over my eyes,
And that she could keep me in the dark if she were actually pregnant? 90
I got back to Athens just the day before yesterday.
I'd been in Lemnos[13] as part of an official embassy.
But here's her cute little maid Astaphium—
I've transacted some business with her before too.

SCENE 2

Astaphium enters from Phronesium's house.

Astaphium (*to slaves inside*)
(*SONG through 129*)

Listen closely at the door and keep close watch over the house: 95
No customer of ours must ever go forth and multiply!
Though he spreadeth his seed among us, make sure
The fruit he bears with him is bitter and barren. I know how men are,
Especially the young ones nowadays!
Five or six buds come in together to visit some of us whores; 100
Their plans are carefully laid out in advance: once they're inside,
One of them plants kiss after kiss on his girl and the others become kleptos.
If they notice anyone on guard, the clowns create a diversion.
They dine at our expense, stuffing themselves like sausages.

---

11 The soldier's name is Greek, not Babylonian (see n. 36 below). He is probably to be thought of as a
    mercenary in the army of the Seleucids who ruled Babylonia following the death of Alexander the
    Great in 323 BCE.

12 Plautus coined the verb *pergraecor* ("to *really* Greek it up"), which reflects a traditional, stereotypical
    Roman view of Greeks as decadent. For the Roman perspective here, cf. 55 and n. 8 above.

13 An island in the north Aegean Sea. Diniarchus' ambassadorship indicates that he is a citizen of high
    status and wealth.

That's how it goes down, and some of you spectators[14] can vouch for every detail.   105
What a heroic campaign, stealing plunder from plunderers!
But, by Castor,[15] we sure do graciously return the favor to these looters!   107-10
They watch us pillage their property, and then voluntarily bring us even more.

Diniarchus (*aside*)

    Ouch! Everything she says stings me especially.

    I've brought plenty of my property here … for surrender.

Astaphium (*to someone inside*)

Yes, I remember. I'll bring him back with me to our house if he's home.

Diniarchus

    Hey, Astaphium! Hold on a minute before you take off.   115

Astaphium

Who's there?

Diniarchus

    Turn around and see.

Astaphium

                Really, who's there?

Diniarchus

    Someone who wants only the best for you.

Astaphium

                 If that's what you want,

Hand it over then.

Diniarchus

        That'll happen. Just turn around though.

Astaphium

                    Oh,

Now you're really annoying me, whoever you are.

Diniarchus

    Wait, you worthless whore!   120

Astaphium

    Leave me alone, you upper-class bore.

    Oh, is that you there, Diniarchus? So it is.

Diniarchus

    Good to see you.

Astaphium

        You, too.

Diniarchus

    Come on over here and give me your hand.

---

14 A direct appeal to the young males in audience, common in Plautus (cf. the more formulaic example, introduced by "where are the …," as at *Menaechmi* 128), who may have vociferously identified themselves.

15 Castor (= Greek Kastor) and his brother Pollux (= Greek Polydeuces), known as the Dioscuri, are gods of athletics in general and horsemanship in particular, and in myth become alternatively human and divine. In Roman comedy, only women swear by Castor.

Astaphium

    Your wish is my command.   125

Diniarchus

    How's it going?

Astaphium (*trying to release herself from his grip*)

               I'm fine as I can see you are.

    We should throw a dinner party now that you're back.

Diniarchus

    Lovely words and a lovely invitation, Astaphium!

Astaphium

                             Please

Just let me carry out my mistress' order.

Diniarchus

                   Off you go. But listen—

Astaphium

                        What do you want?

Diniarchus

Tell me where you're off to and who you're supposed to bring back.

Astaphium

                          Archilis   130

    The midwife.

Diniarchus

        You sneaky woman! You reek of all the training you've digested![16]

    You're caught red-handed, bitch!

Astaphium

                Please do explain.

Diniarchus

    You distinctly said you'd bring back a "him" here, not a "her."[17]

    Your man has suddenly morphed into a woman: you're a bitch *and* a witch.

    So just tell me who this man is, Astaphium—a new lover?   135

Astaphium

    I think you have too much time on your hands.

Diniarchus

                Why's that?

Astaphium

    Your nose is in other people's business, but you're not on their payroll.

Diniarchus

    I owe all that leisure time to you.

Astaphium

              Please do explain.

Diniarchus

               Glad to oblige.

---

16 Literally, "you stink of the lesson you eat," a proverb.

17 I.e., at 114.

Once you bankrupted me, the only business left for me was other people's business.
If that hadn't happened, I'd have plenty of my own business to busy myself with.   140

Astaphium

Did you really imagine you could become a public servant of Venus or Amor[18]
Without bankrupting yourself right out of any and all of your business?

Diniarchus

It's the opposite of what you say. Phronesium is the public servant here.
Our contract was torn up when I couldn't pay my grazing fees and she confiscated
    my herd.[19]

Astaphium

You're just like everybody else who mismanages his affairs: 145
When they can't pay their taxes, they usually blame the tax collectors.

Diniarchus

That whole pecuniary situation at your place turned into a stampede for me.
In lieu of that, how about providing me with a little piece of flatland to plow inside
    here?

Astaphium

Our place is not for plowing—it's a grassy meadow. If you're so set on plowing,
You should go find some boys. They're used to being ploughed.[20]   150
We regulate access to our pasture. *They* collect fees for their plow-land.

Diniarchus

I'm quite familiar with both systems.

Astaphium

                                And that's precisely why you're out of business—
You're a failure in both fields. But which territory do you prefer?

Diniarchus

Tough call: you women are a lot pushier, but they're accomplished liars.
Whatever you give them disappears and is never seen again;   155
When you ladies get something, at least you eat it up or gulp it down.
To sum up: they're degenerates, you're all worthless show-offs.[21]

Astaphium

Everything you say against us or the boys, Diniarchus,

---

18 Amor (= Cupid(o) and Greek Eros), son of Venus and the personification of sexual love.

19 A difficult and thoroughly Romanized passage. Private tax collectors were contracted by the state to
    rent out public land to citizens for grazing their animals. Following up on Astaphium's (figurative)
    mention in line 141 of public service—here different from our sense of the term in that it probably
    refers to slaves employed by the state to perform certain offices—Diniarchus in his conceit alleges that
    he has become financially beholden to his mistress because she violated their agreed upon terms of
    payment.

20 There is a running debate in ancient literature as to whether women or boys make better lovers for men.
    Adult males engaged in homoerotic, as well as heterosexual activity, as long as their status was not
    threatened by such encounters (i.e., they did not allow themselves to be sexually penetrated).

21 Diniarchus' meaning is not clear. Whereas the women conspicuously consume some of their fees for
    prostitution on food and drink (for parties with their customers?), clothes (?), make-up (?), etc., boys do
    not?

Applies only to you.
Diniarchus

How's that?
Astaphium

Here's how:

If you're going to accuse others, you need to be squeaky clean yourself.   160

You, Mr. Smarty-pants, have nothing of ours; we "worthless show-offs" own all
    your stuff.

Diniarchus

Oh, Astaphium! This isn't the way you used to speak with me!

You were so charming back when what's now yours was mine!

Astaphium

When a man's a live one, you get to know him; when he's not, R.I.P.

I once knew you that way.

Diniarchus

So now you're dead to me?   165

Astaphium

Please now! Could anything be more obvious?

You used to be the consummate lover. Now you only bring your mistress
    complaints.

Diniarchus

Damn it, this is all your fault! You just had to rush things along!

Shouldn't you have paced your plundering some, to string out my financial
    extinction a bit?

Astaphium

A lover's like an enemy's town.

Diniarchus

What the hell do you mean?   170

Astaphium

The sooner he's plundered and pillaged, the better for his mistress.

Diniarchus

True, but a friend and a lover are two very different things.

And it's absolutely the case that a longtime friend is the best thing you can have.

Astaphium

If he's still alive.

Diniarchus

Damn it, I'm not dead! I've still got land and houses!

Astaphium

Then, goodness me, why are you standing outside like a stranger or some
    foreigner?   175

Stranger, indeed! You go right in. There's absolutely no one in world

She loves with all her heart and soul as much as you—if you really have property.

Diniarchus

Your tongue and talk may be sprinkled over with honey,

But the hearts and actions of you women have been soaked in bile and bitter
   vinegar:

There's a sweet coating around your words, but you're pure venom on the inside! 180

Astaphium

If lovers don't shower us with gifts … then I haven't learned how to talk.

Diniarchus

If a lover lacks the means to shower you with gifts … then *I* haven't learned how
   to talk. 181a

Astaphium

You shouldn't talk like that, my dearly beloved!

That's for cheapskates who hate themselves.

Diniarchus

You're a bitch … and just as irresistible as ever.

Astaphium

                                  We've looked so forward to your return!

My mistress has been wanting to see you so badly! 185

Diniarchus

Come again?

Astaphium

            You're the only one of all her lovers that she loves.

Diniarchus

                                        Hurray—

For my land and houses! You've rescued me just in time! But tell me, Astaphium …

Astaphium

                                          Yes?

Diniarchus

Is Phronesium inside now?

Astaphium

                     She's inside for you. I don't know about any others.

Diniarchus

Is she well?

Astaphium

                  Oh dear yes! And I think she'll be even better once she sees you.

Diniarchus

Do you know what makes falling in love our greatest downfall? 190

When we're told what we want to hear, even when it's an outrageous lie,

We're foolish enough to take it as the truth, and we foolishly stay calm.

Astaphium

Really now! That's not so!

Diniarchus

                    So you say she loves me?

Astaphium

                              Yes, you—and you alone!

Diniarchus

I heard she's had a baby.

Astaphium

                    Please be quiet, Diniarchus!

Diniarchus

                                        Why?

Astaphium

I shudder terribly whenever someone mentions the childbirth!   195
You almost lost your Phronesium. Please do go in and see her.
You'll have to wait for her to come out, though. She was taking a bath.

Diniarchus

But tell me: how does someone who was never pregnant manage to give birth?
I never noticed her belly swelling—at least as far as I could see.

Astaphium

She was hiding it from you. She was afraid   200
You'd press her to have an abortion and kill the child.[22]

Diniarchus

Then that Babylonian soldier that she's expecting right now
Is the baby's father?

Astaphium

                    Yes, we got a message from him,
And it said he'd be here soon. I'm surprised he isn't here already.

Diniarchus

Should I go in then?

Astaphium

                    Absolutely! Just as if it were your own home.   205
You're still very much one of the family now, Diniarchus.

Diniarchus

When will you be back?

Astaphium

                    Very soon—the place I'm headed for is nearby.

Diniarchus

Come back soon. In the meantime, I'll be waiting inside the house here.

---

22 Plant extracts (and other methods) were used to induce abortions in antiquity. Ancient attitudes toward
abortion were mixed, as today. Infanticide, including the exposure of children, however, seems to
have been widely practiced. See further *The Oxford Classical Dictionary*, 3rd edn. (1996) entries for
"abortion" and "infanticide."

SCENE 3

Left alone on stage, Astaphium launches into a song.

Astaphium

(*SONG through 255*)

    Ha, ha, hee, hee! Ah, to relax

    Now that this tedious bore's gone inside!   210

  All alone at last! Now I'll speak freely,

  And say exactly what I want, and whatever way I please to say it!

My mistress has already sung a dirge over lover-boy's property inside:

All his land and houses have been mortgaged, and Amor holds the deeds.

My mistress does divulge her most important plots to him,   215

Though he's so much more a consultant to her than a comrade-in-arms.

  He gave while he could, now he has nothing. We have what he had,

  He has what we had—nothing. That's the human condition.

  Human fortune changes so fast, life is uncertain.

  We remember his prosperity, he remembers our poverty;   220

  Is it any wonder we've swapped memories?

  He's in need—hey, what are we to do? He had his lovin', fair and square.

  It'd be a crime for us to pity men who mismanage their affairs.

    A proper prostitute should have good teeth,

    And flatter and slaver over every man she meets;   225

    The tongue's for wheedling, the heart's for scheming.

    A hooker should be just like a bramble bush:

  Any man who brushes against her suffers instant loss or pain.

  She should never let a lover plead his case, but when he has nothing to give,

  Just dismiss him for dereliction of duty.   230

No man will ever be a proper lover unless he's an enemy to his money.

He'll get his lovin' as long as money's coming in; when's he's out, he needs new income.

Once he's a have-not, let him calmly give way to the haves.

There's no point in giving unless the giver wants to give again.

The person who easily forgets he's given will get his lovin' at our house.   235

Yes, the proper lover first neglects his affairs and then neglects the loss of his money.

The men are always claiming we're the offenders here,

And that we're greedy. Now how is that so? What is it we're doing wrong?

I submit: has any lover ever truly given his mistress enough?

Has any one of us ever received enough or even asked for enough?   240

    Now when a lover and his gifts are barren,

    We take him on his word alone that it's so,

    And when he has nothing to give, it's not as if we have enough.

    And so we're always seeking new donors

    Who have untapped treasures to donate.   245

    Take for instance this young country fellow, Strabax, who lives over there.

    You'd be hard pressed to find a more charming or generous donor.

  Just last night he hurdled over the garden fence to pay us a visit

Without his father finding out. I'd like to see him.
But he's got a slave who is an utter savage.   250
If he so much as sees any one of us women getting close to their house,
He raises a ruckus and shoos us away like geese in a grain store.
He's such a rube! I'll take my chances and knock on the door.
Anyone watching the door here? Anyone inside?   254-5

SCENE 4

Truculentus answers the door.

Truculentus[23]

Who's that ramrodding our door so violently?

Astaphium

It's me! Look over here at me.

Truculentus

What do you mean "me?"

Astaphium

Doesn't it look like me?

Truculentus

What's all this running up to the house and pounding on it about?

Astaphium

I hope you're well.

Truculentus

I'm sick and tired of your "hope you're well's." Don't want 'em;
I'd rather be sick or fall down a well than accept one of those.   260
Just tell me: what business do you have here at our house?

Astaphium

Such anger! Put a plug in it!

Truculentus

What's that about plugging? You want me to bang her?[24]
Are you trying to lure a simple farmer into one of your sick orgies? Have you no
   shame?

Astaphium

I said "anger," not "bang her!" You're the one who perverted my words.
This guy is way too savage!

Truculentus

Are you going to keep badmouthing me, woman?   265

Astaphium

How'd I insult you?

Truculentus

Well, you're saying I'm a savage.

---

23 His name means "fierce" or "savage" in Latin.
24 For Truculentus' characteristic linguistic confusion, cf. 683-86 and n. 55 below

If you don't leave right this moment or tell me what it is you want,
Damn it woman, I'll flatten you underfoot the way a sow flattens her litter!

Astaphium

This kind of talk reeks of the farm.

Truculentus

                        You pack of apes ought to be ashamed of yourselves,
Coming here to parade yourself about with your bones all gussied up,   270
All proud of the fact you've dyed your dress smoky-black. You're disgusting!
Think you're pretty because you've got some bronze bracelets?

Astaphium

Ohhhh, I like it when you talk tough to me!

Truculentus

                    See if you like this one: I noticed
You're carrying bronze rings around with you—planning to claim some property?[25]
I bet those Victories you're wearing are made of wood.[26]   275

Astaphium

Don't touch me.

Truculentus

              Me touch you? I solemnly swear by this little hoe of mine
That I'd rather canoodle with a broad-horned cow out in the country
And spend the whole night long lying in the straw with her
Than receive a hundred free nights with the likes of you, dinner included!
You think country-living's disgraceful? I'm ashamed to even think of your way
    of life!   280
But just what business do you have at our house, woman?
Why do you run over here every time we come to the city?

Astaphium

I want to meet the women of your house.

Truculentus

                  What women?
There isn't even a single female fly in this house.

Astaphium

There's not one woman living there?

Truculentus

                  They took off for the country. Now get lost. 285

---

25 A reference to a solemn Roman ceremony (*mancipatio*) to mark a transfer of property that involved the use of bronze coins and a scale. Truculentus is mocking Astaphium's choice of jewelry (i.e., of base metal), and also suggesting that she is taking on airs by claiming the right to participate in a ceremony that was probably not extended to slaves.

26 I.e., are counterfeit. Silver coins bearing the image of the Roman goddess *Victoria* (i.e., the personification of victory, worshipped widely in Rome and Italy = Greek Nike) were first minted *ca* 200 BCE, and their use as pendant earrings or on a necklace presumably was still fashionable in Rome. A "Victory" was worth half a *denarius* (a Roman silver coin originally worth 10 *asses*, the *as* being a copper coin of relatively small value). For the possible date of the play, see Introduction pp. 19-20.

Astaphium

Why are you shouting like a crazy person?

Truculentus

If you don't scurry on out of here this instant,
I swear I'll tear that phony, foofy, frizzy, frilly, over-perfumed
Hair of yours right out of your skull.

Astaphium

Why would you do that?

Truculentus

Because you have the audacity to come up to our house all drenched in perfume …
Er, and because your cheeks are all prettied up with that rosy rouge.   290

Astaphium

Goodness me oh my! I only blushed because you were shouting.

Truculentus

Really? You blushed now did you, whore? As if there were any place left
On your entire body where any color could show through!
You painted your cheeks red and covered the rest of your body with fine white
     powder.
You're all sluts.

Astaphium

And just how have "us sluts" ever done you any wrong?   295

Truculentus

I know more than you think I know.

Astaphium

Pray tell—
What do you know?

Truculentus

I know our master's son Strabax is being ruined in your house,
And that he's being lured into double-dealing and indecency!

Astaphium

If I thought you were sane, I'd yell "Abuse!"
No man is ever ruined here in our house. The men destroy themselves,   300
And after that happens, they can walk away from here intact if they want to.
I don't happen to know that young man of yours.

Truculentus

Oh, is that so now?
The garden wall between our houses would beg to differ. You know, the one
That loses a brick or two each night as he travels the path of perdition to your place?

Astaphium

It's an old wall. There's nothing odd about old bricks falling down.   305

Truculentus

So it's a case of old bricks falling down by themselves?
If I don't tell my master everything you're up to,
May no human being ever trust me again!

Astaphium

Is your master a savage just like you?

Truculentus

Well, he didn't create his wealth by enriching hookers.

That took hard work and thriftiness.   310

And now it's being secretly transferred next door for you whores

To gobble up, guzzle down, and smear all over your bodies! *I should keep quiet?*

You can be damn sure I'm going to the forum to tell the old man everything!

I won't let this stir up a hornet's nest of troubles for my back forty.[27] (*exits*)

Astaphium

My goodness! If this guy subsisted on a mustard-only diet,   315

I don't think he could be sourer. He certainly is faithful to his master, though.

He's quite the savage, but I do hope that all our coaxing, cajoling

And whatever else we pull out of our prostitute's bag of tricks can tame him.

I've seen even the wildest beasts charmed before.

Now I'll go back to my mistress. Oh, look: my bore is back.   320

He looks gloomy. He must not have met up with Phronesium yet.

SCENE 5

Diniarchus emerges from Phronesium's house.

Diniarchus

For fish, life is one continuous bath.

But fish have nothing on this bathing beauty Phronesium here.

If women spent as much time in bed as they do in their baths,

Their lovers would all become bath operators.   325

Astaphium

Can't you put up with waiting just a little?

Diniarchus

Damn it, I'm exhausted from waiting!

In fact, I'm so tired I could really use a bath myself right now.

But please go in, Astaphium, and tell her I'm here—

And get her to hurry up. She's bathed enough.   330

Astaphium

Okay.

Diniarchus

Are you still there?

Astaphium

What do you want?

Diniarchus

May the gods damn me

For calling you back! Didn't I just tell you to leave?

---

27 I.e., for his backside (through beating/whipping).

Astaphium

Yes. But why'd you call me back then, you worthless and silly man?
You just created a mile's worth of delays to deal with. (*she goes in*)

Diniarchus

I really wonder why she stood out front here for so long.   335
She's lying in ambush for someone. The soldier perhaps?
They're zeroed in on him like vultures
That know three days in advance when a meal's coming their way.
They're fixated on him all right, and have even gone slack-jawed over it.
Once he's arrived, no one will pay any attention to me.   340
It'll be as if I've been dead for two hundred years.
How sweet it is to preserve one's property! I'm utterly screwed!
I lost my inheritance and now I must mourn its passing.
But what if a big fat legacy happened to come my way?
Since I've now seen both the bitter   345
And the sweet side of having money,
Damned if I don't watch it like a miser and guard it so closely
That within a few days of getting it ... I'll be broke again.
That's how I'd silence my current critics anyhow.
Hey, look! Their floodgates are opening up!   350
How those ol' door bolts do suck up everything that comes their way!

SCENE 6

Phronesium, accompanied by female attendants, enters from her house.

Phronesium[28]

Oh, come now, sweetheart, don't be afraid! You don't think my door
Has teeth, do you?

Diniarchus

                    Ah, it's spring, beautiful spring!
She's all in blossom! The bloom of her perfume, how radiantly she radiates!

Phronesium

Where are your manners, Diniarchus? You've just returned from Lemnos now   355
And you don't have a nice kiss for your girlfriend?

Diniarchus

Waah! Damn! Now, I'm in for a beating—and a really bad one at that!

Phronesium

Why'd you turn away?

Diniarchus

                    Greetings, Phronesium.

---

28 Her name is based on a Greek word for "wisdom" (*phronesis*). Prostitutes in Roman comedy often
    have names of neuter formation (here marked by the -*ium* ending), though they are usually treated as
    feminine. The etymological meanings of their names typically highlight their roles as sexual objects (cf.
    Erotium, "Love-thing," in Plautus' *Menaechmi*), whereas Phronesium's name points to her empowering
    intelligence. See further Introduction pp. 21-24.

Phronesium

Greetings! Now that you're safely back, will you be dining with us today?

Diniarchus

I have a commitment.

Phronesium

                    Where?

Diniarchus

                          Wherever you tell me I do.   360

Phronesium

I'd love it if you dined here.

Diniarchus

                     And I'd love it even more!

And you'll spend the day with me, right Phronesium dear?

Phronesium

I would if I could.

Diniarchus (*to an imaginary slave, as if he were at a banquet inside*)

                  Quick, go get my sandals!

Take the table away!

Phronesium

                Really! Are you out of your mind?

Diniarchus

I feel so sick, I couldn't possibly drink now.   365

Phronesium

Hold on! I'll do something for you. Don't go away.

Diniarchus

                        Ah, that's like a bucket of cold water.

I'm coming back to my senses. Take my sandals away! Give me a drink!

Phronesium

Oh, really! This is just like you! Tell me now,

How was your trip?

Diniarchus

                Absolutely perfect, seeing that it's brought me

Straight back here to you and given me a chance to see you.

Phronesium

                               Hold me!   370

Diniarchus

Gladly! This is sweeter than sweet, sweet honey!

This is exactly why I'm luckier than Jupiter.[29]

Phronesium

Give me a kiss.

Diniarchus

                How about ten kisses?

---

29 For the god Jupiter, see Appendix I p. 335.

Phronesium

That's why you're so poor:
You promise me more than I ask you for.

Diniarchus

If only you were as frugal with my property as you are now   375
With your kisses!

Phronesium

If I were able to spare
Anything for you, I would certainly do it.

Diniarchus

Are you all neatly cleaned up now?

Phronesium

I think so.
Why? Do I seem dirty to you?

Diniarchus

No, of course not.
But there was a time (back when I was still a live one)   380
That we liked to get dirty with each other.
But what's all this I heard you're doing when I arrived?
You devised a new scheme while I was away?

Phronesium

What do you mean?

Diniarchus

Let me first express my heartiest congratulations
On your being blessed with progeny and your coming through it so well.   385

Phronesium (*to slaves*)

Move away from here now and close the door.
Now that you're the only one left to hear what I have to say
(And you know I've always confided my most important plans to you):
I haven't actually had a baby and I was never pregnant.
I was just pretending to be pregnant. I won't lie about it.   390

Diniarchus

Who'd you do it for, love of my life?

Phronesium

The Babylonian soldier.
He kept me like a wife for a year
While he was here.[30]

Diniarchus

I'd suspected as much.
But why? What did you hope to gain by pretending?

---

30 I.e., the mercenary soldier undertook no campaign for a year and apparently rented Phronesium's
exclusive services during that time.

Phronesium
> I wanted something to lasso him in and tie him up with,   395
> To make sure he'd come back to me again.
> He recently sent me a letter saying
> He'd come and find out just what I think of him.
> And he said he'd give me all his property
> If I didn't kill the baby and raised it instead.[31]

Diniarchus
> I'm glad to hear that.   400
> So what's the plan?

Phronesium
> When the ninth month
> Was fast approaching, my mother ordered the maids
> To fan out in every direction
> And look for a boy or a girl that could be passed off as mine.
> Here's the gist of it: do you know our   405
> Hairdresser Syra?

Diniarchus
> The one who's based near the temple?
> I know her.

Phronesium
> She went around to the families she works for to track down a child.
> She secretly brought me one
> That she claimed had been given to her.

Diniarchus
> Oh, what a sleazy business!
> So the mother who gave birth to it first is no longer the mother,   410
> But the mother who rebirthed it is—you?

Phronesium
> You've got it down pat.
> Now according to the soldier's message,
> He'll be here soon.

Diniarchus
> So in the meantime,
> You're taking good care of yourself just as a "new mom" should?

Phronesium
> Of course.
> What could be finer than giving birth without going through the labor?   415
> You know what they say: everybody should excel at their craft.

---

31 For infanticide in the ancient world, see n. 22 above. A Roman father formally recognized a newborn as his own by lifting it up (*tollere*) off the ground. In the event of his absence, he could transfer that power to the child's mother.

Diniarchus

    But what'll happen to me when the soldier comes?

    How am I supposed to live without you?

Phronesium

                         When I have what I need from him,

    It'll be easy for me to throw some sort of a tiff

    And create a major rift between the two of us.   420

    Then, my dearest, I'll be with you

    All the time.

Diniarchus

              By which you of course mean you'll *be with* me all the time?

Phronesium

    I need to do a sacrifice on behalf of the baby,

    Since it's five days old now.[32]

Diniarchus

              Yes, you should.

Phronesium

    Do you want to give me some little gift for it?   425

Diniarchus

    Oh, I feel like a winner again, my love,

    When you ask me for something!

Phronesium

              That's just how I feel when I get it.

Diniarchus

    It'll be here, pronto. I'll send my slave over with it.

Phronesium

    Yes, definitely do that.

Diniarchus

             Whatever he brings, I hope you like it.

Phronesium

    By god, I'm sure you'll give careful thought   430

    To seeing it's a gift that I'll like.

Diniarchus

    Anything else you'd like from me?

Phronesium

                Only that you visit me

When you have a chance. Goodbye (*enters her house*).

Diniarchus

                  Goodbye.

---

32 A reference to the Athenian ceremony of the Amphidromia, according to which on the fifth (some
sources say seventh or tenth) day after its birth a child was named, which amounted to a formal
declaration of intent to raise it (cf. n. 31 above). It is especially ironic that Diniarchus should provide
funds in celebration of this occasion, as he is in fact the baby's father.

By the immortal gods! For her to do what she just did for me!
That was not the act of a mistress,   435
But the sort of thing only a close confidante or a soul mate does!
She confided in me about passing a child off as her own![33]
That's something not even a sister tells her very own sister!
She's revealed the innermost part of her heart to me!
She'll never be unfaithful to me, as long as she lives!   440
How could I not be in love with her? How could I not want the best for her?
I'd sooner stop loving myself than I would her.
Why shouldn't I send her a gift? Yes!
I'll have five minae[34] sent over to her in honor of the occasion,
And at least another mina's worth of food.   445
Why shouldn't she have the best when she wants only the best for me?
Better her than me—seeing as I'm my own worst enemy.

SCENE 7

Phronesium enters with two attendants and the baby. There apparently
is a couch on stage (cf. 478ff.).
(SONG through 464)

Phronesium
   Nurse the baby. How wretched
And heart-wrenching motherhood is! There's nothing but pain for us mothers!   449-50
When I ponder it over in my heart, it's a terrible lie that's told about us women:
We are given far too little credit for being as wicked as we naturally are!
   I'm talking about myself, based wholly on my own experience.
My mind is full of fear, my heart is assailed   454-55
With apprehension—that my scheme will die together with the baby!
Now that I'm said to be a mother, I want it to live all the more.
I've already dared this deception—and one even greater's to follow.
I've followed a shameless path in search of profit,
And adopted someone else's troubles as my own.   460
Never embark upon a deceitful endeavor
Unless you can bring the utmost care and craftiness to it.
You all can see how I've come out here in costume
To play the part of an exhausted, post-partum mom.
If a woman doesn't put the final polish on the evil plot she's started,   465
This means a migraine's in store for her, along with melancholy and absolute
   misery.
But she quickly comes to despise any good she undertakes:
You can find very few women who tire of scheming,

---

33 Palming off a suppositious child on a husband was a crime in ancient Rome.
34 For the value of five minae, see Appendix II p. 337.

And just as few who follow through on any good they've started.
For a woman, doing ill is a far better burden to bear than doing good.   470
I'm a nasty one, thanks to my mother's training and my natural malice:
I pretended I'm pregnant for the benefit of the Babylonian soldier,
And I want the soldier to know that malice of mine was carefully calculated.
I believe he'll be here very soon. Now I've intentionally taken appropriate measures
To appear post-partum and confined to bed.   475
Give me some myrrh and light a fire on the altar, so I can worship Lucina.[35]
Put it here and get out of my sight! Oh, Pitheceum,
Come, help me, help me lie down! Yes, like that—ah, just right for a new mom.
Bring me my sandals, throw a blanket over me, Archilis.
Where are you, Astaphium? Bring herbs and sweetbread inside here.   480
Bring me water for my hands! My goodness, I wish the soldier would come!

SCENE 8

The soldier enters with a retinue and gifts for Phronesium.

Stratophanes[36]

Don't expect me to trumpet my battle-prowess, spectators.
I toot my own horn with my actions, not my words.
I'm well-aware there's a mountain of military men who are liars:
One could mention Homerides[37] and a hundred others,   485
Who've been exposed for telling monstrous lies and martial tall-tales.[38]
                    ****
I don't care for someone who wins the praise of listeners, not witnesses.[39]
One eyewitness is more valuable than ten pairs of ears.
Listeners can only say what they've heard; eyewitnesses see the plain truth.   490
Nor do I care for the man urban wags laud, but the rank and file never mention,
Nor the man whose tongue is sharper than his sword—off the battlefield, that is!
Doers of deeds bring more boons to the populace than fancy flappers of jaws.
True valor easily earns clear-voiced eloquence-itude for itself.
In my book, an eloquent citizen without valor is no better than a professional
     mourner,   495

---

35 A Roman goddess of childbirth, sometimes identified with Juno (see Appendix I p. 335).

36 His appropriately blustery name means "Light of the Army" in Greek.

37 Stratophanes is confused here. Homer was the 8th century BCE epic poet of the *Iliad* and *Odyssey*. The Homeridae were a guild of professional rhapsodes who recited Homer's poems. The otherwise unattested name Homerides seems to clumsily conflate "Homer" and "Homeridae," and Stratophanes also mistakenly believes that the traditionally blind bard Homer was a soldier.

38 In the course of Stratophanes' bumbling speech here (cf. n. 37 above), he seems to be alluding to contemporary controversy surrounding Roman commanders' highly competitive claims to celebrate military triumphs in a period of enormous military expansion. Cf. Introduction p. 2.

39 Ancient narrators are often careful to distinguish between events they have only heard about from others and those they have personally observed (i.e., by "autopsy"), though Stratophanes' insistence on eyewitness accounts here is characteristically over-the-top.

Who only knows how to laud others but cannot praise herself.
I'm here in Attic Athens[40] to visit my mistress, and to see how she's doing.
I pressed my bod' up against hers nine months ago and now she's pregnant.
Phronesium (*to Astaphium*)
See who's speaking close by.
Astaphium (*to Phronesium*)
                                        Your soldier Stratophanes is nearby,
My dear Phronesium. Now pretend to be weakened by childbirth.
Phronesium
                                                            Shhh!   500
Think an expert so accomplished as me in the art of deception needs advice?
Stratophanes
It seems the woman's already had the baby.
Astaphium
                                                Want me to approach him?
Phronesium
                                                                Yes.
Stratophanes
Oh, good, Astaphium's coming over here to meet me.
Astaphium
                                                Greetings, Stratophanes!
I see you're safe and—
Stratophanes
                        Yes, yes. But tell me, has Phronesium had the baby?
Phronesium
Yes, a beautiful baby boy.
Stratophanes
                        Aha! So, does he take after me at all?
Astaphium
                                                        You have to ask? 505
He shouted for a shield and a sword the instant he was born!
Stratophanes
That's proof he's mine!
Astaphium
                        Yes, he's your spitting image.
Stratophanes
                                                Woohoo!
Is he big? Has he joined the army already? Did he return from battle laden with
    spoils?
Astaphium
He was only born five days ago.

---

40 Attica is the name of the region surrounding (and including) the city of Athens.

Stratophanes

                So what?

By Hercules, he should have accomplished something after so many days!   510

Why'd he leave his mother's uterus if he wasn't ready for battle?

Astaphium

Follow me to her so you can congratulate her.

Stratophanes

                            Right behind you.

Phronesium

Now where is that girl who left me and went away? Where is she?

Astaphium

I'm right here, and I have someone you've missed—Stratophanes!

Phronesium

                                  Oh, where is he?

Stratophanes

Mars greets his wife Neriene[41] upon the occasion of his arrival from abroad.   515

I congratulate you on getting through it well and being blessed with progeny.

You have borne us both a great glory!

Phronesium

Oh, hello. You almost deprived me of light and life

When you buried that sword of yours inside my body to satisfy your lust!

I'm still quite ill from that.   520

Stratophanes

Now, now. All your labor wasn't for nothing:

You bore a son who'll fill your house with spoils.

Phronesium

Ah, *HELLO*! It's much more urgent that our granary is filled with grain!

Otherwise, we'll be wiped out by hunger before he wins those spoils.

Stratophanes

Now cheer up.

Phronesium

                Please kiss me … ah! I can't lift my head.   525

Oh, the pain is so intense! I can't even walk …

On my own.

Stratophanes

              If you told me to kiss you in the middle of the ocean,

I wouldn't hesitate for an instant, honey-bun!

That you know from experience. And know now, my Phronesium,

That I love you. Look! I've brought you two Syrian maids.   530

They're all yours. You (*to slave*), bring them here.

They both were once princesses in their country, a country I personally purged.

Take them—my treat.

---

41   The (obscure) wife of Mars (see Appendix I p. 335) in Roman mythology.

Phronesium

> Doesn't it bother you that I already have so many maids to feed?
You think I want another swarm of them raiding my pantry?

Stratophanes

Hmmm ... maybe that wasn't the perfect gift. Give me that little bag, boy.   535
Look, my darling, I've brought you a little pashmina from Phrygia.[42]
Take it.

Phronesium

> This little gift's for me? *This* is for all that labor I went through?

Stratophanes (*aside*)

God, I'm all but ruined now! That baby is worth his weight in gold—mine, that is.
And that doesn't even take the purple into account.[43] I brought you incense
From Arabia and frankincense from Pontus.[44] Take them, my darling.   540

Phronesium

Yeah, yeah, I got them. Take these Syrian slave-girls away from here.

Stratophanes

Do you love me just a little?

Phronesium

> Goodness no, and for good reason!

Stratophanes (*aside*)

> None of this was enough for her?

Not even one nice word for me!
Those gifts I gave her could be sold for twenty minae!
Now I know for sure she's really mad at me.   545
I'd better leave. Hey, darling: it's all right with you
If I go to a dinner I was invited to, isn't it? I'll come back here for bed.
Why the silent treatment? (*aside*) I'm clearly in for it now. But what is *that*?
Who's this guy leading a big parade of stuff?
It appears they're bringing it here, but I'll know for sure soon enough.   550

---

42 Phrygia was a district of Asia Minor (now Turkey) that included Troy.

43 Purple dye (here for the pashmina) extracted from shellfish was widely used by the Romans to mark
high status and wealth.

44 A northern region of Asia Minor (modern Turkey) extending along the south coast of the Black Sea.

SCENE 9

Cyamus and other slaves of Diniarchus enter with gifts.
(SONG through 630)

Cyamus[45]

> *Come on! This way, together now, you liquidators,*
> *Eliminators, and exterminators of our stuff!*
A man in love can't help but be worthless and pillage himself in disgraceful ways.
> *How do I know this, you ask?*
>> *At our place there's a lover doing disgraceful things*   555
>>> *By treating his property like pooh*
>>> *To be promptly removed from the house.*   556a
>> *He's quite clean, or maybe he just fears an inspection.*
But he clearly wants his house clean—or should I say cleaned out?
Since he's determined to self-destruct, I'll support his cause on the sly,
And see he reaches his ultimate goal as swiftly as possible.   560
Now regarding that mina for provisions: I've had it reduced by five nummi—
That is, I skimmed off a tithe for Hercules.[46]
I'm no different from a man who diverts river water for his own use:
If the water isn't diverted, it would just run off into the sea.
So too, this stuff's headed for the sea and a meaningless, watery death there.   565
>> *When I see this all happening*
>>> *I pilfer, filch and*   566a
>>> *Plunder the plunder.*
>> *A prostitute is just like the sea:*
She absorbs all the gifts you give her, but never overflows.
You can count on this at least: what she keeps becomes invisible.   570
Give her anything imaginable, and neither giver nor receiveress sees it again.
That's the M.O. of this prostitute who's sweet-talked my master into poverty—   572-3
>> *She's just about cut him off from property, friends, life and dignity.*
Ah look, she's right over there. I bet she heard what I was saying.   575
She's pale, like someone who's had a baby. I'll speak to her as if I don't know a thing.
Good day to you.

Phronesium

> *Same to you, Geta.*[47] *How are you doing? Are you well?*

Cyamus

I'm well and am here with someone not so well, but I have something to make you
> *well-er.*

---

45 His name means "bean" in Greek, and is probably meant to comically highlight his role as a cook (cf.
    615).

46 For the value of five nummi, see Appendix II p. 337. Roman merchants regularly dedicated a tithe (i.e.,
    ten percent) of their profits to Hercules. The "tithe" of five nummi skimmed off by Cyamus here for
    himself dates the play to *ca* 190 BCE or earlier. Cf. Introduction pp. 19-20.

47 Phronesium is pretending not to know his name (as symptomatic of her feigned condition).

My master, the light of your life, told me to bring you all these gifts
You see these guys carrying, and five minae of silver on top of it all.   580

Phronesium

    The great affection I feel for him hasn't been for nothing!

Cyamus

    He told me to beg you to be pleased with these.

Phronesium

I'm very pleased and glad to get them. Have them carried inside, Cyamus.

Astaphium

    Didn't you hear what she told you?

Cyamus

    I don't want the containers carried off—just the contents.   585

Astaphium

My, you're shameless, Cyamus!

Cyamus

                     I'm shameless?

Astaphium

                          Yes, you are.

Cyamus

                              In all honesty,

You think I'm shameless? You're a den of disgrace yourself!

Phronesium

    Please tell me, where is Diniarchus?

Cyamus

                     At home.

Phronesium

    Tell him that because of these gifts he's sent me
I love him more than any other man in the world,   590
    And I value him more than anyone else,
    And do tell him to come see me here.

Cyamus

But who's that gloomy guy with the stink-eye? What's eating him up?
    Whoever he is, he's really
Down in the dumps!

Phronesium

    He damn well deserves it. He's worthless. You remember   595
That soldier who lived with me here, don't you? He's the father of my child.
    He keeps an eye on me, comes to visit,
    Lingers, listens and watches to see who I'll destroy next.

Cyamus

                             Yes, I know the bum.

    That's really him?

Phronesium

           Sure is.

Cyamus

                The way he growls when he looks at me!
He just groaned from the pit of his stomach.   600
Watch: now he's gnashing his teeth and pounding on his thigh!
The way he beats on himself, you'd think he was a soothsayer.[48]

Stratophanes

It's time to uncork the full force of my rage and rancor! Answer me:
Where are you from? Who owns you? How dare you be so rude to me!

Cyamus

                                        I felt like it. 604-5

Stratophanes

Don't speak to me like that!

Cyamus

                    How's this then? I DON'T GIVE A RAT'S ASS ABOUT YOU.

Stratophanes

And what about you? How dare you say you love another man!

Phronesium

                                        I felt like it.

Stratophanes

You did now? We'll see about that. So you're in love with that effeminate fornicator
With the curly ringlets, that shade-huggin',[49] *tom-tom beatin'*[50] *bum?*   609-10
And just because he gave you some supplies, vegetables and a vinaigrette?

Cyamus

                              What's the meaning of this?
You shameless mountain of lies? How dare you badmouth my master!

Stratophanes

Just one more word out of you and I'll chop you into chunks with this sword.

Cyamus

Just touch me once and I'll rip open your middle like a lamb.
You may have your renown on the battlefield—mine's in the kitchen.   615

Phronesium

If you knew what was good for you, you wouldn't harass the visitors
Who bring me much-welcome gifts. Especially when your gifts are so worthless.

Stratophanes

So I've lost the contest here as well as all my gifts?

Phronesium

                                   There's no question about that.

---

48 A prophet (*hariolus*) might beat himself into an inspired frenzy before revealing his prophecies.

49 Ancient intellectuals were stereotypically portrayed as pale aesthetes who lacked the swarthy suntan of men who engaged in vigorous (outdoor) public activity.

50 The eastern goddess Cybele (Magna Mater) was imported to Rome in 204 BCE. She and her devotees—mostly eunuch priests who played small drums—were viewed with suspicion and disapproval by Roman traditionalists. Cf. Introduction pp. 31-32.

Cyamus
If you've lost everything, why sit here and annoy us then?
Stratophanes
Damned if I don't drive this fellow away from here today!
Cyamus
Come here. No, over here. 620

Stratophanes
Still making threats, you scumbag? I really am going to rip you into chunks now.
How dare you! The idea of you coming here and approaching her!
And acting like you know my mistress!
Defeat me in battle or you'll die instantly.
Cyamus
Defeat you in battle?
Stratophanes
Stop! Do what I say! 625
Now I'll chop you into chunks: tis' noble to die by chopping.
Cyamus
Here's the catch: that sword of yours is quite longer than my knife.
Do allow me to fetch a BBQ spit. If I must go to war with you, warrior,
I must first go home and round up a referee who's fair.
(aside) I'd better just disappear while I can with my stomach in one piece! 630
Phronesium
Bring me my sandals. Take me inside this instant.
My poor head is aching from all this wind. (*exits*)
Stratophanes
But what about me? Don't you think I've got a headache over my gift of the two
maids?
Walk away, will you? So that's how it is!
There's no more obvious way I could be shut out than the way 635
I'm shut out right now! Fine, go ahead and make a spectacle out of me!
It wouldn't require much encouragement to get me
To shatter this damn house's ankles to bits!
Does the behavior of these women change with the wind or what?
Since she had the baby, she's taken on airs. 640
Now it's as if she's saying: "I neither ask nor forbid you
To go inside my house." I'm not going in and I don't want to.
I guarantee you that within a few days she'll be saying I'm a man of steel.
Enough chatter. (*to retinue*) Follow me this way.

SCENE 10

Strabax enters from the wing leading to the country.

Strabax[51]

My father sent me off to the farm earlier this morning   645
To give the cows their meal of acorns.
After I got there—praise be to the gods!—a guy showed up
Who had bought some Tarentine[52] sheep from my father
And owed him the money for them.
He asks for my father. I tell him he's in town   650
And I ask him what he needs.
The guy pulls a money-bag from off his neck
And gives me twenty minae. I'm glad to get it,
And I put it in my own money-bag. He takes off, and I brought
My sheep-turned-twenty-minae to town in this money-bag of mine here!   655
Mars[53] must have gotten mad at my father,
Seeing as his sheep are not far from the wolves.
No doubt about it, I'll use this money to knock the blocks right off
Those citified and prettified lover boys and boot them out on the street!
My plan is to rip up my father by the roots first   660
And then proceed to rip off my mother too.[54]
Now I'll deliver this money to the woman I love more than my own mother.
Knock-knock! Anybody inside? Will somebody open the door?

Astaphium

What's this now? Strabax, dear! You're not a stranger! Please,   664-5
You must come right in.

Strabax

                              I must?

Astaphium

Yes, of course. You're a member of the family.

Strabax

                                        I'll do it,
So you don't think I'm a slow-poke. (*goes inside*)

Astaphium

                              Oh, how charming of you!

---

51 His name means "Squinter" in Greek, perhaps a feature stereotypically associated with rustics.

52 Tarentum (= the modern city of Taranto) in southern Italy, colonized by Spartans in the 8th century BCE.

53 For the god Mars, see Appendix I p. 335.

54 Strabax here brazenly flouts the essential Roman concept of *pietas* (cf. English "piety"), which required absolute obedience and respect toward parents. Such subversions of traditional morality are not uncommon within the festival context of Roman comedy.

SCENE 11

Truculentus enters from the wing leading to the forum.

Truculentus

It seems strange that young master Strabax
Isn't back from the country—   670
Unless he secretly slithered into this here cesspool of sin.

Astaphium

Damn! If he sees me, he'll start hollering at me again!

Truculentus

I'm a lot less savage than I was, Astaphium.
In fact, I'm not savage at all. No need to be afraid.
What do you say?

Astaphium

                    What do you want?

Truculentus

                                    I was hoping for a little lip-itude.   675
Tell me—no, *order* me to do whatever you want, however you want it.
I've retired my old ways. I'm a totally new character now.
I can even take on a whore and give her some lovin'.

Astaphium

Oh my, what charming news! Tell me though,
Do you have—

Truculentus

                    Money in hand, you mean perhaps?   680

Astaphium

How charming, you understand *exactly* what I meant!

Truculentus

Oh, you! I've become quite witty from coming to town so often.
I'm a genuine cud-up[55] now!

Astaphium

Come now, please! I think you meant to say that you're a "cut-up."
You know, that you like to tell funny jokes.   685

Truculentus

Fine, whatever—pretty much the same thing as being a cud-up.

Astaphium

Please come in with me now, darling.

Truculentus

                                    Here—take this.
It's a do-me payment, so you'll spend the night with me.

Astaphium

Geeze! A "do-me payment"? What sort of beast is this here?

---

55 The rustic-minded Truculentus commits a malapropism: he means to say, "I'm a real wit" (*cauillator*),
but mistakenly says "I'm a real cabbage-head" (*caullator*).

Don't you mean a *down payment*?
Truculentus

                                   Country dialect. It's like in   690
Praeneste[56] when you ask for a stork and they just give you the bird.
Astaphium

Please do come in.
Truculentus

                I'll wait here for a while
To see if Strabax is back from the country.
Astaphium

                              Strabax just returned from the country.
He's already inside the house—
Truculentus

                  Before stopping in to see his mother?
What an utterly worthless person!
Astaphium

                  Careful now—don't regress.   695
Truculentus

Careful now or … I'm shutting up.
Astaphium

                    Please take my hand and come inside.
Truculentus

Here. (*aside*) Well, off I go into this dive,
Where my money's in for some very rough treatment.

SCENE 12

Diniarchus enters.

Diniarchus

Of all the beings already born or destined to be born, there's no one
I'll ever want the absolute best of everything for more than Venus!   700
Great gods! I'm so happy … so happy I could fly!
The news Cyamus brought back to me was pure joy!
My gifts are not just acceptable—they're adored here at Phronesium's house!
Sweet as that is, there's an even sweeter sugarcoating:
The soldiers' gifts are unwelcome and despised! Now this is sheer delight! 705
The ball's in my court: if she spurns the soldier, the woman's mine!
In this case, my loss is also my salvation: if I weren't lost, I'd be utterly done for.
I'll keep watch on all the doings there, who's going in and who's coming out.
I'll figure out what my fate will be from a distance here.

---

56 A very old town (= modern Palestrina) in the region of Latium near Rome. Truculentus literally says "in
Praeneste a *ciconia* (= "stork" in Rome) is a *conea* (the Praenestean dialectical equivalent)." The joke
here hinges on the fact that "the stork" in Latin slang also indicated some sort of derisive gesture made
with one's fingers.

Having shifted all I have to this house, the reality is I'm broke and down to
   begging.   710

SCENE 13

Astaphium enters from Phronesium's house.
(SONG through 729)

Astaphium (*to slaves inside*)
   I'll take care of my tasks out here just fine. Make sure you do the same inside.
   Nourish your own advantage, as you should, be sure to drain him dry!
Pull out all the stops while the time is right, he wants it, and he still has the cash;
Charm your lover that way, and he'll rejoice even when he knows he's been used.
   In the meantime I'll stay here and take up the rearguard   715
   As he continues to export his entire estate to you.
   While that's happening, I won't allow anyone to come in and annoy you.
So on with the show as you like.
Diniarchus
Astaphium! Tell me who's being used now.
Astaphium
                        You scared me! You're here?

Diniarchus
   Am I annoying you?
Astaphium
                Well, yes—more than you were.   720
   Anyone we can't use annoys us.
But please pay attention and I'll tell you something.
Diniarchus
   What? Is it about me?
Astaphium
                I won't try to hide it:
What a haul she's making in there!
Diniarchus
               What? She's got a new lover?

Astaphium
   She's tapped into a fountain of untapped treasure.
Diniarchus
                    Who is he?   725

Astaphium
I'll tell you, but you've got to keep quiet about it. Know Strabax here?
Diniarchus
                        Of course.

Astaphium
He's the new net-profit at our house, our latest cash crop.
He botches up his business badly, but always with a nice smile!

Diniarchus

He's cooked, just like me!
I squandered my goods and I've got only frowns to show for it, not to mention a closed
door.

Astaphium

You're a fool if you think your words can undo what's already done.   730
Even Thetis put an end to mourning for her son.[57]

Diniarchus

You're not letting me in now?

Astaphium

Now why would you be any more welcome than the soldier?

Diniarchus

Because I paid her more.

Astaphium

And we let you in more when you did.
The paying customers are enjoying their turn now.
Congratulations on having learned your lesson. Now give others a chance to go to
school.   735

Diniarchus

I'm all for others learning, but can I have a refresher course so I don't forget
everything?

Astaphium

But what about your teacher while you're refreshing?
She'd like some memory-work too.

Diniarchus

Huh?

Astaphium

In the form of tuition payments. Remember?

Diniarchus

I most certainly made one of those today! I had five minae of silver delivered to her
And an additional mina's worth of supplies!

Astaphium

Yes, I can confirm it arrived.   740
And thanks to you, they're all enjoying themselves.

Diniarchus

Oh no! My enemies
Are devouring my stuff in there! I'd rather die than put up with this!

Astaphium

You're an idiot.

---

57 The sea-nymph Thetis was the mother of the Greek hero Achilles who, as an immortal, had
    foreknowledge of his death in the Trojan War and grieved accordingly. Astaphium, however, may have
    Thetis confused with the more usual example of the eternally grieving mother, Niobe, all of whose
    children were slain by the gods Apollo and Artemis (= Roman Diana: see Appendix I p. 335) owing to
    her boastfulness about them.

Diniarchus

        Why? Enlighten me, Astaphium.

Astaphium

                                      Because I'd rather

Have my enemies envying me than vice-versa.

It's pure agony for a loser to envy a winner.   745

Those who are envied are the haves, those who envy the have-nots.

Diniarchus

And it's not possible for me to have a half-share of my own supplies?

Astaphium

If you wanted a half-share, you should have delivered half to your house.

We keep a record of accounts received here the same way they do in Hades:[58]

We warmly welcome them into our house, but they can never leave.   750

Goodbye.

Diniarchus

        Stop!

Astaphium

           Let go of me.

Diniarchus

                      Let me go in—

Astaphium

                                    To your own house, yes.

Diniarchus

But I'd much rather go into yours.

Astaphium

                            No can do—you're so demanding!

Diniarchus

Just let me try—

Astaphium

                      I'll let you wait. That try would be too trying for us.

Diniarchus

Tell her I'm here.

Astaphium

                    Get lost, she's busy. That's the way it is, so don't deceive yourself.

Diniarchus

Are you coming back or not?

Astaphium

                    I'm being called by someone with a lot more power than you.   755

Diniarchus

Just one word—

---

58 Hades is the underworld to which the dead are eternally confined. All sales are definitely final at Chez
Phronesium.

Astaphium
> Say it.

Diniarchus
> Are you letting me in?

Astaphium
> Get out of here, you liar!

You asked for one word and you just said five—all of them lies.

Diniarchus

She's gone inside and I'm shut out. Should I have to put up with this?
Damn it, you skank! I'll start shouting and make a spectacle out of you
Right here in the street for taking money illegally from so many men![59]   760
I swear I'll have your case brought before the magistrates,
And demand quadruple damages from you! You witch,
You child-snatcheress! Damn it, I'll expose all your shameful shenanigans!
What's to stop me, now that I've lost everything?
I'm shameless, and I couldn't care less about what sort of shoes I wear.[60]   765
But why am I shouting here? What if she told them to let me in?
If she did, I'd solemnly swear not to oblige her.
What crap! If you pound on a sharp stick, you just hurt your hands.
Why get angry at someone over nothing, especially when she thinks nothing of you?
By the immortal gods, what's that?   770
It's old Callicles, my father-in-law-to-have-been, and he's got two maids in custody.
One's her hairdresser, the other's his own slave.
I don't like this at all. I thought I had just one thing to fret over!
Now I have to worry about all my old mistakes being discovered.

SCENE 14

Callicles enters with Syra and his maidservant.

Callicles[61]

I'd badmouth you? I'd prefer you'd badmouth yourself.   775
I think you both know from experience that I'm a calm and gentle person.
I questioned you both when you were strung up and being whipped.[62]
Oh yes, I remember each and every detail of your confessions.
Now I want you to confess the same things here without the torture.
You've both got the character of a snake, and I swear   780
I'd sooner kill you and cut out your forked tongues than listen to your doublespeak!
Unless you'd prefer to be led off to the men with the little bells?[63]

---

59 A reference to the ancient Italian practice (*flagitatio*) of publicly shaming a debtor into payment.
60 Roman patricians were distinguished by their right to wear red shoes.
61 A generically aristocratic-sounding name (lit., "of beautiful renown") in Greek.
62 In the ancient world, the testimony of slaves was admissible only if it was exacted under torture.
63 Roman executioners had bells that became symbolic of their profession.

Maid

These straps on our arms hurt so much, we have to confess.

Callicles

Tell the truth and the straps will come off.

Diniarchus (*aside*)

Now I'm confused about what's up,   785

But I do know about my past mistakes—and that makes me very afraid.

Callicles

First of all, you two must stand apart. Yes, just like that.

No signals or nods, now. I'll be a wall between you. You first.

Maid

What am I supposed to say?

Callicles

Tell me what happened to the child my daughter

Gave birth to, *my* grandson! Let's hear the main points.

Maid

I gave it to her.

Callicles

Quiet now.   790

Did you take the boy from her?

Syra[64]

Yes.

Callicles

You be quiet now.

That's enough confessing from you, I don't want to hear any more.

Syra

I'm not denying anything.

Callicles

But you are creating a darkish hue for your shoulder blades.

Their accounts agree so far.

Diniarchus (*aside*)

Poor, poor pitiful me!

Everything I'd hoped to keep secret is coming out now.   795

Callicles

Tell me, you: who told you to give her the child?

Maid

My senior mistress.[65]

Callicles

What about you? Who told you to take the child?

---

64 Her name indicates she was Syrian (slaves were often generically named after their country of origin).

65 I.e., Callicles' wife.

Syra

My junior mistress[66]
Told me to bring it to her and keep everything secret.

Callicles

So tell me what you did with the child.

Syra

I took it to my mistress.

Callicles

What did she then do with it?

Syra

She took it to my mistress immediately.   800

Callicles

Which mistress, damn it!

Maid

She has two.

Callicles

Answer only when I ask you something!
It's you I'm interrogating.

Syra

The mother gave it as a gift to her daughter.

Callicles

That's more than you said earlier.

Syra

You're asking me more.

Callicles

Answer me quickly:
What did the girl who received it do?

Syra

Passed it off.

Callicles

As whose?

Syra

Her own.

Callicles

As her own son?

Syra

As her own, yes.

Callicles

Almighty gods, help us!   805
How much easier it is for one women to give birth to a child than another!
Thanks to another's labor, this one gave birth painlessly!
What a blessed child. He has two mothers and two grandmothers.

---

66 I.e., Phronesium.

I shudder to think how many fathers he has! Such is the nature of female behavior!

Maid

Surely the blame here belongs to men much more than women: 810

A man, not a woman, got her pregnant.

Callicles

I understand that too.

Fine chaperone you were!

Maid

"Where there's greater strength, there's greater power."

He's a man, he's stronger. He overtook her and took what he wanted.

Callicles

And he sure as hell brought a lot of trouble on you too!

Maid

You hardly need to remind me of that. I've had firsthand experience of it.   815

Callicles

I haven't had any success today in making you tell me his name.

Maid

So far. But that'll change: though he doesn't show himself, the man is here.

Diniarchus (*aside*)

Damn! I'd better turn into a statue and not budge an inch.

The whole thing's out now and they'll be trying me for a capitol offense.[67]

I did it! It was my stupidity! I'm terrified of what they'll say next about me.   820

Callicles

Tell me who raped my virgin daughter.

Maid

Hey, wall-prop![68] I can see you and I know what you did.

Diniarchus (*aside*)

I can't tell if I'm dead or alive, and I have no idea what to do!

Should I go or should I stay? I'm t-t-totally t-terrified!

Callicles

Going to name him or not?

Maid

Diniarchus—the man you betrothed her to first.[69]   825

Callicles

Where is he?

---

67   While potentially subject to serious legal consequences in both Rome and Greece, the rape of an unmarried (free-born) girl might be tolerated if the rapist agreed to marry his victim. Cf. Introduction p. 34.

68   Literally, "patron of the wall" (*patronus parieti*), and so a playful allusion to the Roman social patronage system, under which patrons, in return for political support, owed certain responsibilities (such as legal support) to their clients. Diniarchus, in his fear and discomfort, has pressed himself tightly against some part of the stage's wooden backdrop.

69   Cf. 849.

Diniarchus

　　　　　Right here, Callicles. I beg you by these knees of yours I'm grasping:
Find the wisdom to pardon my utter stupidity!
Pardon me for an offense I committed under the influence of wine.

Callicles

I don't buy it. You're passing on the blame to a speechless mute.
If wine could speak, it would defend itself here.　　　　　830
It's the custom of men to have control over wine, not vice-versa—
Decent men, that is. But a person who's bad by nature
Is bad regardless whether he's a drinker or abstains altogether.

Diniarchus

I know I must listen to what I don't want to hear because I'm guilty.
I acknowledge my guilt and I'm at your mercy.　　　　　835

Maid

Callicles, don't do something you'll regret later.
The defendant is pleading his case unshackled: it's the witnesses you've tied up.

Callicles

Untie them. Come now, off with you both. Each of you go on home.
Tell your mistress to hand over the child when someone comes for him.
As for you: let's both go to court.

Diniarchus

　　　　　Why take me to court? You're my judge.　　　840
I beg you, Callicles, please give me your daughter's hand in marriage.

Callicles

Me let you marry her? I think you settled that issue a while back.
You didn't wait for me to let you marry her: you just took her for yourself.
So go ahead and keep her now that you've taken her. But you're looking at a major
　　fine.
On account of your stupidity, I'm deducting six talents[70] from her dowry.　　845

Diniarchus

Fair enough.

Callicles

　　　　　You'd best retrieve that son of yours from that house.
And take your wife away from my house as soon as you possibly can.
I'm off now. Now I have to send a message to that crony of mine
Telling him to make some other arrangement for his son.

Diniarchus

I'd better ask her for the child now, so she doesn't refuse to hand him over later.　850
That shouldn't be a problem, since she's the one who divulged every last detail to me.
But aren't I lucky! Here she comes outside right now.
What a long jab she has! She pierces my heart with it from way over there!

---

70 For the (very substantial) value of six talents, see Appendix II p. 337.

SCENE 15

Phronesium enters from her house.

Phronesium

A prostitute's as bad as grimy spinach if she can't promote her own interests over
    a drink.

Her body may be soaked with wine, but her head should stay sober. 855

I'm quite upset that my hairdresser's been so badly mistreated.

She told me the child has been discovered to be Diniarchus'.

Diniarchus (*aside*)

Ah, I can see her and hear her words—the woman who controls my property and
    progeny.

Phronesium (*aside*)

There's my lover who appointed me guardian of all his personal goods.

Diniarchus

Woman, I was looking for you.

Phronesium

                What's up, my sweetheart? 860

Diniarchus

Cut the "sweetheart" crap! I'm done now with all that.

Phronesium

I most certainly know what you want, what you're hoping for, and what you're after:

You want to see me, you're hoping for some lovin', and you're after the child.

Diniarchus (*aside*)

By the immortal gods! How blunt! She got the gist of it in just a few words!

Phronesium

I do understand that you have a fiancée, and a child from her, 865

And you have to marry her now, and that your affections are elsewhere …

And that you're about to leave me utterly abandoned.

But consider the mouse, a very small, yet smart little creature:

Mice never entrust their life to a single mouse-hole,

But always have another escape-plan if one is blocked up. 870

Diniarchus

Let's discuss these things more later, when I have some free-time.

Now back to the child—

Phronesium

              Oh please let him stay at my house

For the next few days!

Diniarchus

           Absolutely not!

Phronesium

              Please!

Diniarchus

                Why should I?

Phronesium

It's in my best interests.
Let me keep him just for three days, while I'm bamboozling the soldier.
If I get anything out of it, you'll get your cut too.   875
But if you take him away, all hope of fleecing the soldier will pass with the wind.

Diniarchus

Okay, I'm with you. There's no possibility of doing otherwise, even if I wanted to.
Go ahead, use the child and take care of him. You have the money for that.

Phronesium

Oh I love you so much for this favor! Whenever a war breaks out at home,
Just come see me. You can always be my booty-buddy[71] at least.   880

Diniarchus

Goodbye, Phronesium.

Phronesium

Don't you mean to say "light of my life?"

Diniarchus

You'll hear that phrase from time to time during our rendezvous.
Anything else?

Phronesium

Just take care.

Diniarchus

I'll come see you when I have the chance.

Phronesium

He's really got up and gone away. Now I can speak freely here.
That saying, "your wealth is where your friends are," sure rings true.   885
Thanks to him, there's still hope of swindling the soldier today.
Oh, I do love that soldier more than I do myself—that is, while I get what I want
        from him.
But even if we take a lot from them, we usually have little to show for it:
Such are the triumphs of prostitution.

Astaphium

Be quiet now!

Phronesium

Why? What is it?

Astaphium

The child's "father" is coming.

Phronesium

Let him come here, if it's just him.   890

---

71 I.e., he can come have sex with her *and* lavish her with gifts; in Roman slang, a prostitute is commonly
    referred to as her customer's "friend" (*amica*). The phrase here (*amicus manubiarius*, "plunder pal")
    also probably alludes to contemporary Roman disputes about the proper distribution of war-spoils in a
    period of great military expansion. Cf. Introduction pp. 2, 22.

Astaphium

　　It is.

Phronesium

　　He can come to me, as he wishes.

Astaphium

　　　　　　　　　　　　　He's headed straight to us.

Phronesium

　　As the gods are my witness, I'll finish him off in style today!

SCENE 16

Stratophanes enters.

Stratophanes

　　I'm bringing a mina's worth of gold in reparations to my mistress,
　　A little icing on the cake to make my previous gifts more welcome.
　　But look over there: mistress and maid in front of the house. I'll approach them.　895
　　What are you doing?

Phronesium

　　　　　　　　　Don't speak to me.

Stratophanes

　　　　　　　　　　　　Why so harsh?

Phronesium

　　Could you just stop bothering me?

Stratophanes

　　　　　　　　　　What's wrong, Astaphium?

Astaphium

　　She's mad at you and rightly so.

Phronesium

　　　　　　　　　　That's true. And I don't treat him

　　Poorly enough.

Stratophanes

　　　　　　　　Sweetheart, if I did anything wrong earlier,
　　I've brought a mina's worth of gold to make up for it. Look if you don't
　　　　believe me.　　　　　　　　　　　　　　　　　　　　900

Phronesium

　　My hand does not believe in the existence of anything it's not holding.
　　The baby needs food, so does the woman who bathes it.
　　For the nurse to produce milk, she needs an endless supply of fine wines.
　　We need firewood, we need charcoal,
　　We need baby clothes, pillows, a cradle,　　　　　　　　　905
　　Blankets for the cradle, oil, and flour. The kid eats all day!
　　We don't get through a single day without needing something else!
　　The offspring of soldiers can't be raised like baby birds!

Stratophanes

　　Look here then—take this to fill those needs.

Phronesium

I'll take it, even though it's not enough.

Stratophanes

                             I'll add a mina to it later.

Phronesium

                                            Still short.   910

Stratophanes

I'll give you whatever you tell me to. Now give me a little kiss.

Phronesium

Let go of me! You're so annoying!

Stratophanes

                        I'm getting nowhere. Where's the love? Time's wasting.

Little by little, I've lost more than ten minae worth of … lovin' today.

Phronesium (*to Astaphium*)

Here's the money. Take it inside.

Strabax (*enters from Phronesium's house*)

                          So where in the world is my mistress?

I'm not getting' anything here or in the country. I'm rotting away: 915

Lying here on the bed waiting for her only makes me miserable … and so hard!

Look, there she is. Hey honey, what are you up to?

Stratophanes

                               Who's this guy?

Phronesium

Someone I love more than you.

Stratophanes

                     Than me?

Phronesium

                Yes.

Stratophanes

                     In what way?

Phronesium

In a way that'll make you stop annoying me.

Stratophanes

                      You're going to take my money and run?

Phronesium

I've already stored it away inside.

Strabax

                     Come here, honey. I'm talking to you.   920

Phronesium

I was just coming to you, my darling.

Strabax

                     I'm serious now, damn it!

I know I look stupid, but I do expect some pleasuring here.

I know you're pretty and all, but you'll be sorry if I don't get that pleasuring soon.

Phronesium
Are you looking for a hug and a nice kiss?
Strabax
Whatever, so long as I get pleasured.
Stratophanes
So I'm supposed to watch her cuddle with other men right before my eyes?   925
Damn it, I'd rather die here right now! Hands off him, woman,
Unless you'd like for both of you to die at the hand of my sword.
Phronesium
You'd better empty your wallet, soldier, if you want some lovin':
Only gold, not iron, will discourage me from loving him, Stratophanes.
Stratophanes
How in the hell can a pretty and sophisticated woman like you love a man
like *him*?   930
Phronesium
I just remembered a proverb an actor once uttered in the theater:
"All human beings can be either thick-skinned or finicky depending on the profit to
be made."
Stratophanes
But the idea of embracing a man so sloppy and so filthy!
Phronesium
However sloppy and filthy he may be, he's handsome and smart to me.
Stratophanes
I gave you gold—
Phronesium
Me? You gave your child food.   935
If you want to spend time with *this* lady, it's time for another mina of gold.
Strabax (*to Stratophanes*)
You're headed straight to hell in a hand-basket—better hang on to some travel-
money.
Stratophanes
What do you owe him?
Phronesium
Three things.
Stratophanes
Specifically?
Phronesium
Perfume, a night, some kissing.
Stratophanes
That's tit for tat. But, now, even if you do love him,
Can't you share just a little of your delicates with me?   940
Phronesium
And just what is it I should share with you? Tell me?

Stratophanes

Go on playing word games. I'll use force to win my love.

Phronesium

                                        Careful, big fellow.
Don't end up hurting yourself with those big iron teeth of yours.

Stratophanes

She lets anybody in her house! Take your hands off her!

Strabax

Take that, action-man, and go right to hell, by Hercules!   945

Stratophanes

I gave her gold!

Strabax

            I gave her silver.

Stratophanes

                        But I brought her a purple pashmina!

Strabax

And I gave her sheep and wool and I'll keep giving her whatever she asks for.
You're better off competing against me with minas rather than menaces.

Phronesium

You're such a charming person, Strabax dear. Please keep after him.

Astaphium

An idiot and a crazy person are competing to lose everything. We're saved!   950

Stratophanes

Come on, you squander something first.

Strabax

                        No, you first—and then die!

Stratophanes

Here's a talent of silver—it's in Philips,[72] take it for your own.

Phronesium

Ah, better! Now you're one of the family, but you'll have to support yourself
    independently.

Stratophanes

Put your money where your mouth is, and open up your money-belt. Afraid of
    something?

Strabax

You're a tourist. I live here, and so I don't walk around with a money-belt.   955
I bring her flocks in a bag tied around my neck. (*to Phronesium*) I sure gave it to
    him!
I stripped him clean down to the bone!

Stratophanes

                        No, no—I'm the one who gave!

---

72 For the value of a Philip, see Appendix II p. 337.

Phronesium

Oh, please go inside: you can be with me. And you, too.

Stratophanes

What? How can you say that? You'll be with him and I'll be in line for seconds?
But I gave—

Phronesium

Yes, you gave *back then*. He's about to give now. I have yours, I'm awaiting his. 960
But I'll satisfy you both to your heart's content.

Stratophanes

All right. Seeing how things are, I've got to take what I'm offered.

Strabax

One thing's for sure: you're not sharing my bed!

Phronesium

What a lovely day of hunting, with everything done just the way I wanted!
All my business has turned out so fine! I can do just the same for you: 965
If anyone's in the mood for love, be sure to let me know.
How about some applause for Venus' sake? This play's been made under her
supervision.[73]
Spectators! Fare well! Stand up and applaud!

---

73 The appeal to Venus is highly ironic, given the utter absence of love (romantic or sexual) in this satirical
play. It is also possible that the reference is metatheatrical, if the play was performed before a temple of
Venus. Cf. Introduction pp. 4-5.

Adelphoe

("The Brothers")

CHARACTERS WITH SPEAKING PARTS

MICIO, *a sixty-four year old bachelor and Athenian citizen*
DEMEA, *older brother of Micio, a farmer living in the Athenian countryside*
SANNIO, *an Athenian pimp*
AESCHINUS, *older son of Demea who was adopted by Micio and raised in the city*
PARMENO, *slave of Micio*
SYRUS, *older slave of Micio*
CTESIPHO, *younger son of Demea who lives with his father in the country*
SOSTRATA, *Athenian widow and neighbor of Micio*
CANTHARA, *elderly nurse of Sostrata*
GETA, *a (male) slave of Sostrata*
HEGIO, *an elderly Athenian citizen related to Sostrata*
DROMO, *younger slave of Micio*
PAMPHILA, *daughter of Sostrata (her voice is heard from inside at 486-87)*

SCENE

Athens: before the houses of Micio and Sostrata. One stage wing leads to the forum/city-center, the other to the country.

PROLOGUE[1]

Since our playwright is well-aware that his work has drawn
Unfair scrutiny and that his critics are bent
On panning the play we're about to perform,
He's decided to testify on behalf of himself and his work:
You'll be the judges of whether it deserves praise or scorn.   5

---

1   The Roman comic playwrights introduced the use of an impersonal prologist (perhaps the head of the acting troupe) to ancient comedy to speak on behalf of the play and the playwright. Terence's prologues are distinct for their focus on his critics and other literary/dramatic issues strictly extraneous to the performance at hand. See further Introduction pp. 10-11.

There's a comedy by Diphilus[2] entitled *Synapothnescontes*.[3]
Plautus[4] did a Latin version of it called *Commorientes*.
In the Greek original, a young man snatches a prostitute
From a pimp at the beginning of the play.
Plautus decided not to touch that scene, so our playwright picked it up   10
And translated it into his *Adelphoe* word for word.[5]
This is the play we're about to perform fresh today.
You can decide whether this is a case of theft
Or just amounts to rescuing a scene that had been carelessly abandoned.
Now another claim being made by his spiteful critics   15
Is that elite individuals[6] are collaborating with him to write his plays.
They allege this as if it were a vicious insult,
But our playwright considers it a supreme honor that he has won the support
Of men who lend their support to all of you and to this nation—
The very same men who unbegrudgingly help each and every one of you   20
In times of war and peace, and in all your daily business.
Now don't expect to hear the plot of the play at this point.
The old men who appear in the opening scene will divulge some of it;
The rest you'll get from the action. Now remember:
Your goodwill and fairness will inspire our playwright to boost his output!   25

SCENE 1

Micio enters from his house, yelling at a slave.

Micio

Storax! Aeschinus didn't come back from dinner last night!
And not one of the slaves who were supposed to escort him home did either.
What people say is definitely true: if you fail to come home
When you're supposed to, you're better off if every last thing
Your angry wife can conceive of about your absence is true.   30
But it's not the same where devoted parents are concerned:
The wife just imagines that you're hot for someone,
Or that someone's hot for you, or you're out drinking
And having the time of your life while she's suffering miserably at home.
Parents? The things I imagine when my son doesn't come home   35

---

2   Popular Greek New Comedy playwright (cf. Introduction p. 4) who provided the source play for a few
    surviving Roman comedies.

3   Greek for "Partners in Death;" *Commorientes* in 7 is the Latin version of the title. Nothing survives of
    either play.

4   For the Roman comic playwright's life and career, see Introduction pp. 7-9.

5   On the practice of "contaminating" Greek literary sources, see Introduction p. 11.

6   According to the biographical tradition, Terence was born in Carthage in North Africa and brought to
    Rome as a slave, where he was subsequently freed and acquired the patronage of influential Romans.
    See further Introduction p. 9.

Just about worry me to death! Has he caught pneumonia?
Did he fall down somewhere and break something?
Really! The very idea that a person would ever conceive of
Taking something into his heart more precious than his own self!
And he isn't even my own son, he's my brother's!   40
My brother and I have been polar opposites since we were kids.
I've had an easy and leisurely life here in the city,
And—what some people consider paradise—
I've never been married. My brother? Just the opposite.
He lives in the country, he works hard, he scrimps and he saves,   45
He has a wife and they had two sons.
I adopted the older of the two, this Aeschinus I was just talking about.
I've raised him since he was a child and loved him as my own.
I take sheer joy in him, and he's the most precious thing in my life.
I also take pains to see that he feels the same way about me.   50
I provide well for him, I look the other way, and I don't impose
My paternal authority[7] all the time; I've actually trained my son
To keep me in the loop about just the sorts of things
Youngsters are always trying to hide from their fathers.
To my thinking, a boy who's been trained to con his father,   55
And dares to do it, has no qualms about snowing others.
I believe we can discipline our children best by generosity,[8]
And by cultivating a sense of respect—not just fear.
My brother disagrees with me on that and has no stomach whatsoever
For my views: "What are you doing, Micio?   60
Why are you ruining the boy we both care so much for?
Why's he's whoring about? Why's he out drinking? Why give him
So much spending money for that, and for a wardrobe? You're such a fool!"
He's far too strict, and goes way beyond what's reasonable.
Now in my opinion, he's making a big mistake in assuming   65
That authority based on intimidation has more weight
Or lasts longer than when it's rooted in friendliness.
My thoughts on this matter?
A person who only does his duty under duress
Does so as long as believes someone's watching;   70
If he thinks he can get away with something, his true character resurfaces.

---

7   I.e., Micio is the antithesis of the traditionally stern Roman father (*paterfamilias*): see further
    Introduction pp. 26-27. There is also a metatheatrical dimension (cf. Introduction pp. 8-10) to his claim
    here to promote absolute transparency in his father-son relations (52ff.), as lovesick young men in New
    Comedy by convention deceive their fathers in an effort to gain access to their beloved.

8   The literal meaning of the Latin word *liberalitas*, "possession of the qualities of a free-born person"
    reflects an ancient presumption that free-born persons were necessarily superior to slaves in morality,
    appearance, and intelligence. Its translation here by "generosity" is meant in the broadest sense, i.e., in
    terms of liberality, openness, munificence, etc.

The person you've won over with kindness is sincere,
And wants to give back what he got, whether you're there watching him or not.
Proper paternal training results in a son who does what's right on his own,
And not just because someone else threatens him.   75
That's the difference between a father and a master.[9] If a father can't do this,
He should own up to the fact that he has no true authority over his children.
But is this the very person I was talking about? It sure is!
He looks pretty grumpy. My guess is that I'm in for his usual scolding.
You're looking well, Demea.   80
Good to see you.

SCENE 2

Demea enters from the wing leading to the forum.

Demea

                  Er, yes. Good timing—I've been looking for you.

Micio

Why so grumpy?

Demea

                You wonder why I'm grumpy
When we have Aeschinus to deal with?

Micio (*aside*)

                        What did I tell you?
So what's he done?

Demea

                What's he done? Let's see: he has no shame,
He has no respect for anything and thinks he's completely above the law!   85
Let's forget about everything he's done in the past.
Want to know the latest stunt he's pulled off?

Micio

                        Yes, tell me.

Demea

He ripped off the door of someone's house and broke right in.
He practically beat the owner and his entire household to death,
And he snatched a woman out of there that he's hot for!   90
Everyone's saying his behavior is utterly disgraceful!
Everyone I run into tells me about it, Micio!
It's the talk of the whole town! If he needs a role model,
Hasn't he noticed how his brother keeps his nose to the grindstone
Out there on the farm, and shows proper respect for frugal and sober living?   95
He's nothing like Aeschinus! And what I say about him

---

9   The Roman *paterfamilias* (cf. n. 7 above) did in fact have legal authority over his children that
    amounted to ownership as in the case of slavery, and he could even have his children executed with
    impunity. Cf. Introduction p. 26.

Really applies to you, Micio: you're the one that's spoiled him!

Micio

What's more unfair than a person who's never done anything in life?
Nothing can possibly be right unless he's experienced it himself.

Demea

What do you mean by that?

Micio

                                    That you're way off base here, Demea.   100
Listen to me. It's not a disgrace for a young man
To whore around or go out drinking.[10] It simply isn't.
Same for breaking down doors. If you and I never did that sort of thing,
It was only because we were poor. Do you now consider
What you couldn't do then because of poverty a badge of honor?   105
That's just not reasonable. If we had had the means to do these things,
We would have. And if you just acted like a human being,
You'd let him do them now when he has the excuse of youth,
Rather than encouraging him to do them later when it's inappropriate—
You know, after he's happily tossed your sorry corpse out of the house!   110

Demea

Holy Jupiter![11] You're going to drive me to the nut-house!
IT'S NOT A DISGRACE FOR A YOUNG MAN TO DO THESE THINGS?

Micio

                                          Now, listen to me
Before you start pounding the same things into my head over and over again.
You gave your son up to me for adoption.
He's my son now, Demea. If he makes a mistake,   115
The brunt of it falls squarely on my shoulders.
Catered parties, booze, scented hair-gels[12]—it's all out of my pocket.
He has an affair? I'll finance it for as long as I can;
When I can't, he'll probably be locked out of her house.
He broke some doors? They can be fixed.   120
He tore some clothing? I'll see it's mended. Thanks to the gods,
I have the means to take care of this, and it hasn't been a problem for me yet.
So either stop preaching or get a mediator of your choice:
I'll prove that you're one who's got it mostly wrong here.

Demea

                                      Good lord!

---

10 Micio's condoning of Aeschinus' behavior here is not (as modern audiences may assume) entirely out of step with Roman moral tradition. See further Introduction p. 20.

11 For the god Jupiter, see Appendix I p. 335.

12 The use of scented hair-oil in Roman comedy is associated with (usually extramarital) sexual activity, esp. in connection with banqueting where prostitutes are present.

Learn to be a father from those who've mastered the concept![13]   125
Micio
You're his biological father—I'm his spiritual one.[14]
Demea
Spiritual? You—
Micio
                    Watch it. If you're going to go on and on, I'm leaving.
Demea
So that's how it is?
Micio
                    Expect me to listen to the same thing over and over again?
Demea
I'm concerned.
Micio
          I'm concerned too. But, Demea,
Let's divide that concern up in half. You be concerned about one son,   130
I'll be concerned about the other. Your concern about them both
Is pretty much the same thing as asking for Aeschinus back.
Demea
                                        But no, Micio—
Micio
That's the way I see it.
Demea
              All right, then! If that's what you want,
Go ahead and let him spend, squander and flounder! Doesn't matter to me.
Now if so much as one word about—
Micio
                    Demea!   135
Are you about to lose it again?
Demea
                    Don't you believe me? Am I asking for my son back?
It's hard for me, it's not like I'm just some stranger here. If I object … okay, I'll stop.
So I should concern myself with just one son? Fine. Thanks to the gods,
He's just the son I wanted. Someday, that son of yours will realize that …
I don't want to say anything more about him. (*exits*)   140
Micio
What he said isn't exactly on the mark—but it's not totally off either.
I am bothered by these things, but I certainly don't want him

---

13 When Demea here says (lit.) "learn to be a father from those who truly know how [i.e., to be a father]," does he mean from those who have learned from the experience of parenting or, more likely, (biological) fathers who know how to parent properly by virtue of their blood relationship to their children? Cf. Micio's response (126 and n. 14 below) and Introduction pp. 26-31.

14 Micio literally says, "you're his father by birth (*natura*), I'm his father by/because of *consiliis*, where the range of the meaning of the Latin noun *consilium* includes "advice," "counsel," "sense," "reason."

To know that's the case. It's just the sort of person he is:
Calming him down means standing up to him and discouraging him,
Even if that provokes a barely human reaction.   145
But if I were to add to his anger or somehow encourage it,
I'd be just as crazy as he is. And yet it's true
That Aeschinus is doing us some harm here.
What prostitute hasn't he hooked up with or spent money on?
And get this: he recently told me   150
He wanted to get married! I thought he was tired
Of the lifestyle or maybe the "passions of youth" were flaming out.
I was glad—but here we go again. Whatever's up,
I'd like to talk to him and find out about it. Maybe he's at the forum. (*exits*)

SCENE 3

*Aechinus enters from the wing leading to the forum with Parmeno
and a prostitute, followed closely by Sannio.*

Sannio

Help, help, people please help me! Help an innocent and   155
Defenseless man!

Aeschinus (*to the girl*)

Easy now—stand right over there.
You don't need to look back. You're safe. He won't touch you while I'm here.

Sannio

I'll get her no matter what you all—

Aeschinus

He may be a scumbag, but he's not about to risk getting another pounding today.

Sannio

Come on now, Aeschinus! You can't claim you didn't know what to expect
from me.   160
I'm a pimp for god's sake!

Aeschinus

I know.

Sannio

A pimp indeed, but as honest as they come.
As for your forthcoming apology about not having meant to treat me like this,
Here's what I make of it![15] Trust me, I know my rights and I'll exercise them!
You'll pay for mistreating me, and I don't mean with just words.
I know all your kind's "I didn't mean for it to happen; you have my solemn word 165
You didn't deserve such treatment." No I didn't, but I certainly did get it!

Aeschinus (*to Parmeno*)

Go on ahead now and open the door. Hurry!

---

15 Sannio makes some sort of defiant gesture here.

Sannio

Just going to ignore me?

Aeschinus (*to the girl*)

Go inside now.

Sannio

I won't allow this!

Aeschinus

Over here, Parmeno.
You're too far off. Stand here beside him—yes, just like that.
Now keep your eyes glued right on mine.   170
The instant I give you the signal, punch him in the mouth.

Sannio

I'd like to see him try.

Aeschinus

Hey, watch it!

Parmeno

Let go of the lady! (*strikes Sannio*)

Sannio

I don't deserve this!

Aeschinus

Watch it or you'll get another one.

Sannio

Hey! Ouch!

Aeschinus

I didn't give the signal—but that's a mistake you're welcome to make.
Go in now. (*to the girl*)

Sannio

What's going on here, Aeschinus? Are you the local king?   175

Aeschinus

If I were, I'd have it decreed that you be awarded just what you deserve.

Sannio

What business do you have with me?

Aeschinus

None.

Sannio

Know what sort of man I am?

Aeschinus

Not interested.

Sannio

Have I ever laid a finger on anything of yours?

Aeschinus

Oh, you'd know about it if you had!

Sannio

Why should *you* have this girl instead of me? I paid for her in cash.
Answer me that.

Aeschinus

It'd be better if you didn't make a big scene out here in public.   180
If you keep on annoying me, I'll have you hauled off into the house,
And you'll be buried alive with whips until you're declared dead.

Sannio

Whips? For a free citizen?

Aeschinus

Count on it.

Sannio

You're despicable! And they claim there's liberty and justice for all here!

Aeschinus

If you're finished ranting now, pimp, I'd appreciate it if you'd listen up.

Sannio

Who's the one ranting here?

Aeschinus

Enough of that: back to the point.   185

Sannio

Back to what point?

Aeschinus

I have something of interest to you. Care to hear it?

Sannio

Yes, if it's a fair deal.

Aeschinus

Hah! A pimp who's concerned about fairness!

Sannio

Fine. Yes, I'm a pimp—corrupter and defiler of all the youth, a liar,
Blah, blah, blah.[16] The fact remains: I haven't done you any wrong.

Aeschinus

Damn! So I can expect that soon?

Sannio

Please, back to that deal.   190

Aeschinus

You bought her for twenty minae[17] (and damn you for that!).
I'll give you just as much in cash.

Sannio

Suppose I don't want to sell her to you.
Will you force me to?

Aeschinus

Absolutely not.

Sannio

Well, I was afraid—

---

16 Sannio metatheatrically (cf. Introduction pp. 8-10) refers to the typical characterization of pimps in
     Roman comedy (cf. the terms of abuse hurled at the pimp Ballio in Plautus' *Pseudolus*, 357-69).

17 For the value of twenty minae, see Appendix II p. 337.

Aeschinus

I don't think
She should be sold at all, seeing as she's a free person. I'm claiming her.[18]
Take your pick: the cash or a date in court?   195
Think it over until I get back, pimp. (*exits*)

Sannio

Holy Jupiter!
It's no surprise victims of crime are driven to the point of insanity!
He dragged me out of my house, beat me up, and stole my girl!
He must have landed over five hundred blows on my poor body!
How'd he square things up? He demands I sell her to him at cost!   200
Since he's done so much for me, I'll let it be. He's just demanding his due.
Come on now, Sannio, you know you want it—the cash, that is. Ah, but I'm
    a clairvoyant:
The instant I agree to a price, he'll produce witnesses to say I sold her.
The cash? It was all a dream, and I can just hear the old "Come back tomorrow!"
I could put up with that if he paid—yes, even when I'm a victim here.   205
But I understand how things are: when you take up this line of work,
Young men will abuse you, and you just have to put up with it in silence.
But no one's going to pay me. It's pointless for me to try to balance the books!

SCENE 4

Syrus enters from Micio's house.

Syrus (*to Aeschinus inside*)
Shush! I'll meet with him in person and see he accepts the offer and even says
He got a fair deal. What's this I'm hearing   210
About you and my master having some kind of fight, Sannio?

Sannio

If you can call it a fight—
It was the most one-sided contest I've ever seen!
It wore us both out: I got the pounding, and the pounding eventually got to him!

Syrus
It was your fault.

Sannio
What should I have done?

Syrus
You should have been more accommodating to him.

Sannio
Letting him use my face as a punching bag wasn't obliging enough?   215

Syrus
You know, sometimes disregard for money at just the right time yields the most
    profit.

---

18   This is a bluff to encourage Sannio to sell her.

Come on, were you afraid that if you gave in just a little and were more
  accommodating
To the young man, you wouldn't be paid back with interest?
Could you be any stupider?

Sannio
                    I don't invest in the future.

Syrus
  Geeze, Sannio! Don't you know anything about baiting a hook?   220

Sannio
  I'm sure that way's better, but I've never been smart enough
  Not to prefer taking whatever cash I could get in the here and now and then running.

Syrus
  Come on, I know you better than that! What are twenty minae to you
  When you have a chance to help him out? I've also heard you're off to Cyprus[19]—

Sannio
                                                        What?

Syrus
  —and that you've bought up a lot of merchandise and booked a ship.   225
  I imagine that's a load on your mind. But you'll take care of this when you get
    back, right?

Sannio
  I'm not moving an inch. (*aside*) Damn! That's what they were counting on!

Syrus (*aside*)
                                                        He's scared

  I've thrown a monkey wrench in his plans![20]

Sannio (*aside*)
                                The nastiness of it! He's snuck up on me
  At the worst possible time! I bought several ladies
  And a lot of other local merchandise to take to Cyprus.   230
  I'm in for a huge loss if I don't get them all to market there.
  But if I let this business here slide until I get back from Cyprus,
  It's no good. The deal will have gone stone-cold: "Back at last?
  Why'd you let it go? Where've you been?" I'd be better off letting her go
  Than staying here for a while now or going to court later.   235

Syrus
  Have you made an estimate of how much you stand to make?

Sannio
  Is this honorable behavior? That Aeschinus would even attempt such a stunt!
  The nerve of him snatching the girl away from me by a sneak attack!

---

19 A large eastern Mediterranean island, perennially an important trade center owing to its strategic
    location.
20 Literally, "I've put a stone in his sandal," a proverb.

Syrus (*aside*)

    He's falling apart. I have one last offer. How's this grab you?

    Rather than risking a total loss,   240

    Why not split the difference?

    He can scrape ten minae together from someplace.

Sannio

                      Good lord!

    Now I have to worry about just getting my investment back?

    Has he no shame? He's loosened up every tooth in my mouth

    And thanks to his fists, my whole head is swollen up like a ball!   245

    To top it all off, he wants to cheat me! Nope—I'm not going there!

Syrus

                           As you like.

    Anything else before I go?

Sannio

           Yes, damn it, there is something!

    Regardless of what's happened, and rather than going to court,

    Let me recover what's mine—the amount I paid for her, at least.

    I know that up to now we haven't been friends,   250

    But you'll see I never forget someone who does me a favor.[21]

Syrus

                       I'll do what I can.

    But there's Ctesipho! He's in a good mood

    About his girlfriend.

Sannio

        What about my request?

Syrus

                Just wait a minute.

SCENE 5

Ctesipho enters from the wing leading to the country.

Ctesipho

    It's a joy to receive a favor from anyone when you need it,

    But a favor from someone who's supposed to help you out is an absolute delight! 255

    Oh my brother, my dear brother! What's the best way to praise you?

    No words of mine could ever express the full extent of your goodness!

    The one thing I have over everyone else in the world

    Is a brother who's a master of every human virtue!

Syrus

    Hey, Ctesipho!

---

21 Latin *amicitia* (cognate with *amare*, "to love"), is used of both friendship based on genuine affection (as in 67 above) and also political and interpersonal alliances that depend on reciprocal exchanges of favors (so here).

Ctesipho
> Syrus! Where's Aeschinus?

Syrus
> Right here at home—waiting for you.

Ctesipho
> Ah!   260

Syrus
What is it?

Ctesipho
> What is it? It's only because of him I'm still alive, Syrus!

What a guy! He put my interests ahead of all his own!

The insults, the infamy, the trouble and the crime—he took the fall for it all!

That beats everything! What's that? Did the door creak?

Syrus
> Hold on! It's him coming out.

SCENE 6

Aeschinus enters from Micio's house.

Aeschinus
Where's that criminal?

Sannio (*aside*)
> He's after me! Has he got any money? That's it!   265

I don't see a cent!

Aeschinus
> Excellent, just the person I'm looking for. What's up, Ctesipho?

Everything's fine now. There's no reason to be glum.

Ctesipho
Absolutely no reason whatsoever, seeing as I've got you for a brother, Aeschinus!

My dear brother! I'm afraid to praise you further to your face—

You might mistake my sincere gratitude for mere flattery.   270

Aeschinus
Don't be silly, Ctesipho! It's not as if the two of us are strangers.

It just bothers me that I found out so late and things had almost reached the point

That no one could have rescued you no matter how much they wanted to.

Ctesipho
I was ashamed.

Aeschinus
> Now that's silliness, not shame! Almost going into exile

Over a little thing like that! It's awful to even mention it! May the gods forbid it!   275

Ctesipho
It was my mistake.

Aeschinus
> What's the latest from our friend Sannio?

Ctesipho

He's calmed down.

Aeschinus

I'm off to the forum to pay him off. You should go see her inside, Ctesipho.

Sannio (*to Syrus*)

After him, Syrus!

Syrus (*to Aeschinus*)

Yes, let's go. He's in a big rush to get to Cyprus.

Sannio

Not so big a rush

As you'd like. I've got time to stay here some.

Syrus

Settle down—you'll get paid.

Sannio

But will I be paid in full?

Syrus

Yes. Just quiet down and follow this way.

Sannio

Right behind you.   280

Ctesipho

Hey, Syrus!

Syrus

What?

Ctesipho

Please pay that utterly despicable person off as soon as possible.
I'm afraid that if he gets any angrier, this whole story will leak to my father—
And that'd be the end of me!

Syrus

Won't happen. Cheer up, and in the meantime, go enjoy yourself with her inside.
And have the couches[22] and everything else set up for us.   285
I'll seal the deal and come back here with some groceries.

Ctesipho

Yes, please do that. Since everything's turned out so nicely today, let's party!

SCENE 7

Sostrata enters from her house with Canthara.

Sostrata

My dear nurse, please tell me what's happening!

Canthara

What's happening?

Everything will be just fine. She's started her first contractions just now, dear.

---

22 Greeks and Romans both reclined on couches while dining.

You act as if you've never witnessed a birth or had a baby yourself.   290

Sostrata

Oh me oh my! We're all alone! We've got no one! Geta isn't even here.

I've got no one to send for a midwife or to go get Aeschinus!

Canthara

But he'll be here soon: he never lets a day go by

Without coming.

Sostrata

Yes, he's the only cure for all my ills.

Canthara

Under the circumstances, things turned out as well as they could have, mistress. 295

If she had to get raped, it's best that a young man like him was involved.

He's got such a good character and heart, and he's from such a fine family.

Sostrata

You've got that right. I only hope the gods preserve him for us!

SCENE 8

Geta enters from the wing leading to the forum.

Geta

Now it's reached the crisis point! If everyone in the world got together

To find a way to get us out of this mess, there's really nothing all of them   300

Could do for my mistress, her daughter, or for me! It's so awful!

There's no escape! All of a sudden, we're walled in on every side

By violence, poverty, injustice, isolation, and disgrace!

What a world we live in! The evil, the unspeakable acts—and the filthy bum!

Sostrata

Oh dear! What's Geta so worked up about here? Why's he rushing about

   like this?[23]   305

Geta

Could nothing restrain him, nothing constrain him? His honor, his solemn oath,

His compassion for her? Not even the imminent birth of the child?

An innocent girl he forced into disgrace that she didn't deserve?

Sostrata (*to Canthara*)

                                I'm not quite

Following what he's saying.

Canthara (*to Sostrata*)

                 Please, Sostrata, let's get closer.

Geta

                          Ahh!

I'm so steamed up about this, I'm nearly out of mind!   310

There's nothing I want more than to have that whole family right in front of me:

---

23 Geta is playing the stereotypical New Comedy role of the "running slave" who enters breathlessly with urgent news. Cf. Terence, *Eunuch* 36.

I'd spew out every last ounce of my anger at them while it's still fresh!
I'd consider it punishment enough, provided I get to punish them my way.
I'd snuff out the geezer who fathered this beast first!
Then I'd rip Syrus apart for leading him on in it all— 315
I'd hoist him up by his midsection, pound his head into the ground,
And then pave the road with his brain bits!
And the young man himself? I'd rip out his eyes and toss his body off a cliff!
The rest? I'd wail on them, flail at 'em, trample 'em and impale 'em!
But I need to share the bad news with my mistress at once.

Sostrata
Let's call him back. Hey, Geta! 320

Geta
Let me go, whoever you are.

Sostrata
It's Sostrata.

Geta
Where? I've been looking all over for you.
Very fortunate to see you at last! We meet just in the nick of time!
Mistress—

Sostrata
What's wrong? Why are you shaking?

Geta
— it's horrible!

Canthara
Why all the panic, Geta?
Catch your breath.

Geta
We're completely—

Sostrata
Yes, completely what?

Geta
—finished.
It's over.

Sostrata
Please, out with it! What's over?

Geta
Now—

Sostrata
Now what, Geta? 325

Geta
Aeschinus—

Sostrata
What about him?

Geta
—is no longer like family to us.

Sostrata

Oh no,

I'm finished! Why?

Geta

He's fallen for another girl.

Sostrata

No, no, dear no!

Geta

And he's not even trying to hide it! He snatched her from a pimp in broad daylight.

Sostrata

Is this for sure?

Geta

Yes, absolutely. I saw it with my own eyes, Sostrata.

Sostrata

Oh,

This is awful! I don't know what to believe anymore or who to trust!   330
Our Aeschinus did this? He was the lifeline of us all, our single hope and source
    of strength!
He's the one who swore he couldn't live a day without her,
And said he'd put the baby in his father's lap
And beg him to allow him to marry my daughter.

Geta

Stop crying, mistress. We need to make a plan for the future.   335
First: are we going to put up with this or tell someone about it?

Canthara

What! Are you insane?

You think this should be public knowledge?

Geta

No, I don't like that at all.

First of all, the facts show that he's parted company with us,
And if we disclose the matter publicly, I'm sure he'll deny it.
It would just create doubts about your reputation and your daughter's lifestyle.   340
Even if he did confess, it wouldn't be good for her to marry him
When he's in love with someone else. So we should probably just keep quiet.

Sostrata

No, absolutely not!

I won't!

Geta

What'll you do?

Sostrata

Tell people.

Canthara

Oh dear, Sostrata, give this very careful thought!

Sostrata

Things couldn't get any worse than they already are.

First, she has no dowry. On top of that, she's lost what's second best to that: 345
She can't be given in marriage as a virgin now. Here's our only plan:
If he denies it, the ring that he left will serve as evidence.[24]
Since I know that I'm free from all blame in this,
And that no bribes or anything else unbecoming of her or me has happened,
I'll go to court.

Geta

      All right, your suggestion's better.

Sostrata

            You must go   350
Right this moment and tell our relative Hegio every last detail.
He was a very close friend of my late husband Simulus and treated us very well.

Geta

To be sure, no one else treats us well now. (*exits*)

Sostrata

         Hurry now, Canthara dear!
Run and get the midwife so she'll be here when we need her! (*enters her house*)

SCENE 9

Demea enters from the wing leading to the forum.

Demea

Damn it all! I've been told my son Ctesipho   355
Was in on the breaking and entering with Aeschinus!
What else can I look forward to, if the son
Who still shows some promise can be corrupted by his brother?
I suppose I should go looking for him in a dive somewhere.
I'm sure his sleazy brother talked him into going there.   360
Look, there's Syrus headed this way. I'll find out from him where my son is.
That convict's part of the gang, and if he realizes
I'm on the look-out for him, he won't tell me a thing.
I won't give away what I'm after.

Syrus (*enters from the wing leading to the forum with other slaves*)

         We just told every
Last detail of the whole story to Micio.   365
I've never seen a person happier!

Demea (*aside*)

        Holy Jupiter,
What a stupid man!

Syrus

        He had only the highest praise for his son,
And thanked me for having come up with the plan.

---

24 Roman males gave their brides-to-be iron engagement rings.

Demea (*aside*)

I'm going to explode!

Syrus

                  He counted the cash out on the spot,

And laid out an additional half-mina for expenses—   370

And that's been spent in accordance with my precise instructions.

Demea (*aside*)

                                       Gag!

Here's your man, if you need to pull off a job without a hitch!

Syrus

Oh, Demea. I didn't know you were here. What's up?

Demea

What's up? The way you people operate! It's beyond me!

Syrus

Yes, I won't lie to you! It's silly … no, it's downright insane!   375

Gut the rest of those fish, Dromo!

But let that biggest eel romp around in the water for a while.

We'll de-bone it when I get back.

Not 'til then, now.

Demea

                How utterly disgraceful!

Syrus

                              Yes, I don't like it either,

And I'm always making noise about it. See that those salted fish   380

Are nicely soaked, Stephanio.

Demea

                  Oh, almighty gods!

Is spoiling his son Micio's goal? Is he hoping to win a medal for it?

Oh, this is terrible, just awful!

I can already picture the day when poverty will compel Aeschinus

To become a mercenary!

Syrus

                  Oh, Demea!   385

Now that's true genius: not only seeing clearly

What's right on your plate today, but even getting a glimpse of

What'll be there tomorrow!

Demea

                  Tell me now: is that stripper[25] in your house?

---

25 The girl is described as a *psaltria*, i.e., a musician trained on a small harp-like instrument (*psalterium*). Prostitutes were usually trained to provide musical entertainment as well as perform sexual acts at dinner parties. The unnamed girl is also apparently an expert in lascivious dancing (cf. 752), and so I translate "stripper" here and throughout, though I am aware that modern exotic dancers are not necessarily also prostitutes.

Syrus
Take a look inside yourself.
Demea

He's going to keep her in his house?
Syrus

Yes,
He's that crazy.
Demea

Is this all really happening?
Syrus

It's all because of his father's   390
Ridiculous mellowness and deplorable leniency!
Demea

My brother disgusts me,
And I'm ashamed of him.
Syrus

There's quite a difference between the two of you,
Demea, an enormous difference! And I'm not just saying that because you're here.
You're wisdom personified, every inch of you from head to toe.
He's a complete airhead. You'd never let your son   395
Do these sorts of things, would you?
Demea

Let him? It's more like I'd
Have sniffed it out six months in advance of its starting!
Syrus
You don't have to remind me about your ever-watchful eye!
Demea

I really
Want for him to stay just the way he is.
Syrus (*aside*)

Be careful of what you ask for.
Demea
Tell me: have you seen him today?
Syrus

Who? Your son?   400
(*aside*) Now I'll pack him off to the farm. I think he's been busy in the country.
Demea
Are you sure he's there?
Syrus

Yep. I went with him there myself.
Demea

Great!
I was afraid he was hanging around here.
Syrus

And he was quite angry too!

Demea
    About what?

Syrus
                He went right after his brother in the forum
    About the stripper.

Demea
              Really?

Syrus
                    Oh yes—and he didn't mince words.   405
    Now just when the money was being counted out,
    Our guy happens to show up out of the blue. He started shouting:
    "Aeschinus! How could you do this? How could you bring such undeserved disgrace
    Down upon our family?"

Demea
                I'm going to cry out of joy!

Syrus
    "You're not just wasting money—it's your life that's at stake!"   410

Demea
    Bless him! I can still have hope! He does his ancestors proud!

Syrus
                        (*aside*) Amazing!

Demea
    And he's full of good old-fashioned aphorisms like that, Syrus!

Syrus
                        (*aside*) Uggh!

    He's had an excellent teacher at home.

Demea
                I do my best.
    I never miss a teaching opportunity! Bottom line:
    I tell him to look at other people's lives as if looking into a mirror   415
    And to pick out proper role models:
    "You must do this!"

Syrus
            Right on target!

Demea
              "Avoid that!"

Syrus
                  Brilliant!

Demea
    "This is a badge of honor!"

Syrus
              Just the thing!

Demea
                "That's shameful!"

Syrus

How righteous!

Demea

           Then I continue—

Syrus

                    You know,

I really don't have the time to listen right now. I've come into some very
    fine fish,   420
And I've got to be careful they don't spoil.
You see, Demea, it's just as disgraceful for us slaves
Not to do the things you just said as it is for you masters.
So I try to share pearls of wisdom with my co-slaves just the way you do it:
"This one's too salty!" "That one's burned!" "This wasn't cleaned enough!" 425
"That's just right: remember to do it that way next time!"
I make every effort to impart all the wisdom I have to offer to them.
Bottom line: I tell them to look into dishes as if looking into a mirror, Demea,
And I advise them on what needs doing.
I realize the things that we slaves do are trivial,   430
But what're you gonna do? It is what it is.
Anything else you'd like to see?

Demea

                      Yes—for you people to develop some common sense!

Syrus

Going off to the country?

Demea

                Right away.

Syrus

                      Yes, why bother staying here in town

Where no one even listens if you cast out one of your pearls? (*enters Micio's house*)

Demea

Yes, I'm definitely off to the country, since the person I came here for is there. 435
He's the one I care about, *he's* the one I'm concerned with!
My brother can worry about the other one, if that's the way he wants it.
But who's that off a ways there? Is that our relative Hegio?
If I can trust my eyes, it is him! Yes indeed,
This gentleman's been a friend to our family since I was a boy!   440
Good lord! How few citizens of his moral fiber are still around today!
You'd be sorely disappointed if you expected any trouble for the state
To arise from a man of his caliber!
What a delight to see a relic of that generation still among us!
Yes, it's a pleasure to be alive these days after all!   445
I'll wait here and have a chat with him.

SCENE 10

Hegio enters with Geta.

Hegio

By the immortal gods, Geta! What a despicable act!
I can't believe what I'm hearing!

Geta

It's what happened.

Hegio

But for such low-class behavior

To have come from a family like that!
Oh, Aeschinus, that's not something your father would do!

Demea (*aside*)

He's obviously   450

Heard about the stripper. His very own father couldn't care less,
And though we're not even blood relatives, he takes it so to heart!
My goodness, I wish Micio could be somewhere around here to hear this!

Hegio

They won't get away with this, if they don't do the right thing!

Geta

Our entire future is on your shoulders, Hegio!   455
You're all we've got. You're our protector, you are our father.[26]
When our elderly master died, he put us entirely in your hands.
If you abandon us, we're finished.

Hegio

Don't even say that!
I won't abandon you and my sense of duty would never allow it.

Demea (*aside*)

I'll go up to him. Greetings to you, Hegio.   460

Hegio

Just the person I was looking for. Hello, Demea.

Demea

What's up?

Hegio

It's about your older son Aeschinus,
The one you let your brother adopt—
He's not behaving with the decency one expects of a gentleman.[27]

Demea

How's that?

---

26 The Roman social hierarchy was built around a rigidly stratified system of patrons and their dependent
    clients. In his relationship with his clients, the *patronus* took on many of the prerogatives of the all-
    powerful Roman father.

27 Literally, "in the manner of good (*bonus*) and freeborn (*liberalis*) man." Cf. n. 8 above.

Hegio

            You knew our friend Simulus, didn't you?   465

Gentleman about our age?

Demea

            Yes, of course.

Hegio

                       Your son

Has raped his young daughter.

Demea

                What?

Hegio

                     Hold on.

You haven't heard the worst of it, Demea.

Demea

                       How could it possibly get worse?

Hegio

Trust me, it does. This much at least we could somehow put up with:

Nightime, lust, wine, youth—all the usual contributing factors—   470

That part's excusable.[28] When he had realized what he had done,

He went to the girl's mother all on his own. He cried, he begged, he pled,

He pledged and swore up and down that he'd marry the girl.

They forgave him, they shielded him, they trusted him.

The young girl became pregnant as a result of the assault.   475

It's now the ninth month, and our fine young man (may the gods save us!)

Has gotten himself a stripper to live with! He's completely abandoning the girl!

Demea

Are you certain about all of this?

Hegio

                   The girl's mother is available to testify.

So is the girl, and her condition is obvious.

And then there's Geta—he's a decent and hardworking fellow,   480

By slave standards at least. He's the one putting food on the table

And supporting the whole family. Tie him up, take him away and interrogate him.[29]

Geta

It's the honest truth, Demea. You can even put me on the rack.

And in the end Aeschinus won't deny it. Bring him in here for a face-to-face.

Demea

I'm ashamed. I don't know what to do or what I should say   485

To him.

Pamphila (*from within*)

            Oh, the pain, the pain is tearing me apart!

---

28 Literally, "It's human" (*humanumst*). Cf. 687.

29 The testimony of ancient slaves was admissible only if it was extracted under torture.

Help me, Juno Lucina,[30] oh please help me now!

Hegio

Tell me now: is she giving birth?

Geta

Yes, Hegio!

Hegio

Look,
Demea, she's appealing to your sense of family honor:
How about freely granting her what you can be forced to do?   490
I pray to the gods that all turn outs in a way that becomes your family.
But if you all have other ideas, Demea,
I'll do everything I can to protect the girl out of respect for her dead father.
We were kin, and were raised together from early childhood.
We were inseparable in times of war and in times of peace,   495
We bore the weight of poverty together.
And so I'll strive, struggle and pull out all the stops for them:
I'd sooner lay down my life than ever desert them!
What do you say to that?

Demea

I'll go find my brother, Hegio.

Hegio

Fine, Demea. But take this closely to heart: 500
Your life is free of all burdens,
And you're rolling in money, power, prosperity, and privilege.
And so *you* especially should be fair and respect justice—
That is, if you all want to be known for your integrity.

Demea

Come back later: everything called for by justice will be done.   505

Hegio

As it should be. Geta, take me inside to Sostrata. (*they exit*)

Demea

It's not as if I didn't predict all this! I only wish that this were the end of it!
But I know this kind of liberal thinking
Will just lead to even bigger trouble someday!
I'll go find my brother and rehash this all to him.   510

---

30 For the goddess Juno, see Appendix I p. 335. With the exception of Alcmena in Plautus' *Amphitryon*,
    pregnant female characters do not appear on stage in ancient theater, but are sometimes heard, as here,
    giving birth off stage (i.e., as if within a stage house).

SCENE 11

Hegio enters from Sostrata's house.

Hegio (*to Sostrata inside*)

Cheer up now, Sostrata, and try to give her whatever comfort you can.

I'll catch Micio in the forum if he's there,

And tell him every last detail of what's happened.

I'll give him a chance to do his duty if that's what he intends to do.

If he has other plans in the matter, he needs to tell me   515

So that I can take appropriate action this instant. (*exits*)

SCENE 12

Ctesipho enters from Micio's house with Syrus.

Ctesipho

My father's really gone off to the country?

Syrus

A while ago.

Ctesipho

Really?

Syrus

He's at the farm and

I'm sure he's doing some chore there at this very moment.

Ctesipho

If only!

Not that I wish him any ill, but I'd love for him to wear himself out

To the point that he couldn't get out of bed for the next three days!   520

Syrus

I'm all for that—and something even better if it exists.

Ctesipho

Right with you there.

And I'm dying to finish the livelong day the way I started it—partying!

The reason I hate that farm so much is that it's so close to here:

If only it were farther away …

He'd be overcome by nightfall before he could get back here.   525

You can be sure he'll hustle back when he sees I'm not there.

He'll ask me where I was: "I haven't seen you all day long!"

What'll I say?

Syrus

Nothing coming to you?

Ctesipho

Not a thing.

Syrus

You are so pathetic!

Don't you have clients,[31] friends, guests—anybody?

Ctesipho

Yes, but why?

Syrus

So you could be "engaged" with them.

Ctesipho

When I wasn't really? Impossible!

Syrus

Possible!   530

Ctesipho

Maybe for the daytime. But what excuse can I have to spend the night here?

Syrus

Agghhh, if only it was the local custom to do business at night!
But you should just take it easy. I've got his personality down pat.
The instant he's about to explode I can make him as tame as a sheep.

Ctesipho

How?

Syrus

He loves hearing you praised: I'll make you into a god in his eyes   535
By reciting a list of all your virtues.

Ctesipho

Mine?

Syrus

Yours. Tears roll down his cheeks

As if he were a happy little boy! But look at that!

Ctesipho

What?

Syrus

Speak of the devil![32]

Ctesipho

It's my father?

Syrus

In the flesh.

Ctesipho

Syrus, what do we do?

Syrus

Go inside. I'll take care of it.

Ctesipho

If he asks, you haven't seen me. Are you even listening? (*withdraws into the background*)

Syrus

Can you just stop now?

---

31 Cf. n. 26 above.

32 The actual Latin proverb here is "the wolf in the story!" (*lupus in fabula*).

SCENE 13

Demea enters from the wing leading to the forum.

Demea

    I'm so unlucky! My brother is absolutely nowhere to be found.   540
    And while I was out searching for him, I ran into one of the hired hands
    Who said my son was not at the farm. I have no idea what to do now!

Ctesipho

    Psst, Syrus?

Syrus

            What?

Ctesipho

                    Is he looking for me?

Syrus

                          He sure is.

Ctesipho

                                I'm finished!

Syrus

                                      Calm down!

Demea (*still not noticing Ctesipho and Syrus*)

    Damn! What's with all this bad luck? I can't figure it out,
    But it seems I was born for this one thing—putting up with crap!   545
    When there's trouble for us, I'm the first to sense it, the first to get wind of it,
    And I'm the first to report the bad news … and I bear the brunt of it all by myself!

Syrus (*aside*)

    Now *that's* funny! The guy who knows absolutely nothing thinks he's first to know!

Demea

    I'm back to see if my brother's returned.

Ctesipho

                          Syrus, come on!
    Don't let him just crash right in here!

Syrus

                        Will you just be quiet?   550
    I'll take care of things.

Ctesipho

                  I'm sure as hell not going to trust you again today!
    I'll lock her up with me in some storeroom. That's the safest thing to do. (*exits*)

Syrus

    Get to it then. I'll get rid of him.

Demea

                  There's that bum Syrus!

Syrus (*pretending not to see Demea*)

    Even the most patient person in the world couldn't put up with all this!
    I'd like to know just how many masters I have! What a pain!   555

Demea (*aside*)

What's he yapping about? What's he up to? Tell me, my good man: is my brother
home?

Syrus

What the hell's this "my good man" about? I'm practically dying here.

Demea

What's wrong?

Syrus

You even have to ask? Ctesipho nearly pummeled the stripper and me
To death!

Demea

Huh? What are you saying?

Syrus

Just look at how he split my lip.

Demea

Why'd he do that?

Syrus

He said I egged him on to buy her.

Demea

Didn't you just tell me   560

You'd taken him to the farm?

Syrus

I did. But he came back all angry later.

He didn't hold anything back! Imagine someone shameless enough to beat up an
old man!

I used to carry him around in my arms when he was just so small!

Demea

Outstanding, Ctesipho! You're a chip off the old block! You are now officially a
man!

Syrus

Outstanding, eh? If he's got any brains, he'll keep his hands to himself in the
future.   565

Demea

How brave of him!

Syrus

Quite brave indeed, overwhelming a terrified girl

And a poor slave like me who can't fight back. Oh it's beyond brave all right!

Demea

Couldn't have turned out better! He realizes as much as I do you're the ringleader.
But is my brother inside?

Syrus

No.

Demea

I wonder where I can find him?

Syrus

I know where he is, but I'll never tell you.

Demea

What's that?

Syrus

That's how it is.   570

Demea

You're about to have your brains bashed in.

Syrus

I don't know
The name of the man he's meeting, but I know where his place is.

Demea

Tell me about his place then.

Syrus

Do you know the butcher's market down this way?

Demea

Yes, of course.

Syrus

Go up that way right down this street. When you get there,
There's a steep hill in front of you. Hurry on down that   575
And then here's a shrine on *this* side. Right nearby there's an alley.

Demea

Which one?

Syrus

Right where there's a big wild-fig tree.

Demea

Right.

Syrus

Continue *that* way.

Demea

But that alley is a dead-end.

Syrus

Oh, geeze! Oh boy, my bad!
And I'm supposed to be a *homo sapiens*![33] Go back to the marketplace.
You're less likely to get lost that way, and you'll get there faster.   580
Do you know the house of Cratinus the rich guy?

Demea

Yes I do.

Syrus

Once you're past it,

---

33 The standard Latin word for "human being" (*homo*) here bears the loaded sense "a rational human being."

Go left straight *this* way. When you get to Diana's[34] temple, go to the right.
Before you reach the city-gate, right around the reservoir,
There's a bakery and then a factory. He's there.

Demea

What's he doing there?

Syrus

He's having some solid oak couches for outdoor use made.   585

Demea

So you people can party in the garden too! How lovely! I really need to go find him.
(*exits*)

Syrus

Yes … do go away! I'll see you get all the exercise you need, death-chow![35]
I'm annoyed Aeschinus is so late coming back. Lunch is spoiling.
Ctesipho's totally wrapped up in his rendezvous, and so I'm all on my own.
I'll go in now and sample the choicest of the hors d'oeuvres,   590
And as I slowly sip a few cups of fine wine, I'll string out the day.

SCENE 14

Micio enters with Hegio from the wing leading to the forum.

Micio

There's really no reason I should get so much praise for this, Hegio.
I'm just doing what I should: righting a wrong we're responsible for.
Did you think I'm one of those people who feel a wrong has been willfully
    committed
Against them if you complain about a wrong they've committed themselves?   595
Then they make an accusation *against you* on top of it all! Are you thanking me
    for not doing that?

Hegio

No, not at all! It's never even entered my mind that you're not the man you are.
But please come with me to see the girl's mother, Micio,
And tell her in person what you just told me—
That all the confusion here is the brother's fault and that the stripper is his girl. 600

Micio

If you think that's the right thing and what we should do, let's go.

Hegio

That's the right idea,
And you'll put her mind at ease. The stress and worry are wearing her down,
And you'll have done what you should. But if you disagree,
I'll tell her myself what you said.

---

34 For the goddess Diana, see Appendix I p. 335.

35 I.e., food offered up to the spirits of the dead in funeral ritual.

Micio

Not necessary—I'll go.

Hegio

Thanks.

People in less fortunate circumstances often tend to be hypersensitive   605
And more likely to take offense at everything.
Their lack of influence makes them think they're always under attack.
So an apology to her in person would carry more weight.

Micio

What you say is right.

Hegio

Then follow me in here.

Micio

Absolutely.

SCENE 15

Aeschinus enters from the wing leading to the forum.
(SONG through 617)[36]

Aeschinus

This is ripping my heart out!   610
For all this trouble to be thrown my way from out of the blue!   610a
I don't know what to do or how to act!
My limbs are tied up from fear, my mind's paralyzed!
I can't even hold on to a rational thought!
Uggh!   613a
How am I supposed to untangle myself from this mess?
I'm surrounded by so much suspicion, and I richly deserve it!   615
Sostrata assumes I bought the stripper for myself!
The old lady told me that much.
I happened to see her when she'd been sent to get the midwife.
I go up to her and ask how Pamphila's doing and if the baby's coming soon,
And if she's off to get the midwife. "Get away! Get away, Aeschinus!   620
We've had enough of your lies and false promises!" she says.
I reply: "What? Please tell me what you mean?" "Goodbye," she says,
"And enjoy the girl you like so much." I sensed their suspicion, but restrained
    myself
From saying anything to that gossip-hag and having her spill the beans.
What can I do now? Say she's my brother's? That's exactly what we don't want   625
Made public. It's possible that it wouldn't turn out that way though ...
But I'm really afraid they won't believe what happened.
There's so *much* plausible evidence against me: *I* grabbed her, *I* paid, *I* took her home.

---

36 A rare instance of song in Terence. Cf. Introduction p. 36.

True, this was all my fault—and not telling my father every detail, no matter what!
I could have talked him into letting me marry her.   630
I've just been stalling up to now: time to wake up, Aeschinus!
The first thing to do is go to them and clear things up about me.
Here's the door. I'm done for! Just knocking on this door makes me shiver.
Hey, it's me, Aeschinus! Somebody open up the door right now!
Somebody's coming out. I'll hide over this way.

SCENE 16

Micio enters from Sostrata's house.

Micio (*to Sostrata inside*)

                                 Do as I said, Sostrata.   635

I'll find Aeschinus and tell him what's been decided.
But who's that knocking at the door?

Aeschinus (*aside*)

                             It's my father! I'm done for!

Micio

                                         Aeschinus!

Aeschinus (*aside*)
What's he doing here?

Micio

                   Was that you pounding on the door?

(*aside*) Dead silence. Why don't I mess with his head a little?
Seems fair, since he didn't volunteer to tell me about all this himself.   640
Aren't you going to answer me?

Aeschinus

                     No, not that door, as far as I know.

Micio

As I'd expect. I was wondering what business you had here.
(*aside*) He blushed! Everything's okay.

Aeschinus

                    But please tell me, father,
What business brings you here?

Micio

                  None of my own, really.
A friend of mine dragged me away from the forum here just now   645
To help him out.

Aeschinus

                With what?

Micio

                 Let me tell you:
Some women of very modest means live here.
I don't suppose that you know them—well, I'm sure you don't.
They haven't lived here very long.

Aeschinus

And so?

Micio

There's a young girl and her mother.

Aeschinus

Keep going.

Micio

The girl's father is dead.   650

This friend of mine is her closest relative,
And so the law requires her to marry him.[37]

Aeschinus

Oh no!

Micio

What's the matter?

Aeschinus

Nothing. Everything's fine. Continue.

Micio

He came to take her away with him—

He lives in Miletus.[38]

Aeschinus

What? He's taking her away with him?

Micio

That's right.

Aeschinus

All the way to Miletus?

Micio

Yes.

Aeschinus

(*aside*) I'm gonna be sick.   655

What about the two of them? What do they say?

Micio

Not much, as you'd expect.

But the mother cooked up a story about a child being born
That's fathered by another man—but she won't reveal his name.
She says he was her daughter's first, and so she shouldn't be married to my friend.

Aeschinus

What? Doesn't that seem entirely reasonable?   660

Micio

No.

---

37 This is Greek, not Roman law. In Athens, an orphaned female with no brothers had to marry her nearest eligible male relative. Alternatively, the male relative could supply her with a dowry to marry someone outside her family.

38 Large coastal city in southern Asia Minor (modern Turkey), colonized by Greeks at an early date.

Aeschinus

    What do you mean no? Is he going to take her away from here, father?

Micio

    Why shouldn't he?

Aeschinus

                You and your friend have behaved so cruelly,

And without any pity whatsoever, and if you'll allow me

To be even more frank, father, this is behavior unbecoming of a gentleman![39]

Micio

    How so?

Aeschinus

            You even have to ask? What about the feelings of the poor fellow   665

Who had relations with her first?

The wretch could be terribly in love with her right now;

What if he has to watch her snatched up in person

And taken away before his very eyes? That would be a terrible injustice, father!

Micio

    How do you figure? Who's the person that betrothed her and gave her away

      to him?   670

Who'd she marry? When was the wedding? Who consented to all this?

Why'd he marry someone else's woman?

Aeschinus

                     Should a grown-up girl

Have to sit at home

And wait until a relative showed up there?

This is what you should have said, father, and what you should have stood up for. 675

Micio

    Nonsense! Was I supposed to argue against the case of the person I came

      to help?

But how's any of this our concern, Aeschinus?

What do we have to do with them? Let's go. What is it?

Why are you crying?

Aeschinus

             Father, listen to me, please!

Micio

                                  I know everything, Aeschinus.

And because I love you, everything you do touches me deeply.   680

Aeschinus

    And precisely because I want to deserve your love for as long as you're alive, father,

I'm terribly hurt by this bad behavior of mine,

And deeply ashamed to face you.

---

39 Literally "not belonging to a free-born person" (*inliberaliter*); cf. n. 8 above.

Micio

I believe that. I know you're an honorable person.[40]
But I'm afraid you're a bit too careless.
In what sort of city do you think you're living now?   685
You raped a girl you had no legal right to touch.[41]
This was your first big mistake—a very big mistake, though an excusable one.[42]
Other men from respectable families have done the same. But afterwards now,
Didn't you stop and consider, and, for your own benefit, didn't you think
About what should be done and how to do it? If you were ashamed to tell me
   yourself,   690
How was I to find out? Nine months passed while you hesitated.
You've done just about everything possible to wrong yourself, the poor girl and
   your son.
Come on! Did you think the gods would fix everything for you as you snored away?
Or that the bride'd be transported to your house without your having to do a thing?
I'd hate to see you being so irresponsible like this in other matters!   695
Calm down—you can marry her.

Aeschinus

                          Really?

Micio

                                        Yes, just take it easy now.

Aeschinus

You're not just playing with me now, are you father?

Micio

                                        Why would I play with you?

Aeschinus

                                                    I don't know.
But I'm really nervous because I want this all to be true so badly!

Micio

Now go home and pray for the gods' help in carrying off the wedding. Go, go!

Aeschinus

What? The wedding right now?

Micio

                          Right now.

Aeschinus

                                        Right now?

Micio

                                                    As soon as possible.   700

---

40 Literally, "I know you have the character of a free-born (*liberalis*) person;" cf. n. 8 above.

41 While potentially subject to serious legal consequences in both Rome and Greece, the rape of an unmarried (free-born) girl might be tolerated if the rapist agreed to marry his victim. See further Introduction p. 34.

42 Literally, his behavior was "human" (*humanus*) cf. n. 28 above.

Aeschinus
May all the gods blast me, father, if I don't love you more than my own eyes![43]
Micio
What? Even more than her?
Aeschinus
No—the same.
Micio
Hurray for that.
Aeschinus
But where's your Milesian friend?
Micio
Lost. Long gone. His ship has sailed. You'd better hurry!
Aeschinus
You should go, father:
You're the one to ask the gods for their blessing. I have no doubt whatsoever
They'll listen more to you since you're a much better man than I am.   705
Micio
I'm going inside to prepare what we need. If you're smart, you'll do as I said. (*exits*)
Aeschinus
What do you make of this? Is this what it means to be a father or a son?
If he were my brother or a close buddy, he couldn't have done any more for me![44]
How can you not love him? And don't you just want to hug him? Oh my!
Because of his kindness, I'm damn near terrified I'll accidently do something   710
He wouldn't like. This calls for total caution.
I should go right in, so I don't become the one who holds up my own wedding.

SCENE 17

Demea enters from the wing leading to the forum.

Demea
I'm so worn out from all that walking! May almighty Jupiter blast you, Syrus,
Along with all your damn directions!
I dragged my ass all over this town! To the gate, to the reservoir …   715
Where haven't I been? And there wasn't any factory there,
And no one said they'd seen my brother!
Now my plan is to plant myself down right here until he comes back.

---

43 A Latin proverb to express the highest possible degree of love. Cf. 903.

44 The phrase used here of Micio's behavior, i.e., *morem gerere* ("to indulge someone"), would sound very odd to a Roman audience with reference to a father's relationship with his son. More commonly, it is used of a dutiful wife's selfless dedication to her husband.

SCENE 18

Micio enters from his house.

Micio (*to slave(s) inside*)
I'll go and tell them we're all ready here.

Demea
But there he is—in the flesh! I've been looking for you for hours.   720

Micio
What for?

Demea
            I've got some horribly disgraceful news for you
About that fine young man of yours.

Micio
                        Here we go again …

Demea
                                It's shocking
And very serious.

Micio
            Just hold on now!

Demea
                        You just don't know what he's about.

Micio
                                Yes, I do.

Demea
You moron! You're imagining I mean the stripper.
I'm talking about a crime against a girl who's a free-born citizen!

Micio
                                I know.   725

Demea
Oh, so you know and you let it go?

Micio
                        What am I supposed to do?

Demea
Why don't you scream and tear your heart out?

Micio
                        I'd of course prefer—

Demea
A child's been born.

Micio
                May the gods bless it!

Demea
                                The girl has nothing.

Micio
I know.

Demea
> And so he'll have to marry her without a dowry!

Micio
> > Obviously.

Demea
What happens now?

Micio
> > Well, whatever the situation calls for: 730
The girl will move from over there to here.

Demea
> > Holy Jupiter!
How can that be the right thing to do?

Micio
> > What else should I do?

Demea
What else should you do? If you're not actually upset by what's happened,
A decent human being would at least pretend to be!

Micio
> > No, I've had her betrothed to him,
Everything's been settled, and the ceremony is happening.   735
I've calmed everybody's fears. Isn't *that* what a decent human being would do?

Demea
But, Micio, do you approve of what's happened?

Micio
> > If I could change the way things are?
No, I don't. But since I can't change them, I bear it all with a level head.
Human existence is just like a game of chance:
You cast the dice and if you don't get exactly what you need the most,   740
You use all your skill to make the best of what chance has tossed your way.

Demea
You—making the best of it? Yes, you *skillfully* wasted twenty minae on the stripper!
You need to do whatever you can to get rid of her somewhere—
And if no one will pay for her, give her away!

Micio
That's not happening, and I actually don't even want to sell her.   745

Demea
What'll you do with her?

Micio
> > Keep her at home.

Demea
> > By the almighty gods!
A hooker and the lady of the house under the same roof?

Micio
Why not?

Demea

    Are you sane?

Micio

          Oh, I definitely think so.

Demea

May the gods save me when I see this stupidity of yours!

I think you're doing this so *you* can have unlimited lap-dances!   750

Micio

Why not?

Demea

    And the new bride will train under her supervision?

Micio

                               Of course.

Demea

And you'll be doing the rope-dance[45] with the both of them?

Micio

Absolutely!

Demea

    Absolutely?

Micio

    And you can join in if we need a fourth.

Demea

                            Ugggh!

Aren't you ashamed of these things?

Micio

              Now, really, Demea!

Drop your usual rage, and in honor of the occasion of your son's wedding,   755

How about putting on a bright and cheery face?

I'm going to meet with them and then I'll come back here. (*exits*)

Demea

                    Jupiter in heaven!

Such a lifestyle! Such morals! Such utter insanity!

Welcoming in a wife without a dowry, a stripper-in-residence,

A den of conspicuous consumption, a young man spoiled rotten by extravagance, 760

And one crazy old man of a father!

Salvation herself[46] couldn't save this family, even if she wanted to!

---

45 None of the particulars of this dance is known. The Romans (or at least the conservative Roman moral
    tradition), in contrast to the Greeks, generally scorned dancing as an exotic and decadent activity.

46 Many personified abstractions were worshipped in Roman religion. There were temples and shrines of
    the personified deity *Salus*, "Salvation" or "Safety" (especially in relation to the welfare of the state), in
    Rome and elsewhere. Cf. *Menaechmi* 2 and n. 2.

SCENE 19

Syrus enters from Micio's house.

Syrus

My goodness, Syrus, you've treated yourself to some deluxe service!
And to perform your duty with such sheer elegance!
Off you go now ... but seeing as though I got so stuffed inside,   765
I think I'll go for a little stroll outside here.

Demea

Would you look at that?

A shining model of discipline!

Syrus

Oh, look! Our old man
Is right here. What's happening? Why so glum?

Demea

You scumbag!

Syrus

Hold on there, chief. Are you spouting out words of wisdom now?

Demea

If you were my slave—

Syrus

You'd be quite rich, Demea,   770

And your finances would be on a rock solid foundation.

Demea

—I'd make an

Example out of you for everyone.

Syrus

Why? What'd I do?

Demea

You even have to ask?

You bum! Here in the thick of all this chaos and major crime,
With none of it satisfactorily resolved—you're drunk!
As if this were an occasion for celebration!

Syrus

I sure regret my coming out here!   775

SCENE 20

Dromo speaks from the entrance to Micio's house.

Dromo

Hey, Syrus! Ctesipho wants you to come back in.

Syrus

Go away!

Demea

What's he saying about Ctesipho?

Syrus

Nothing at all.

Demea

Just a minute now, you ex-con.

Is Ctesipho inside?

Syrus

No!

Demea

Why'd he mention him then?

Syrus

He meant somebody else—some wannabe-hanger-on.
You know him?

Demea

I will soon enough.

Syrus

What are you doing? Where are you going?

Demea

Let go!   780

Syrus

Don't—please.

Demea

Get your hands off me, you human punching-bag!
Or do you want me to smash your brains to bits right here?

Syrus

There he goes.
That's one extremely unwelcome party crasher, especially for Ctesipho!
Well, what should I do now?
Until this commotion settles down, I might as well go off into a corner
    somewhere
And try to sleep off my little binge. Yes indeed.   785

SCENE 21

Micio enters from Sostrata's house.

Micio

Just as I said, Sostrata, we have everything ready for whenever you want it.
Who's making all that racket at the door of my house?

Demea

Damn! What can I do, how should I act? Should I shout? Should I just complain?
Oh sky, oh earth, oh seas of Neptune![47]

Micio

There you are!   790

---

47 For the god Neptune, see Appendix I p. 335.

He's found out everything! That's why he's shouting. Game over.
There's plenty of trouble brewing. Time for reinforcements.

Demea

It's him!

The equal-opportunity corrupter of our children!

Micio

Can't you just repress that rage and get control of yourself?

Demea

I've repressed it and I'm in control. You won't hear any more outbursts from me. 795
Let's focus on the reality. We agreed—and you came up with the idea—
That my son wouldn't be your concern,
And yours wouldn't be mine? Right?

Micio

I won't deny we agreed that.

Demea

Then why is mine drinking at your house? Why are you putting him up?
Why'd you buy him a girlfriend, Micio?   800
And what justification is there for you *not* to reciprocate in our agreement?
I don't make your son my concern, so stop concerning yourself with mine!

Micio

You don't quite have it right.

Demea

I don't?

Micio

I'm sure you know the old saying:
"Among friends, everything is joint property."

Demea

How clever! It's a little too late for that kind of talk, don't you think?   805

Micio

Listen to me for just a minute, Demea, if you don't mind.
First of all, it's the bills our sons are racking up that's gnawing at you.
Please give this some serious thought:
Originally, you were raising the two of them as your means allowed,
Because you thought your property would suffice for both,   810
And at that time you naturally assumed I'd get married.
Go ahead and stick to that original plan:
Save, invest, pinch pennies, strain and struggle
To leave them a nice inheritance, and chalk it up to your own glory.
As for my property, let them enjoy it as the windfall it is.   815
Your net wealth won't suffer;
Consider whatever I provide in addition as pure profit.
If you're willing to look at this pragmatically, Demea,
You'll save yourself, me, and the boys a lot of grief.

Demea

Forget about the money: the behavior of them both—

Micio

                                            Hold on!   820

I know, I was getting to that. There are many indications
Of every person's character, Demea, that allow us to conclude
That one person should be let off scot-free, and another shouldn't,
Even in an instance where they've done exactly the same thing wrong.
It's all about the difference between the doers, not the deed.   825
I've seen signs in our boys that make me confident they'll turn out
Just the way we want them to. I see common sense, intelligence,
An appropriate level of respect, mutual affection. You can see
Their honorable character and spirit,[48] and you can rein them in any time you
    want to.
You may very well be fearful about their being a little too casual   830
When it comes to money. Demea, my brother,
Human beings get smarter about everything as we get older, with one exception:
The single defect that only increases in us with age
Is our overriding obsession with money.
They'll get a bit sharper about that over time.

Demea

                                    I just hope   835
Those fine ideas and permissiveness
Of yours don't completely bankrupt us, Micio.

Micio

                                 Settle down,
That won't happen. Let go of all that for now and follow my lead today.
And take that frown off your face.

Demea

                           Yes, naturally I'll have to do
What the occasion calls for. But first thing tomorrow morning   840
My son and I are taking off from here for the farm.

Micio

                        Take him in the middle of the night even!
Just be cheerful today.

Demea

                  And I'll be dragging
That stripper along with me!

Micio

                    You'll be quite a hero in your son's eyes if you do,
And he'll be tied to the land there forever—
Just make sure she's tied down there, too.

---

48 I.e., their character and spirit is *liber*: cf. n. 8 above.

Demea

                               Oh, I can guarantee that: 845

I'll have her knee-deep in soot, smoke and flour
From grinding and cooking all day. On top of that,
I'll have her out bundling straw in the middle of the day!
I'll see she's as dried out and blackened as a lump of coal!

Micio

                                      Fine.

Now I think you're making sense. And I'd also make your son   850
Sleep with her, even if he doesn't want to.

Demea

Mocking me again? You're so lucky to have that comic temperament of yours!
Now it's my belief that—

Micio

                Don't start!

Demea

                  Yes, yes, I'll stop now.

Micio

Go inside then, and pass the day the way we should. (*exits*)

SCENE 22

Demea's monologue before entering Micio's house.

Demea

No one has ever plotted out his life's plan so successfully that he never faces   855
New challenges and discoveries brought about by circumstances, the passing
   of time,
Or experience itself. Inevitably, you discover you don't know what you thought
   you did,
And the principles we first formed don't hold up in the face of everyday practice.
That's where I am. As I approach my life's homestretch,
I have decided to renounce the frugal life I've lived up to this very moment.   860
Why? The realities of human existence have taught me to place nonchalance
And leniency above all else. To see the wisdom in this, just compare my brother
   and me.
For him, life is a leisurely and endless stream of parties.
He's generous, easy-going, never offensive and has a smile for everybody.
His prime responsibility is to himself, he spends money on himself,   865
And everyone respects and likes him. Me? I'm the typical farmer:
Boorish, gloomy, cheap, fierce, stubborn—and married. And what misery *that*
   has been!
The birth of my sons? More stress. Phew! I wore myself down wanting to earn
As much as I could for them, and ground my life away in search of more stuff.
And now at the end of my life what are the fruits of all my labors?   870
Their contempt! Meanwhile, my polar opposite enjoys the benefits of fatherhood

Without lifting a finger. They adore him, they avoid me. They confide in him,
They worship him and his company, while I'm left all alone.
They want him to live forever, but are looking forward to my death.
It took all my energy to raise them, but he's won them over at minimal cost to
    himself.   875
I get all the misery, he experiences all the joy! All right then, I'm up for a little
    experiment.
I'll be the anti-me, and see if I can talk a smooth game and act generously like him.
He's challenged me after all.
I want to be loved and respected by my children as much as he does.
If the path to that is generosity and indulgence, don't count me out!   880
Bankruptcy? That's of least concern to the person who's oldest.

SCENE 23

Syrus enters from Micio's house.

Syrus
Hey, Demea: your brother doesn't want you to wander too far off.
Demea
Who's there? Oh, it's our own Syrus. Hello. How's it going? What's up?
Syrus
Er … all's well.
Demea
    Excellent! (*aside*) So far I've added three new phrases to my repertoire:
"Oh, it's our own Syrus," "How's it going?" "What's up?"   885
You're proving to be an honorable[49] slave
And I'd gladly do you a good turn.
Syrus
        Er, thanks.
Demea
        I really mean it, Syrus,
And soon you'll get first-hand experience of what I'm saying.

SCENE 24

Geta enters from Sostrata's house.

Geta (*to Sostrata inside*)
I'm off to see how soon they want the young lady to be brought here, Mistress.
Oh look, it's Demea. Hello.   890
Demea
What's your name?

---
49 Cf. n. 8 above.

Geta

        Geta.

Demea

                Yes, Geta. After much thought today,
I've concluded that you're an extremely valuable person.
To my thinking, the truly worthwhile slave is the one
Who cares for his master first and foremost, just as I've seen is the case for you,
    Geta.
And that's exactly why I'll gladly do you a good turn,   895
If the opportunity for that arises. (*aside*) I'm practicing being friendly right now,
And I think it's going pretty darn well!

Geta

                        That's so generous of you to say.

Demea (*aside*)

One by one, I'm finally winning over the masses!

SCENE 25

Aeschinus enters from Micio's house.

Aeschinus

They're just about killing me with all their excitement about the "solemn
    ceremony!"[50]
They're going to blow the whole day on preparations!   900

Demea

How's it going, Aeschinus?

Aeschinus

                 Oh! Father, I didn't realize you were here.

Demea

Yes, damn right I'm here—as your natural father and your father in spirit,[51]
The person who loves you more than his own eyes![52]
But why aren't you off getting your wife?

Aeschinus

                    I'd like to, but everything's delayed
Until they get a musician and a chorus to sing the wedding hymn.   905

Demea

Hey, do you mind listening to an old man?

Aeschinus

                    What is it?

---

50 Donatus, a fourth century CE commentator on Terence, notes that the desire to hold an elaborate
    marriage ceremony here is comically incongruous given the fact that Pamphila has already given birth.

51 Demea strongly asserts that he is Aeschinus' biological father *and*—as if to refute Micio's earlier claim
    (cf. 126 and n. 14 above)—also his father "in spirit" or "feeling(s)" (*animo*).

52 Cf. 701 and n. 43 above.

Demea

Just skip all that stuff—

The wedding hymn, the reception, the torches, the musicians,
And have the garden wall torn down just as quickly as you possibly can.
Bring her over that way and make one house out of two.
Bring the mother and the whole household over too.

Aeschinus

I like the idea!   910

You're the greatest, father!

Demea (*aside*)

Fantastic! Now I'm "the greatest!"

My brother's house will be wide open to the public,
He'll take in a mob there, and it'll cost him a fortune! Ask me if I care?
I'm "great" and my popularity is on the rise!
So have that fat cat brother of mine count out twenty minae for it all.   915
Syrus! You need to go and get to it.

Syrus

To what?

Demea

Demolitions!

And you, Geta, go off and bring the ladies.

Geta

May the gods bless you, Demea.

It's obvious that you want the best for our family
From the bottom of your heart. (*Syrus and Geta exit*)

Demea

I think you all deserve it.

What do you say?

Aeschinus

I agree entirely.

Demea

It's certainly better   920

Than having her brought here in public view—and she's just given birth
And is very weak.

Aeschinus

I can't imagine a better plan, father

Demea

That's what I'm known for! But look, Micio's coming out.

SCENE 26

Micio enters from his house.

Micio (*to slave(s) inside*)
My brother said to? Where is he? You said to do this, Demea?
Demea
I certainly did. We should use this and every other possible means   925
To make us all into one big family here, complete
With devotion, support and unity.
Aeschinus
Please, let's do that, father!
Micio
I don't have a problem with it.
Demea
And it absolutely is the right thing for us to do.
Now for starters, his bride has a mother.
Micio
True. What of it?
Demea
A good and decent woman.
Micio
That's what they say.
Demea
She's up there in years.   930
Micio
I'm aware of that.
Demea
She's long past her child-bearing years,
And she has no one to take care of her. She's all alone.
Micio (*aside*)
Where's he going with this?
Demea
The right thing for you to do is marry her—and you should encourage him to,
   Aeschinus,
Micio
Me? Marry?
Demea
Yes, you.
Micio
Me?
Demea
I do mean you.
Micio
Ridiculous!

Demea (*to Aeschinus*)

                                                                 If you were a real man,[53]

He'd do it.

Aeschinus

          Father, please!

Micio

                      Why are you even listening to him, you ass?

Demea

                                               It's no use: 935

This is how it's going to be.

Micio

                  You're nuts!

Aeschinus

                        Please do it for me, father!

Micio

You're nuts! Let go of me!

Demea

                  Come on, do it for your son.

Micio

                                     This is insane!

You want me to be a bridegroom for the first time at the age of sixty-four,

And to marry a decrepit old bag? *That's* what you're asking me to do?

Aeschinus

Yes. I already promised them.

Micio

                    You promised them! Be generous with what's yours, sonny! 940

Demea

Come on, what if he asked for an even bigger favor?

Micio

                                What could possibly be bigger?

Demea

Do it for him.

Aeschinus

                Don't be such a curmudgeon!

Demea

                        Promise you'll do it!

Micio

                                      Get off my back!

Aeschinus

Not until you're persuaded.

---

53 Another pregnant use of the word *homo* (cf. n. 33 above).

Micio

Now this is pure coercion!

Demea

Be generous, Micio.

Micio

All right. Even though this seems perverse, ridiculous, silly
And utterly out of character for me, I'll do it, seeing the two of you are so hell-
bent on it!   945

Aeschinus

Thank you! How can I not love you?

Demea (*aside*)

Everything's going my way. What should I ask for next?
There's still the matter of Hegio. He's their closest relative,
He's related to us by marriage, and he's poor. We should do something for him.

Micio

Like what?

Demea

There's that small plot of land you rent out just a little ways from town:
Let's give it to him for keeps.

Micio

You call that small?

Demea

Big, small—   950

It's got to be done regardless. He's been like a father to the girl, he's a good man,
And he's one of us. It's the right thing to do. After all, Micio, if I may borrow
That expression of yours from a while back: "the single defect that only increases
In us with age is our overriding obsession with money."[54] That's a blemish
We all should avoid!

Aeschinus

A true saying, and we should practice what we preach, father! 955

Micio

All right then. The plot of land will be Hegio's, since Aeschinus wants that.

Aeschinus

Yes!

Demea

Now you truly are my brother in both body and soul!
(*aside*) And I get to cut his throat with his own sword!

---

54 Cf. Micio' words at 832-34.

SCENE 27

Syrus enters from Micio's house.

Syrus

Your orders have been carried out, Demea.

Demea

You're a good man! And so, doggonit, I'm of the opinion
That Syrus here should be set free. It's the proper thing to do.

Micio

Him? Free?   960

Why *him*?

Demea

Lots of reasons.

Syrus

Oh Demea! You really are a gentleman!
I've devoted my life to taking care of the both of them since they were children.
Teacher, advisor, mentor—I've done it all to the best of my ability.

Demea

And the proof is in the pudding! Yes, shopping on credit,
Rounding up whores, and throwing a party in the middle of the day!   965
These are not the accomplishments of the average person.

Syrus

You are a delightful man!

Demea

And on top of that, he was an accomplice in buying the stripper today.
He took care of everything. He should be rewarded, and it'll inspire
The other slaves to do better.[55] Aeschinus wants it too.

Micio

You do?

Aeschinus

Yes.

Micio

If it's what
You really want. Hey, Syrus, come over here to me. You officially are free.[56]   970

Syrus

Thank you, all. And special thanks to you, Demea.

Demea

I'm delighted.

---

55 Slaves were not infrequently emancipated in Rome, and the possibility of manumission was used
    as motivation for slaves to serve their masters well. Demea, however, is quite sarcastic here: cf.
    Introduction p. 30.

56 Manumission in Rome or Greece could be accomplished through a simple speech act, as it is here with
    the formula *liber esto*.

Aeschinus

So am I.

Syrus

I know. I only wish my wife Phrygia[57] could be free along with me!
That would make my happiness everlasting!

Demea

She's a fine woman for sure.

Syrus

And she was the first to breastfeed your grandson
Today.

Demea

Then, in all seriousness, darn it,   975
It's only right that she should be freed on account of being the first to do that!

Micio

Freed for *that*?

Demea

Yes, for that. And I'll even pay you what she's worth.

Syrus

May the gods always give you everything you want, Demea!

Micio

You've had one very fine day, haven't you Syrus?

Demea

That's for sure, Micio,
Provided you do what you should by providing him with a little spending
    money.   980
Just a loan—he'll pay you right back.

Micio

How about less than a little?

Aeschinus

He's a good guy!

Syrus

I swear I'll pay it back.

Aeschinus

Come on, father!

Micio

I'll think it over.

Demea

He'll do it.

Syrus

You're the greatest!

---

57 Phrygia was a district of Asia Minor (now Turkey) that included Troy. Slaves were often generically
   named after their place of origin.

Aeschinus

Father! You're wonderful!

Micio

What happened to you? Why this sudden change in your outlook?

What's with all the whimsy and the instant generosity?

Demea

I'll tell you.   985

It was to show that the reason the boys consider you to be so approachable

And jovial is not because your life is truly just and good at the core,

But only because you agree with whatever they want, spoil them,

And lavish money on them, Micio. Now if my way of living is so repulsive to you,

Aeschinus, just because I don't indulge you in whatever you do, regardless of   990

Whether it's right or wrong—I'm through here. Buy, squander, do whatever you
    want!

But when you're not seeing things clearly because of your age,

Or pulled along too much by your desires and too little by your brains,

If you want me to grab hold of you and straighten you out or provide some support

When it's needed, I'll be there for you.

Aeschinus

We admit it, father: 995

You know what's best. But what about my brother? What happens to him?

Demea

I'll let

Him keep her, but this is the last time.

Micio

That's fair.

All

Applause, please!

Eunuchus

("The Eunuch")

CHARACTERS WITH SPEAKING PARTS

PHAEDRIA, *a young Athenian citizen*

PARMENO, *a slave of the family of Phaedria and Chaerea*

THAIS, *a prostitute/brothel-owner living next door to the family of Phaedria and Chaerea*

GNATHO, *a parasite (i.e., a professional dinner-guest and flatterer) of Thraso*

CHAEREA, *younger brother of Phaedria*

THRASO, *a mercenary soldier*

PYTHIAS, *a slave (i.e., "maidservant") of Thais*

CHREMES, *a young Athenian citizen, brother of Pamphila*

ANTIPHO, *a young friend of Chaerea*

DORIAS, *a slave (i.e., "maidservant") of Thais*

DORUS, *a eunuch slave purchased by Phaedria for Thais*

SANGA, *a slave and cook of Thraso*

SOPHRONA, *a slave and wet nurse of the family of Chremes and Pamphila*

SENEX, *unnamed father of Phaedria and Chaerea*

SCENE

Athens: before the house of Thais and that of the family of Phaedria and Chaerea. One stage wing leads to the forum/city-center, the other to the harbor.

PROLOGUE[1]

Our playwright, just as much as anybody else, aims to please
As many distinguished citizens as he can, while offending as few as possible,
And so you can add his name to the list of folks who live by this principle.

---

1   The Roman comic playwrights introduced the use of an impersonal prologist (perhaps the head of the acting troupe) to ancient comedy to speak on the behalf of the play and playwright. Terence's prologues are distinct for their focus on his critics and literary/dramatic issues strictly extraneous to the performance at hand. See further Introduction pp. 10-11.

Now if there's a certain someone[2] out there who thinks
He's been harshly attacked, he needs to think again: 5
That wasn't an attack, but merely a response to *his* initial assault.
He's the one who takes good Greek plays and converts them into bad Latin ones
By translating accurately enough but far too literally.
And he's the one who recently mangled Menander's *Phantom*.[3]
And in *The Treasure*[4] he has the defendant argue his case   10
For the disputed gold before the plaintiff even speaks
And explains why he's the rightful owner of the treasure,
And how it found its way into his father's tomb in the first place!
From now on, he shouldn't fool himself into thinking
The quarrel's over and our playwright has nothing more to say to him.   15
I advise him to see the error of his ways and to stop ripping me.
There are many other charges I'm overlooking for now
Which can be brought forward later if he continues to attack me as he has.
The play we're about to perform is Menander's *Eunuch*.[5]
After the *aediles* purchased it,[6]   20
He arranged a little sneak preview for himself.
The presiding magistrate showed up, the rehearsal began,
And our friend shouts out: "A thief, not a playwright, composed this play,
But he's not pulling the wool over my eyes!
There's an old play called *The Flatterer*.[7] Naevius[8] and Plautus[9]   25
Produced versions of it, and *that's where* he's stolen the characters
Of the parasite and the soldier from." If our playwright's guilty as charged,
This is an oversight, not an intent to commit theft!
You can all decide for yourselves if this is so soon enough.
The original version of *The Flatterer* is by Menander.   30
There's a fawning parasite and a braggart soldier in it.
Our playwright does not deny that he transferred these characters

---

2   Luscius of Lanuvium (a small Italian town near Rome) is meant. Luscius, an older contemporary of
    Terence and a rival dramatist, is consistently portrayed in Terence's prologues (cf. *Adelphoe* 1-21) as a
    pedantic critic of the "contamination" of Greek source plays. See further Introduction pp. 10-11.

3   Menander was the most famous playwright of Greek New Comedy (see Introduction pp. 3-4). *Ca* 100
    lines of his *Phantom* remain, while no trace of Luscius' "mangled" version survives.

4   Nothing survives of Luscius' play. Menander and other Greek playwrights wrote plays with this title.

5   Only a few fragments of Menander's version of this play survive.

6   Producers sold the playwrights' scripts to the Roman magistrates (*aediles*) sponsoring the public
    festivals at which the plays were performed. See further Introduction p. 5.

7   No Roman version of this play survives.

8   Naevius, a playwright born in Campania (a region of west central Italy), wrote both comedies and
    tragedies during the last quarter of the 3rd century BCE, but is best known for his epic poem on the war
    between Carthage and Rome (he is said to have served in the Roman army in the last years of the First
    Punic War, which lasted from 264 to 241 BCE).

9   For the comic playwright Plautus' life and career, see Introduction pp. 7-9.

From the Greek play to his own *Eunuch*. But he categorically denies
Any knowledge of the existence of the two previous Latin plays.
And besides, if he's denied the right to use the same characters as other writers,   35
Wouldn't he also be prohibited from scripting in the role of a running slave,[10]
Or from bringing virtuous wives, nasty prostitutes,
A hungry parasite, and a braggart soldier on stage,
Or having a baby passed off as someone's, an old man tricked by a slave,
Or including love, hate, and suspicion at all?   40
The bottom line: you can't say anything that's never been said before.
So you should give us modern playwrights a fair hearing,
And forgive us for reviving a standard practice of our predecessors.
So pay attention and listen in silence,
So that you can fully grasp what *The Eunuch* has to say.   45

SCENE 1

Phaedria enters from his house with Parmeno.

Phaedria
What should I do then? Do I refuse to go even
When she invites me personally? Or is it better for me
To just decide not to tolerate insults from hookers?
She shut me out. She calls me back. Should I go back? No, not even if she begs me!
Certainly that would be the best and boldest thing—if you could do it!   50
But if you start strong but don't follow through,
And, when you can't stand it anymore and no one wants you,
You voluntarily approach her without first drafting a peace treaty,
And show that you love her and can't be without her—that does it, it's all over,
And you're as good as dead! And once she sees you're beat, she'll mess with your
      head.   55
So think it through and through, while there's time.

Parmeno[11]
Master, when something lacks sense or reason,
There's no sense in trying to take control of things by reason.
Love is a bundle of contradictions:
Insults, anxieties, quarrels, truces and war followed by peace again.   60
Expecting to make rational sense
Out of all this chaos is just as futile as
Trying to find a sure-fire system to make yourself insane.
And then there's the thoughts you mull over with yourself in anger:
"I'd go to her when she ... to him ... and me ... and didn't ... just let her ...   65

---

10 The character of the slave who rushes onto the stage to deliver an important message was stereotypical
    in Roman comedy (cf. Geta in Terence's *Adelphoe* 299ff.), as are the other figures and situations
    mentioned in lines 36-39 here.

11 His name means "steady" or "trustworthy" in Greek, a common name for slaves.

I'd rather die! She'll find out what sort of a man I am!"
But damn it, with just one lousy crocodile tear
That she manages to squeeze out by pathetically rubbing her eyes,
She'll douse out every last one of your fiery words, and completely turn the tables,
So that you're the one who pays.

Phaedria

       Such disgusting behavior!   70
I now see that she's trashy and I'm just torturing myself!
I'm sick of it and at the same time I'm burning up with passion. I'm alert and aware,
Conscious and cognizant ... that I'm destroying myself! I've got no idea what to do!

Parmeno

What should you do? How about buying your way out of captivity as cheaply as
 possible?
And if cheaply isn't possible, do it at whatever price you can.   75
But don't torture yourself.

Phaedria

      That's your advice?

Parmeno

          If you're smart,
You won't add to the list of troubles that come naturally with love,
And you'll just try to tolerate these stoically.
But look! The blight on our estate approaches in person:
She mows down everything we're supposed to reap!   80

SCENE 2

Thais enters from her house.

Thais

Oh dear me! Yesterday I turned Phaedria away
And now I'm afraid he's misconstrued my motives
And is brooding.

Phaedria

    I t-t-t-tremble
And sh-shiver all over, Parmenio, the instant I see her.

Parmeno

         Settle down.
Once you get close to that fire, you'll have more heat than you can handle.   85

Thais

Who's talking over there? Oh, you're here, my dear Phaedria?
Why are you standing out here? Why didn't you come right in?

Parmeno (*aside*)

         Huh?
Not a word about shutting him out?

Thais

    Why so quiet?

Phaedria

Obviously, it's because this door is always *so* open to me.
Or maybe it's because I'm número uno at your place?

Thais

Oh, let that go now. 90

Phaedria

What? Let it go? Oh Thais, Thais! I only wish that our love
Could be on equal terms and our emotions evenly matched!
Then you could agonize over things just the way I do,
Or I wouldn't have to care one iota about anything you do to me.

Thais

Phaedria, sweetheart! Please don't torture yourself over that! 95
I swear, it wasn't because there's someone else I'm hot for,
Or like more than you! It was a matter of circumstances. I had no option.

Parmeno

Oh, *now* I see. You're so terribly in love with him you had to shut him out.

Thais

So that's your attitude, Parmeno? Well, let me tell you
Why I had you asked here.

Phaedria

All right.

Thais

First tell me though: 100
Is he able to keep a confidence?

Parmeno

Me? Absolutely!
But listen up. I guarantee my silence according to this principle:
I keep quiet about things that are true and never divulge them.
But as for lies, empty rumors, fabrications—they spill right out of me,
I'm full of cracks, and anywhere you look I'm leaking. 105
So if you want me to keep secrets, just tell me the truth.

Thais

My mother was from Samos[12] and lived at Rhodes.[13]

Parmeno

That can be kept secret.

Thais

At Rhodes then, a certain merchant
Gave her a little girl as a gift.
She'd been kidnapped from Attica.[14]

---

12 An island in the Aegean Sea just off the coast of Asia Minor (modern Turkey). Prostitutes in new
   Comedy are often said to be from Samos (cf. *Menaechmi* 179 and n. 32).

13 A large Greek island close to the mainland of Caria (modern Turkey).

14 The territory around and including the city-state of Athens.

Phaedria

>   She's a free citizen?

Thais

>   I believe so,   110

But we can't be certain yet. She told us the names
Of her father and mother herself, but because of her age at the time
She didn't know the name of her country or anything else about herself.
The merchant added that the pirates he bought her from
Said she'd been abducted at Sunium.[15]   115
The instant my mother took her in, she set herself to teaching the girl everything,
And to raising her like her own daughter.
Most people believed she was my sister.
I came here to Athens with that foreigner I was having an exclusive affair with.
He's the one who left me everything that I have.   120

Parmeno

Two lies: expect a leak.

Thais

>   Why?

Parmeno

>   Because

You weren't satisfied with one man and he wasn't your only financer—
My master here has played a major role in bankrolling you.

Thais

True, but allow me to finish my story.
In the meantime, a soldier who had started up an affair with me went off
    to Caria.[16]   125
It was during that time that I came to know you.
You know for yourself how I've shared all my thoughts with you
And considered you my closest confidante since then.

Parmeno

Parmeno is not going to keep quiet about that.

Phaedria

>   Oh, you have doubts about this?

Thais

Now please listen up. My mother recently died at Rhodes.   130
Her brother is quite greedy where money's at stake,
And when he saw that the girl was good-looking and an accomplished musician,[17]
He expected to fetch a nice price for her.

---

15 Sunium is the name of a promontory at the southern tip of Attica.

16 Area of southwestern Asia Minor (modern Turkey). Carians are known to have engaged in mercenary service from an early date.

17 She most likely has been trained to play a small lyre-like instrument. Prostitutes typically played such instruments at parties, in addition to providing sexual services.

So he put her on the market and sold her. By complete chance,
This soldier-friend of mine was there. He bought her for me as a present,   135
Completely unaware and ignorant of all this of course.
He came back here, but since he realized that I also had a thing going on with you,
He's always manufacturing excuses for not handing her over to me.
He claims he'd like to give her to me,
But is afraid that once I have her I'll leave him,   140
And so he wants a pledge from me that I won't dump him for you.
That's what he says he's afraid of. But I have my own suspicions
That he's got a crush on the girl.

Phaedria
                                    Anything more than that going on?

Thais
No, and I did ask around. Now I have many reasons, my dear Phaedria,
For wanting to take the girl away from him.   145
First of all, she's virtually my sister. Second, I might be able
To reunite her with her family. I'm alone here,
And I don't have any friends or relatives, Phaedria,
And that's why I want to win some allies by doing a favor like that.
Please help me here! It'd make it so much easier   150
If you'd let the soldier be my leading man here
For the next several days. No response?

Phaedria
                                    You bitch!
What do you expect me to say when you treat me like this?

Parmeno
Score one for our side! It finally got to you! You are a man!

Phaedria
Like I didn't know where you were going with all that!   155
"A little girl was abducted from here. My mother raised her up as her own.
She was virtually my sister. I want to return her to her family ..."
Of course, I can see exactly where all this talk is leading:
I'm being shut out, he's being let in.
Why? Obviously you love him more than you do me,   160
And you're afraid the girl he brought with him will lure your big catch away.

Thais
Me? Afraid of that?

Phaedria
                                    What is it you're afraid of then? Tell me, now:
Is he your only bankroller? Have you ever seen
An interruption in the flow of funds from me?

When you told me you wanted a little slave girl from Ethiopia[18]   165
Did I or did I not drop everything at once to find you one?
And then you tell me you want a eunuch
Because all the important women have them!
I found one, and yesterday I paid twenty minae[19] for the pair of them.
Though you spurned me, I didn't forget about these things.   170
And what do I get for it all? More rejection!

Thais

                                        All right, then, Phaedria.
I really do want to take the girl away from him and believe
My idea is the best way to do that.
But I'll do what you say rather than risk making an enemy out of you.

Phaedria

I only wish the words "rather than risk making an enemy out of you"   175
Were heartfelt and sincere! If I could just believe
You really meant what you said, I could put up with anything.

Parmeno (*aside*)

Doesn't take much more than a word and he surrenders.

Thais

Ouch! Me not sincere? Haven't I always given you
Everything you ever asked me for, even in jest?   180
And I can't count on you to give up so much
As just two days to me?

Phaedria

                                        If it's really just two days.
But let's make sure it doesn't turn into twenty!

Thais

Absolutely no more than two or—

Phaedria

                                        I don't like the sound of that "or."

Thais

It won't happen. Just allow me this one thing.

Phaedria

                                        I guess.   185
Do what you want. I have no choice.

Thais

                                You're so sweet! How can I not love you?

Phaedria

I'll go out to the country and torture myself there for the next two days.
That's settled, then. I have no choice except accommodating Thais.

---

18 Dark-skinned Ethiopians generally were considered exotic by both Greeks and Romans and ownership
of them as slaves was a status symbol.

19 For the value of twenty minae, see Appendix II p. 337.

Parmeno, see those two are brought over here.
Parmeno

Sure. (*exits*)

Phaedria
Farewell for these next two days, my dear Thais.
Thais

The same to you, 190

My dear Phaedria. Want anything else?
Phaedria

Do I want anything else?

Yes! That when you're with the soldier your heart is elsewhere.
And that you love me and want me day and night,
Dream about me, long for me, think about me,
Hope for me, have pleasant thoughts about me—and be completely mine! 195
Be my soul just as I am yours! (*exits into his house*)
Thais
Oh dear! Maybe he doesn't put much faith in me
And gauges me by the character of the other women here.[20]
I can say with absolute certainty and honesty
That I haven't lied to Phaedria 200
And no man is closer to my heart than he is.
Everything I've done here I've done for this girl.
I really think I've just about found her brother now,
And he's a quite distinguished young man.
He's arranged to come see me at home today. 205
I'll go inside and wait for him to arrive here.

SCENE 3

Phaedria enters from his house with Parmeno.

Phaedria
See they're brought over here just as I told you.
Parmeno

Will do.

Phaedria

And do it right.

Parmeno
Not a problem.
Phaedria

And fast.

Parmeno

Sure.

---

20 For Thais' monologue here, see Introduction p. 32.

Phaedria

                      Are my orders clear enough for you?

Parmeno

                                      Geeze!

I can't believe you're even asking. This isn't brain surgery!

I just wish you could somehow make as much as you're about   210

To lose in this deal, Phaedria!

Phaedria

                I'm also losing something even more valuable in it—myself.

So don't be so anxious about that!

Parmeno

                      I'm not. I'll see it's all done.

Anything else you'd like?

Phaedria

Talk up our present as much as you can,

And do your best to keep my rival away from her.   215

Parmeno

Yes, I remember. No need to remind me.

Phaedria

                          I'm off to the farm—where I'll stay.

Parmeno

Good plan.

Phaedria

          Wait a minute.

Parmeno

                  What do you want?

Phaedria

                          Do you think I can be tough

And resist coming back all that time?

Parmeno

                  You? Hell no!

You'll either charge back here instantly—or once you realize you can't sleep.

Phaedria

I'll exhaust myself by working so hard that I'll sleep whether I want to or not.   220

Parmeno

All you'll do is make yourself lie awake exhausted.

Phaedria

                        Nonsense, Parmeno! Enough now!

By Hercules,[21] I've got to stop being so weak-willed! A little self-control, please!

Like I can't go for three days without her if I have to?

Parmeno

                            Phew!

Three whole days? Careful—don't overdo it!

---

21 For the god Hercules, see Appendix I p. 335.

Phaedria

My decision stands. (*exits*)

Parmeno

Good gods, just what sort of disease is this? The idea that love can so transform
    men   225
That they're no longer recognizable as themselves!
I remember when he was as together, serious and in control as anyone.
But who's that coming this way? Why it's none other than Gnatho,
The soldier's parasite. And he's got the girl for Thais with him.
Ooh la la! She is good-lookin'! She's hotter than Thais herself!   230
Damn if I don't look pathetic today with this broken-down eunuch of mine!

SCENE 4

Gnatho enters from the wing leading to the forum.

Gnatho[22]

By the immortal gods! One person sure can be superior to another!
What a world of difference between a smart man and a fool, as I realized from
    this event:
On my way here today I met a man of my class and status,
A decent enough guy who like myself had devoured his family inheritance.   235
He looks all scruffy, filthy and sick, and is covered in rags and ravaged by time.
"What's with this get-up?" I say. He replies: "I'm one poor bastard
Who lost all that he had. Just look at how far I've sunk. All my friends
And associates—gone!" I was infuriated by the stark contrast with myself:
"You totally worthless bum!" I say, "Have you abandoned all hope?   240
Did you lose your brain along with your stuff? I'm from the same background
    as you.
But look at my face, my healthy glow, my clothes and the shape I'm in.
I've got nothing, yet I have everything. I don't own a thing, but want for nothing."
He replies: "But I can't stand being a laughingstock or someone's punching bag."
"What!" I say, "You think that's how it's done? You're way off base!   245
Long, long ago, a previous generation of our kind[23] made their living that way.
But there's a new style of hunting nowadays that I happen to have invented:[24]
There exists a class of men who want to be the head honcho in all things but aren't.
They're the ones I stalk. My goal is not to make them laugh at me,
But instead I laugh at their jokes and stand in awe of their wit.   250
I applaud whatever they say. And if they then say the opposite, I applaud again.
Somebody says 'no,' I say 'no;' somebody says 'yes,' I say 'yes.'

---

22 The parasite's name appropriately means "The Jaw" in Greek.

23 I.e., parasites.

24 Gnatho is bombastically claiming to be the inventor (Latin *primus inventor*) of this style of ingratiating
    oneself. In the ancient world, such claims were usually reserved for important cultural achievements,
    e.g., the invention of agriculture. Cf. Plautus, *Menaechmi* 451 and n. 54.

I've trained myself to be entirely agreeable. That's the smoothest road to riches
　　nowadays."
Parmeno (*aside*)
Pure genius! He turns fools right into lunatics!
Gnatho
As we chatted, we came upon the market　　　　　　　　　　　　　　255
And the delicatessen owners ran up all happy to see me,
As did the fishmongers, butchers, the rent-a-cooks, and sausage-makers—
All the ones who've made a haul off of me in good times or in bad.
They greet me, congratulate me on my return, invite me to dinner.
When my poor famished friend gets an eye of my celebrity　　　　　260
And how easy it was to make a living this way,
He started to beg me to be his teacher. I told him he could be my disciple,
My hope being that just as the philosophical schools are named after philosophers,
So too parasites may soon be known as Gnathonists.
Parmeno (*aside*)
So this is the end product of all that free time and free food!
Gnatho
　　　　　　　　　　　　　　　　　　　　But I should take　265
This girl to Thais and invite her to my master's dinner.
But there's our rival's slave Parmeno standing before the door here.
He looks glum. All must be well. Evidently, they're getting the cold shoulder.
I think I'll have some fun with this airhead.
Parmeno (*aside*)
　　　　　　　　　　　　　　　　　They're thinking this gift
Makes Thais all theirs.
Gnatho
　　　　　　　　　Greetings, greetings from Gnatho to his dear friend Parmeno!　270
What are you up to?
Parmeno
　　　　　　　　　Standing up.
Gnatho
　　　　　　　　　　　　　So I see.
See anything here you'd rather not?
Parmeno
　　　　　　　　　　　　You.
Gnatho
　　　　　　　　　　　　　　　Right. But isn't there something else?
Parmeno
Why should there be?
Gnatho
　　　　　　　　　Because you look so glum.
Parmeno
　　　　　　　　　　　　　　　　　　　It's nothing.

Gnatho

Be happy then.

What d'ya think of this little purchase?

Parmeno

Not all bad.

Gnatho (*aside*)

That got him.

Parmeno (*aside, having overheard Gnatho's aside*)

No it didn't.

Gnatho

How do you think Thais will like this present?

Parmeno

I think you really mean to say   275

That we've been booted out from here. Listen, everything's subject to change.

Gnatho

I'll be giving you a six-month vacation, Parmeno:

No more running back and forth, no more staying up until dawn.

Now don't I bring you joy?

Parmeno

Me? Yeah, yukity yuk.

Gnatho

It's what I do for friends.

Parmeno

Congrats.

Gnatho

I'm not keeping you, am I? Maybe you were on your way somewhere?   280

Parmeno

Nope.

Gnatho

Then do me just a small favor: help me get admitted here.

Parmeno

Knock it off! Just go right in. Since you've got that girl, the door's wide open for
    you.

Gnatho (*as he goes inside*)

Should I have someone sent out to you from inside?

Parmeno

Just wait until those two days are over!

You're lucky enough to be able to open the door with just one finger now,

But I guarantee that soon you won't get anyone to answer using both heels!   285

Gnatho (*returning*)

Still out here, Parmeno? Now *surely* you weren't posted on guard here

To keep any go-between from secretly passing from the soldier to Thais? (*exits*)

Parmeno

How clever! No wonder the soldier's so fond of you.

But look: there's my master's younger son coming here.
I wonder why he's left the Piraeus.[25] He's supposed to be on guard duty there.   290
Must be something's up. He's in a hurry and looking around for something.

SCENE 5

Chaerea enters from the wing leading to the harbor.

Chaerea
Damn!
The girl's lost and now so am I for letting her out of my site!
Where do I look, where to track her down, who do I ask, which way do I go?
I haven't a clue! The good news is that wherever she is, she won't stay hidden for
    long.   295
What a beautiful face! I hereby delete all other women from my memory!
I'm tired of these everyday beauties.

Parmeno (*aside*)
                                    How about that! There's the other one
Uttering some nonsense about love! Oh, the poor old father of these two!
This is the one who starts foaming at the mouth
Like a stallion when he's in love;   300
The other brother's affairs are puppy love by comparison.

Chaerea
I wish the gods would zap that old man who held me up today,
And me too for stopping and giving a rat's ass about him!
There's Parmeno. Hello.

Parmeno
                        Why so serious? What's the rush?
Where've you been?

Chaerea
                    Me? I have absolutely no idea where I've been or where I'm going!   305
I'm not even sure who I am.

Parmeno
How's that?

Chaerea
            I'm in love.

Parmeno
                Is that so?

Chaerea
                        Parmeno, now you'll show me what you're made of.
You know how you kept promising me: "Just find someone to love, Chaerea.
I'll make sure you know how useful I can be."

---

25 The port of Athens, as today. Eighteen year-old Athenians (i.e., *ephebes*: cf. n. 37 below) undergoing
    mandatory military training were barracked in the Piraeus. Their duties in their second year of training
    included guarding the frontiers of Attica.

That was back when I'd secretly bring my father's whole pantry to you in your
   room.   310

Parmeno
  Stop it, silly!

Chaerea
        You damn well know it happened! So make good on those promises now.
This is a job worth flexing all your muscles for.
This girl is completely unlike our usual types—you know, the ones
Whose mothers make them slump their shoulders and bind their breasts to look
   thin.
If any of them's a bit chubby, they call her a boxer and put her on a diet.   315
Despite her natural gifts, they insist on making her as skinny as a reed—
And that's the way they find lovers.

Parmeno
               And this girl of yours?

Chaerea
                      Totally new look.

Parmeno
                          Ooh la la!

Chaerea
  No need for makeup, tight body and just plain juicy!

Parmeno
                   How old?

Chaerea
                   How old? Sixteen.

Parmeno
  A flower in bloom!

Chaerea
        You absolutely must get her for me, whether you beg, borrow, or steal her!
Makes no difference to me how, as long as I get her.   320

Parmeno
  Well, whose[26] is she?

Chaerea
       Hell if I know!

Parmeno
           Where's she from?

Chaerea
                Ditto.

Parmeno
              Where's she live?

Chaerea
  Ditto again.

---

26 In light of the prevailing view of children as property in the ancient Mediterranean world, this could
mean "whose daughter is she?" as well as "whose slave is she?"

Parmeno

        Where'd you see her?

Chaerea

               On the street.

Parmeno

                     How'd you lose her?

Chaerea

That was precisely what I was stewing over as I came up just now.
I can't imagine there's anyone else in the world
Whose good luck has turned on him like mine has.   325

Parmeno

What's the big calamity about?

Chaerea

             I'm screwed.

Parmeno

                  What happened?

Chaerea

                       You want to know?
Do you know my father's relative Archidemides? About the same age as
My father?

Parmeno

        Yes of course.

Chaerea

            As I was following the girl I ran into him.

Parmeno

Quite an inconvenience.

Chaerea

           Ah, I'd say quite a disaster!
This went way beyond what you'd call an inconvenience.   330
I can honestly swear I hadn't seen the man
Once within the last six or seven months straight until today
When I least wanted to and had no need of him at all!
Hey, tell me: is that a bad omen or what?

Parmeno

              Bad as they come.

Chaerea

He's way off in the distance, but he comes running up the instant he spots me,   335
Hunched over and shaky as he was, lips all droopy, mouth wheezing open.
"Hey, Chaerea! Hey, I'm talking to you!" he says. I stopped.
"You know what I want you to do?" "No, tell me."
"My case is tomorrow." "So what?" "So be sure to remind
Your father to get up early and come give me his support."   340
It takes him an hour to say all this. I ask if there's anything else.
"No thanks," he says. I take off, and when I look for the girl down this way,

I see she'd just that minute turned down
Onto our street here.

Parmeno (*aside*)

       I'm quite sure he means the girl
Thais just received as a present.

Chaerea

          When I got here, she was nowhere to be found. 345

Parmeno

The girl presumably had people escorting her?

Chaerea

Yes, a parasite and a maid.

Parmeno (*aside*)

        That's her! That's the end of that.
Calm down—the crisis is over.

Chaerea

        You must be talking about something else.

Parmeno

I'm talking about your business.

Chaerea

        You know who she is? Tell me!
You saw her?

Parmeno

      I saw her. I know her. I know where she was taken. 350

Chaerea

What! Parmeno, my friend, you know her? You know where she is?

Parmeno

She was brought to Thais the prostitute's house and given to her as a gift.

Chaerea

Who's rich enough to give a present like that?

Parmeno

           Thraso the soldier,
Phaedria's rival.

Chaerea

     That's a role that won't be easy for my brother to play.

Parmeno

You don't know the half of it! Wait until you hear what 355
The gift is he's countering with.

Chaerea

       Tell me what it is!

Parmeno

          A eunuch.

Chaerea

           That ugly creature
He bought yesterday, that geriatric she-man?

Parmeno

    That very one.

Chaerea

                He'll be *so* booted right out the door, along with the gift.

    But I didn't know that Thais was our neighbor.

Parmeno

                                    She hasn't been for long.

Chaerea

    Damn it, I've never seen her! So, tell me: 360

    Is she the beauty everyone says she is?

Parmeno

                        Oh yes.

Chaerea

                        But nothing compared to mine?

Parmeno

                                  That's another story.

Chaerea

    Please help me make her mine, Parmeno!

Parmeno

                      I'll give it all

    I've got to help you here. Anything else you need?

Chaerea

                            Where you off to?

Parmeno

                                      Home,

    To get those items your brother told me to get, and then deliver them to Thais.

Chaerea

    That's one lucky eunuch to be granted access to this house!   365

Parmeno

    How so?

Chaerea

              You're kidding, right? He'll be able to gaze constantly at a fellow slave

    Of consummate beauty. He'll speak with her, spend time with her under the same roof.

    Sometimes they'll share a meal together or sleep close to each other.

Parmeno

    What'd you say if I said you could be that lucky guy?

Chaerea

                            How, Parmeno?

    Tell me!

Parmeno

        You could take his clothes.

Chaerea

                        His clothes? Then what?   370

Parmeno

I could hand you over to them instead of him.

Chaerea

I'm listening.

Parmeno

And say you were him.

Chaerea

Yes!

Parmeno

And you could enjoy all the perks you were just saying he would:
Sharing meals together, spending time with her, touching her, fooling around
together,
Sleeping close to each other. None of these women knows you or even knows who
you are.
Besides, you've got the youthful looks to pass for a eunuch.[27]   375

Chaerea

Brilliant! I've never heard of a better plan!
Come on, then. Let's go right inside. Dress me up and bring me back pronto!

Parmeno

What do you mean? I was just joking.

Chaerea

Nonsense!

Parmeno

Damn! What have I done now?
What's with the pushing? You'll knock me down! Stop it now!

Chaerea

Let's go!

Parmeno

You're going through with it?

Chaerea

For sure!

Parmeno

Careful this doesn't get too hot to handle!   380

Chaerea

It won't. Let me do my thing.

Parmeno

Yeah: you'll do the crime, but I'll do the time.[28]

Chaerea

Really?

---

27 The Greeks and Romans mostly associated eunuchs with the purportedly decadent east, where they
    often guarded royal harems (the roots of the Greek word *eunouchos* are "keeper of the bed"). Well after
    Terence's day, the ownership of eunuchs became especially fashionable among the Roman elite.

28 The Latin literally reads: "your bean will be threshed on me" (an agricultural proverb).

Parmeno

We're doing something terribly wrong!

Chaerea

                              Wrong? Taking me into a whorehouse
And paying back those instruments of torture by tricking them the same way
They're always tricking us? Those women hold us young men in complete contempt
And are always looking for new methods to torture us! That's wrong?   385
Or do you think the thing to do is pull off some scheme at my father's expense?
People who found out about that would blame me. Everyone'll just see this as poetic
    justice.[29]

Parmeno

All right. If you're determined to do it, I'm in. But don't pile all the blame
On me later.

Chaerea

        I won't.

Parmeno

            So you're asking me to do it?

Chaerea

                                Not asking: ordering and commanding.
I'll take full responsibility. Come along.

Parmeno

                I hope the gods are with us! (*they exit into the house*) 390

SCENE 6

Thraso and Gnatho enter from the wing leading to the forum and city-center.

Thraso[30]

Thais sends me hearty thanks then?

Gnatho

Huge ones in fact.

Thraso

            So she's happy?

Gnatho

                        Not so much because of the gift per se
As the fact that you were the giver.
That definitely was the culminating factor!

Parmeno (*emerges unnoticed from the house*)

                            I'm on the lookout for just the right moment
To bring him over. But there's the soldier.

Thraso

                        That's one of my natural gifts—   395

---

29 Chaerea metatheatrically (cf. Introduction pp. 8-10) refers to a standard plot of Roman comedy whereby
    a young man (*adulescens*)—usually aided by a clever slave—schemes against his father in the pursuit of
    his beloved.

30 His name means "The Bold" in Greek.

Every single thing I do wins me gratitude.
Gnatho
By Hercules, I have noticed that!
Thraso
                          Yes. The king[31] for one always expressed
His fondest thanks to me for whatever I did. He wasn't that way to the others.
Gnatho
Often the man of wit usurps glory won through the great efforts
Of others and by his words makes it his own.   400
This describes you.
Thraso
                You got it.
Gnatho
                    The king then held on to you—
Thraso
                                    Oh, yes!
Gnatho
In his eyes.
Thraso
              True! He entrusts his entire army to me.
And all his plans!
Gnatho
              Amazing!
Thraso
                    And then if ever he had his fill
Of people or if at some point the tedium of court business o'erwhelmed him
And he wanted to rest, as if to … you know what I mean?
Gnatho
                                  I do.   405
As if he would hurl all his pain from deep within.
Thraso
                    You got it!
At those times, he'd lead me away as his only guest.
Gnatho
                          Wow!
Now you're talking about a king with discriminating taste!
Thraso
                          Not just discriminating:
Extremely exclusive about the company he keeps.
Gnatho
                      No, I'd say *entirely* exclusive,

---

31 Thraso presumably was serving as a mercenary for one of the various kings who ruled territories in the Hellenistic world that had fractured (cf. Introduction p. 2) after the death of Alexander the Great in 323 BCE.

If he hangs out with you.
Thraso

                                Everyone was jealous of me.   410
There was lots of grumbling behind my back, but I stayed above it all.
They were terribly jealous, and one guy in particular was beside himself.
He was the one in charge of the Indian elephants.[32]
Once when he was being even more annoying than usual, I said to him:
"Hey, Strato! Are you so beastly because you keep wild beasts?"   415
Gnatho

Absolutely brilliant! And so witty! Olé!
You got him right in the jugular! How'd he take it?
Thraso

                                  Completely dumbstruck.
Gnatho

What else could he do?
Parmeno (*aside*)

                      Almighty gods! What a hopeless excuse for a human being!
And what a scumbag the other one is!
Thraso

                           What about the time
I burned the guy from Rhodes[33] at a dinner party, Gnatho?   420
Have I ever told you that story?
Gnatho

                        Never—but please do!
(*aside*) I've only heard it about a thousand times!
Thraso

                          Well, this
Young smartass from Rhodes I'm talking about is at a party with me.
I happen to be with a whore and he starts flirting with her and making fun of me.
So I say to him: "Listen up, derelict!   425
Why are you trolling for meat when you're such a juicy little tenderloin yourself?"[34]
Gnatho

                                Ha, ha!

---

32 Elephants were employed extensively in ancient Mediterranean warfare, and are perhaps best known in association with Hannibal of Carthage's battles with the Romans during the Second Punic War (218-201 BCE).

33 Cf. n. 13 above.

34 The apparently old Latin saw—which Thraso absurdly claims as his own in 429—here is "You're a hare and you're pursuing delicacies?" Hare meat was served as an hors d'oeuvre, and so the meaning here is: "you shouldn't be making sexual advances at the girl when you're quite attractive yourself." Thraso is older than the young man, and, in accordance with ancient (status-based) sexual norms, in his threat assumes that he would sexually penetrate the Rhodian (but not vice-versa), and so suffer no social disgrace in the homoerotic encounter. The braggart soldier in Plautus' *Miles Gloriosus* is similarly portrayed as being ridiculously lustful.

Thraso

What's so funny?

Gnatho

What you said—it's so witty, funny, stylish … just the best!

Now tell me, is that one yours? I thought it might be old.

Thraso

Had you heard it before?

Gnatho

Yes, often, and it always gets a great reaction.

Thraso

It's mine.

Gnatho

And to use it on such a foolish young gentleman! That was killer! 430

Parmeno (*aside*)

I hope the gods blast you!

Gnatho

How'd he take it?

Thraso

It destroyed him.

Everybody there practically died of laughter. From that point on,

They all started being afraid of me.

Gnatho

And with good reason!

Thraso

But listen up: should I clear the air with Thais about the girl?

She suspects that I'm in love with her.

Gnatho

No, absolutely not! 435

You're better off increasing her suspicion.

Thraso

Why?

Gnatho

You have to ask why?

You're aware of how hot and bothered you get when she mentions

Phaedria or says something nice about him, aren't you?

Thraso

Oh, I can just feel it!

Gnatho

We'll I've got just the right medicine to put a stop to that.

The instant she mentions Phaedria, 440

You toss out Pamphila's name.

If she says: "Let's invite Phaedria to join the party," you say:

"Let's call Pamphila in to sing." If she praises his good looks,

You must respond in kind. In short, fight fire with fire.

That'll gnaw away at her. 445

Thraso

That would be the right strategy, Gnatho—if she actually loved me.

Gnatho

Seeing as she's quite eager for your gifts and loves them,
She's been in love with you for quite a while, and for some time now you've
Been able to yank her chain without much effort.
She's afraid you'll get mad at her and transfer the bounty she now receives
    elsewhere.   450

Thraso

So true. I hadn't thought of that myself.

Gnatho

Nonsense! You just hadn't applied your gifted intellect to it.
If you had, you would have put it so much better yourself, Thraso!

SCENE 7

Thais enters from her house with Pythias.

Thais

I thought I heard the soldier's voice just now.
And there he is. Hello, Thraso dearest.

Thraso

                                Oh my dear Thais,   455
My kissywips, how's it going? Do you love me just a teeny, weeny bit
Because of the gift-girl?

Parmeno (*aside*)

                    That is so slick! What an opening
After a long absence!

Thais

                The most, and you deserve it.

Gnatho

Then let's go straight to dinner. What's the hold-up?

Parmeno (*aside*)

                           Oh, there goes the other one—
Any chance *he* was born from human parents?

Thais

                     Ready when you are.   460

Parmeno (*aside*)

I'll go up and pretend I came out here just now.
Are you going out somewhere, Thais?

Thais

                Oh, Parmeno!
Ah, er … very nice of you. I've got to go …

Parmeno

                Where to?

Thais (*to Parmeno*)

Yes, well—don't you see the soldier here?

Parmeno (*to Thais*)

Yes, the sight of him sickens me. Phaedria's gifts for you are here
When you're ready.

Thraso

Why are we lingering here? Let's leave right now.   465

Parmeno

If I may beg for your permission and full cooperation
In allowing us to greet Thais and to give her some presents.

Thraso

Mighty handsome gifts, I'm sure, and on a par with ours!

Parmeno

You'll see for yourself. (*to slaves inside*) Hey, have those two I told you about
Come out immediately. You: step right up here.   470
She comes all the way from Ethiopia.

Thraso

Worth about three minae.[35]

Gnatho

If that.

Parmeno

Where are you, Dorus? Come on over here. Here's a eunuch for you!
Has the appearance of a gentleman[36] and is in the bloom of youth!

Thais

By the gods! He is good-looking!

Parmeno

What do you think, Gnatho?
Anything to find fault with? And what do you think, Thraso?   475
Silence! I'll take that as approval. Test him in literature,
Athletics, music.[37] Demonstrated expertise in everything
A young man of the better classes ought to have!

Thraso

That's quite a eunuch! If it came to it, and even if was I sober I'd ...[38]

Parmeno

And on top of it all, the person who sent this gift doesn't ask   480

---

35 A relatively small value (cf. Appendix II p. 337).

36 He literally is said to have "an appearance indicative of free status" (*facies liberalis*), reflecting an
ancient presumption that free-born persons were necessarily superior to slaves in appearance, morality,
etc.

37 This indicates that he is an *ephebe*, i.e., a free-born Athenian who at the age of eighteen began his
compulsory military training in preparation to assuming his full duties as an adult citizen. His training
also typically included instruction in literature, music and athletics, all of which were chiefly conducted
at the gymnasium, the male cultural center of a Greek city-state.

38 For Thraso's homoerotic desire here and general lustfulness, see n. 34 above.

That you live and die for him alone and exclude all other men from your life.
And he doesn't tell war-stories, show off his scars,
Or always get in your way as a certain someone does.
No, he's quite content if you receive him when it's not a bother,
Or just when you want to see him and you have the time.   485

Thraso

Obviously, this guy belongs to a poor and wretched master.

Gnatho

I'm quite sure no one who had the wherewithal
To purchase another slave would put up with him.

Parmeno

Shut up! By my accounting, you are the lowest of the low on this earth:
Anyone who stoops to flattering him   490
Is capable of stealing offerings from corpses.[39]

Thraso

Are we going now?

Thais

         I'll take these two in and leave
Some instructions. Then I'll be right back out.

Thraso

I'm leaving. You wait for her here.

Parmeno

         It's hardly proper
For a general to be out for a stroll on a public street with his girlfriend. 495

Thraso

I'm not wasting any more talk on you. You're no different from your master.

Gnatho

Ha, ha, ha!

Thraso

      What are you laughing at?

Gnatho

         What you just said to him ...
Oh, and because I thought of what you said to that guy from Rhodes.
But Thais is coming out.

Thraso

      Go on ahead and see that everything's
Ready.

Gnatho

    Will do. (*exits*)

Thais

      Take good care of things here now, Pythias.   500

---

39 Stealing offerings of food or wine from a tomb was a desperate and despicable crime, used here to
    emphasize Gnatho's extreme poverty.

If Chremes happens to show up here,
First ask him to come back later. If that's inconvenient, beg him to wait here.
If that's not possible, bring him straight to me.

Pythias[40]
Will do.

Thais (*to slaves inside her house*)
      Now there was something else I wanted to say.
Oh yes: take special care of that girl,   505
And don't any of you step out of this house.

Thraso
                      Let's go.

Thais (*to attendants*)
                      Follow me.

SCENE 8

Chremes enters.

Chremes
There's no doubt about it. The more I think it over,
The more I'm convinced this Thais is stirring up a lot of trouble for me.
I now see how she's been slyly sabotaging me
Ever since she first asked me to come to her house.   510
Some of you might be wondering: "what business did you have with her?"
I didn't even know her. When I got here, she found a pretext to detain me.
She said she'd done a sacrifice and had a serious matter
That she wanted to discuss with me. Right then I was suspicious
That she had ulterior motives in all this. She laid down right next to me,[41]   515
Made it clear she was available, and tried to chat me up.
When that fizzled out, she resorted to questions like:
"How long has it been since your parents died?" "A long time," I reply.
"Do you have a farm at Sunium?"[42] How far is it from the coast?"
I'm thinking she wants the estate and has plans to steal it from me.   520
Finally, she asks: "Did you have a little sister who disappeared?
Was anyone with her? Did she have anything with her when she disappeared?
Was there anyone who could identify her?" I'm thinking,
Why would she keep asking these things unless she plans to impersonate
My lost little sister? How shameless is that?   525
But if she's alive, she can't be any older than sixteen,
And Thais is a little bit older than I am.

---

40 Her name may be meant to recall the Pythia, i.e, the inspired priestess/prophetess of Apollo (see Appendix I p. 335) at his major cult center in Delphi.

41 Greeks and Romans both reclined on couches while dining, but Chremes here suggests there are erotic connotations in Thais' behavior as well.

42 Cf. n. 15 above.

Now she's sent another message urging me to come.
She needs to say what she wants or stop bothering me.
I sure as hell won't be coming back a third time! Anyone home?   530
It's Chremes.

Pythias
     Oh, you absolutely darling young man!

Chremes (*aside*)
I'm telling you, they're plotting something against me here.

Pythias
             Thais left you
An urgent message to come back tomorrow.

Chremes
         I'm heading off to the farm.

Pythias
Oh, please—

Chremes
     I can't do it.

Pythias
       Then wait here in the house with us
Until she returns.

Chremes
     No way.

Pythias
       Why not Chremes, sweetie?   535

Chremes
Why don't you go to hell!

Pythias
       If your mind's so made up,
Could you at least go meet her where she is now?

Chremes
          All right.

Pythias (*calling into the house*)
Dorias, take him over to the soldier's house right now! (*they exit*)

SCENE 9

Antipho enters from the wing leading to the harbor.

Antipho
Yesterday some of my buddies and I met in the Piraeus
And planned a party for this afternoon. We put Chaerea in charge of it all.   540
We decided on a time and a place, and how much each of us would chip in.
It's past the time, nothing's ready at our designated spot,
And Chaerea's nowhere to be found! I've got no idea what to make of it all.
They picked me to go find him, and I'm here to see if he's at home.
Who's that coming out of Thais' house? Is it him or not?   545

Oh, it's him, but what has he done to himself? What's with the outfit?
What the hell's going on? I'm absolutely shocked and clueless!
Whatever it is, I think I'll move over here and try to figure it out.

SCENE 10

Chaerea enters from Thais' house, still dressed as the eunuch.

Chaerea[43]

Anybody here? Nope. Anybody follow me out from there? Nope.
Is this the time to jump for joy or what? Holy Jupiter![44]   550
Right now I'd gladly face my own execution
Before I let one of life's tribulations rain on my parade!
And the fact there's no nosy person on my tail now wherever I go,
Hounding and pounding me to death with questions like
"Why all the excitement?" "Why so happy?" "Where ya' going?" "Where ya'   555
Coming from?" "Where'd you get the outfit?" "What ya' looking for?" "Are you
    crazy?"

Antipho (*aside*)

I'll go up to him and answer all his prayers.
Chaerea, what's with all the excitement? What's the meaning of this outfit?
Why ya' so happy? What's the idea? Are you in your right mind? Why the icy stare?
Why the silence?

Chaerea

                    Oh, what luck! Hello, my dear friend!   560
There's no one in the world I'd rather see right now than you!

Antipho

Peleeze do tell me what's up.

Chaerea

                    Oh, *peleeze* do me the favor of listening.
Do you know my brother's lover that lives here?

Antipho

                                        Yes—you mean Thais, of course?

Chaerea

That's the one.

Antipho

                I thought so.

Chaerea

                    She received a young girl as a gift today.
I don't need to describe for you how beautiful she is;   565
You're well aware of what a discriminating eye for beauty I have.
This one knocked me out!

---

43 The ebullient Chaerea's name means "Joy" in Greek.

44 For the god Jupiter, see Appendix I p. 335.

Antipho

                        Really?

Chaerea

                                You'd say she's a perfect ten if you saw her.
To cut to the chase: I fell in love. By complete chance,
My brother had a eunuch at home that he'd purchased for Thais,
And not delivered to her yet. Our slave Parmeno made a suggestion   570
That I couldn't resist.

Antipho

                        What was it?

Chaerea

                                You'll find out faster if you shut up.
It was for me to change into the eunuch's clothes and be taken there in his place.

Antipho

    In place of the eunuch?

Chaerea

                        Right.

Antipho

                        And what in the world did you hope to get out of that?

Chaerea

    Duh? Seeing, hearing and being with the girl I'm so hot for, Antipho!
Not a bad pretext and not a bad plan, eh? I was delivered to Thais,   575
Who was very happy with her gift and took me straight into the house.
And then she entrusts the girl to my care.

Antipho

                        What? To you?

Chaerea

                                To me!

Antipho

                                Talk about security!

Chaerea

    She told me not to leave her side and to make sure no man got near her,
And the two of us were ordered to stay alone together in the women's quarters.[45]
I nodded yes and stared sheepishly at the ground.

Antipho

                        Poor Chaerea!

Chaerea

                                "I'm off to dinner," 580
She says, and takes some maids with her. Just a few of the newer ones

---

45 Literally, "the inner part of the house," which suggests a Greek, not Roman, style house is meant. Greek houses are consistently described as having a segregated women's quarter (*gynaikeion*), though it is not certain what part of a house typically served this function.

Were left behind to tend to the girl. They start the preparations for her bath.[46]
I encouraged them to be quick about it. As that's happening,
The girl sits in her room looking up at a painting.[47] The subject of it
Was the story[48] of how Jupiter shot a shower of gold into Danaë's lap.   585
I started to gaze at it too. The fact that so long ago *he* had pulled off
The very same trick made me even more excited:
A god had made himself into a man and secretly penetrated
Another man's roof, and a woman was tricked via a skylight![49]
And what a god it was: "He whose thunder rattles the lofty foundations of
     the sky."[50]   590
Could I, a mere mortal, possibly do the same? I could ... and I did it gladly!
As I'm mulling over all this, the girl is called to her bath.
She left, she bathed, she returned. Then the maids set her down on the bed.
I stood up and awaited my orders. One comes up to me and says: "Hey, Dorus!
Take this fan and create a nice little breeze for her while we take our baths.   595
You can take a bath if you want when we're done." I hiss at her and grab the fan.

Antipho

I'd have loved to see that shameless face of yours at that moment!
You must have had quite the demeanor—and so big an ass as you holding that
     little fan!

Chaerea

She'd barely gotten the words out of her mouth when they all storm out of the room.
They go off to take their bath with the usual hullabaloo slaves make   600
When their master's away. In the meantime, the girl's overwhelmed by sleep.
I secretly take a sideways peek through the fan like this. At the same time,
I look all around, to see if the coast is clear. It was, and so I bolted the door.

Antipho

Then what?

Chaerea

           What do you think, moron?

---

46   The preliminaries leading up to rape here are pathetically conflated with ancient wedding ritual,
wherein the bride was given a purificatory bath (also thought to promote fertility in marriage). Other
similar perversions of marriage ceremony here include the placement of Pamphila on the bed by her
attendants (593) and the bolting of the bedroom doors (603).

47   Ancient literature abounds in descriptions of works of art and the like such as follows here. The device
is called *ekphrasis*.

48   King Acrisius of Argos received an oracular prophecy that his daughter Danaë would bear a son who
was destined to kill him, and so he imprisoned her in an underground chamber (or, in later versions,
a tower). Zeus (= Latin Jupiter: see Appendix I p. 335), in the form of a shower of gold, penetrates the
structure and impregnates Danaë. Her son from this union, the Greek hero Perseus, later fulfils the
prophecy by killing Acrisius.

49   The opening in the roof here, used to collect water in a basin below, is a distinctive feature of the atrium
of Roman (not Greek) houses.

50   The description is a parody of a line of early Roman tragedy. Chaerea here clearly identifies with
Jupiter's omnipotence in sexual as well as meteorological matters. For the rape scene described here,
see Introduction pp. 33-34.

Antipho

                  Okay, you got me there.

Chaerea

                                     An opportunity

Like that handed to me, brief and unexpected as it was, but so longed for!   605
Do you think I was going to pass it up? Then I would have been a eunuch for real!

Antipho

Damn straight about that. But what about our party? What's happening with that?

Chaerea

It's all ready.

Antipho

               Good man! Where? Your house?

Chaerea

                         No, at our freedman[51] Discus' house.

Antipho

That's a long way from here. All the more reason to rush. You've got to change
   clothes!

Chaerea

But where, damn it? I'm practically banished from home now.   610
I'm afraid my brother's there, or even worse, my father's back from the farm by
   now.

Antipho

My place is close by and you can change there. Let's go.

Chaerea

                     Good call.

Off we go. Now about the girl: you and I need to come up with a plan
That'll allow me to have her in the future.

Antipho

             Let's do it.

SCENE 11

Dorias returns from Thraso's house.

Dorias

May the gods save us all! Based on what I just saw, I'm terribly afraid   615
That crazy soldier will create some commotion and maybe even get rough with
   Thais!
It started when that young man Chremes came—he's the girl's brother—
And she asked the soldier to invite him in. The soldier immediately was furious
But didn't dare say no, and Thais just kept pressing him.
She did it just to keep Chremes there a while, since it wasn't the right time   620
To tell him everything that she wanted to about his sister yet.

---

51 I.e., he was formerly a slave in Chaerea's father's house. Even after being emancipated, slaves in the
   ancient world often retained close ties with their owner and provided certain services to him.

Thraso sulked but invited him in. Chremes stayed and Thais started chatting with
  him.
The soldier assumed she was parading a rival right under his nose,
So he decided to pay her back in kind: "Hey, boy," he says,
"How about getting us some entertainment? Go get Pamphila." "No way in the
  world,"   625
Thais says, "is *she* coming to this party." The soldier insisted and it turned into
  an argument.
Meanwhile my mistress quietly takes off her jewelry and gives it to me for
  safekeeping.
That's a clear sign she'll slip out of there as soon as possible. (*stays on stage*)

SCENE 12

Phaedria returns from the wing leading to the country.

Phaedria
On my way to the farm, I started mulling over things the way
People typically do when something's bothering them,   630
And my thoughts just got more and more pessimistic.
The net result: as all this is happening,
I walked right by our farm without noticing, and by the time I realized it,
I'd gone a long ways past! I made my way back in a very foul mood.
When I got to our farm's driveway, I stopped,   635
And I began to think to myself: "Really now! Do I have to stay here alone
For two days without her? And what happens then if I do?
Nothing. What do you mean 'nothing'? Just because there's no chance
Of touching doesn't mean there's no looking, right? That at least
Will be allowed if the other isn't. At any rate, love from the cheap seats 640
Is better than nothing." Now I've walked on by the farm on purpose.
But why's Pythias running out here in a panic all of a sudden?

SCENE 13

Pythias enters from Thais' house.

Pythias
Oh me oh my! Where can I find that contemptible bum? Where do I look?
To think that he'd even dare such a thing!
Phaedria (*aside*)
                      Oh no, I'm afraid of what this means!

Pythias
The scumbag! It just wasn't enough for him to have his way with her! 645
He had to rip up the poor girl's clothes and tear her hair out on top of it all!
Phaedria (*aside*)
What?

Pythias

        Just give me the chance right now,

And I'd swoop down on that criminal and scratch out his eyeballs!

Phaedria (*aside*)

    Clearly there's been some sort of disturbance in there while I was gone. I'll go see.

    What's the matter, Pythias? What's the big hurry about? Who're you looking for? 650

Pythias

    If it isn't Phaedria, and wondering who I'm looking for!

    You and those lovely gifts of yours can just go straight to hell!

Phaedria

                                 What's the matter?

Pythias

    What's the matter! That eunuch you gave us has created complete mayhem inside!

    He's raped the girl the soldier gave to Thais as a present!

Phaedria

                           What are you saying?

Pythias

    I'm done for!

Phaedria

        You're drunk!

Pythias

               If this is being drunk, I'd wish that only upon my worst enemies! 655

Dorias

    Oh, Pythias, how can something so monstrous as this have happened?

Phaedria

    You're crazy! How could a eunuch possibly have done that?

Pythias

    Whatever he was, all the evidence clearly shows he did what he did!

    The girl's all in tears, and can't even say what happened when you ask her.

    But that paragon of manhood? Nowhere to be found! I also have my suspicions   660

    He took some things on his way out of the house.

Phaedria

                      I'd be quite surprised

If that worthless fellow got very far away. He's probably gone back

To our house.

Pythias

        Please go see if he has.

Phaedria

                 You'll know soon enough. (*exits*)

Dorias

    Oh, this will be the death of me! My dear, I've never even heard of something

        so awful!

Pythias

    Oh my! I'd heard they were hot for women,   665

But couldn't perform.[52] Dear me! It never occurred to me,
Or I would have locked him up somewhere and never entrusted the girl to him!

SCENE 14

Phaedria enters from his house with Dorus.

Phaedria
Get out here, you scumbag! Still struggling, you fugitive?
Come on out, you complete waste of money!

Dorus
                                        Please!

Phaedria
                                                Oh,
Just take a look at that twisted expression on the convict's face!   670
What's the meaning of your coming back here? Why the changed clothes?
Well? What do you have to say for yourself? He had his escape all planned out,
And if I'd gotten home just a bit later, Pythias, I would have missed him.

Pythias
Do you really have him?

Phaedria
                        Yes, of course I do.

Pythias
                                        That's fabulous!

Phaedria
Damn right it's fabulous!

Pythias
                        So where is he?

Phaedria
                                        What do you mean? Can't you see him?   675

Pythias
See him? See who?

Phaedria
                        This guy, of course!

Pythias
                                        Who is this person?

Phaedria
The one who was delivered to your house today.

Pythias
                                            None of us ladies
Has ever laid eyes on this one before, Phaedria.

Phaedria
You haven't?

---

52 Cf. n. 61 below.

Pythias

     You didn't really believe that he was the one
That was delivered to us, did you?

Phaedria

         It's the only one I had.   680

Pythias

Oh, no! There's no comparison between this one and the other!
He was handsome and looked like a gentleman.[53]

Phaedria

         He only seemed that way
Just now because he had that flashy outfit on.
As you can see, without it he's disgusting looking.

Pythias

Shush now! That was far from being the only difference!   685
You'd have really enjoyed eyeballing the young man
That was delivered to us today yourself, Phaedria!
This is a lethargic, rumpled up old geezer
With a face like a weasel's.

Phaedria

     So what's the story here?
Are you trying to convince me I don't know what I actually did myself? 690
Hey you: did I buy you?

Dorus

     Yes.

Pythias

     Tell him to answer me too.

Phaedria

Ask your question.

Pythias

     Did you come to our house today? (*Dorus shakes his head*) No.
See. But that other one did—he was sixteen years old.[54]
Parmeno brought him.

Phaedria

     First things first. Explain to me
Where you got the clothes that you're wearing. Silence!   695
Are you going to tell me or not, you mutant of a man?

Dorus

         Chaerea came—

Phaedria

My brother?

---

53 Cf. n. 36 above.

54 As Chaerea must be at least eighteen (cf. n. 25 above), Pythias is mistaken or exaggerating about his youthful appearance.

Dorus
> Yes?

Phaedria
> When?

Dorus
> Today.

Phaedria
> How long ago?

Dorus
> Just now.

Phaedria
With anyone?

Dorus
> With Parmeno.

Phaedria
> Did you already know him?

Dorus
No. I hadn't ever even heard of him before.

Phaedria
How'd you know he's my brother then?

Dorus
> Parmeno   700

Said he was. He was the one who gave me the clothes.

Phaedria
> Damn!

Dorus
Then he put on my outfit and the two of them left together.

Pythias
Now do you believe I'm not drunk and am telling the truth?
And isn't it clear to you that the girl was raped?

Phaedria
> Come on now, you fool!

Surely you don't trust what *this* one says!

Pythias
> Who needs trust? The evidence is clear. 705

Phaedria
Come a little this way. Hear me? A little more … that's close enough.
Now answer me once again: did Chaerea take your outfit away from you?

Dorus
Yes.

Phaedria
> And put it on himself?

Dorus
> Yes.

Phaedria

           And was delivered here in your place?

Dorus

                    Yes.

Phaedria

  Mighty Jupiter! What a sleazy and shameless person!

Pythias

                Oh no!

  You still don't believe that we've been horribly mistreated?   710

Phaedria

  I'd be shocked if you didn't believe everything he said. (*aside*) I don't know what
    to do.

  (*to Dorus*). This time say no! Can I possibly twist the truth
  Out of you today? Did you see my brother Chaerea?

Dorus

               No.

Phaedria

               I can see

  He won't confess without torture.[55] Follow me this way. "Yes" one minute, "no"
    another!

  (*to Dorus*) Beg me for mercy.

Dorus

            Please, I beg you, Phaedria!

Phaedria

                Now go inside. 715

Dorus

  Ow, ow, ow!

Phaedria (*aside*)

     I don't see any other way of saving face here.

  (*aloud*) You're done for, airhead, if you try to make a fool of me again. (*they go
    inside*)

Pythias

  As sure as I'm alive and breathing, this is one of Parmeno's tricks.

Dorias

  Yes, that's true.

Pythias

     You can be sure I'll find a way to pay him back as he deserves.

  What do you think we should do now, Dorias?

Dorias

              You mean about 720

  The girl?

Pythias

     Do I say something or do I keep quiet?

---

55 The testimony of ancient slaves was admissible only if it was extracted under torture.

Dorias

If you're smart,
You'll let on that you don't know a thing about the eunuch or the rape.
That way you'll steer clear of any trouble for yourself and you'll be doing her a
favor.
Just say that Dorus has taken off.

Pythias

That's what I'll do.

Dorias

Is that Chremes?
Thais will be here soon.

Pythias

Why's that?

Dorias

Because when I left Thraso's, the two of them   725
Had already started arguing.

Pythias

Here, take this jewelry. I'll find out what's up from Chremes.

SCENE 15

Enter Chremes coming from Thraso's house.

Chremes

Oh, my! I've been fooled! That wine got the best of me!
While I was at dinner, I thought I was perfectly sober.
But once I got up, my legs and my brain said otherwise.

Pythias

Chremes!

Chremes

Who's there? Ah, it's Pythias. Wow, you look so much prettier   730
Than you did just a while ago!

Pythias

Right—and you sure are much cheerier.

Chremes

There's eternal truth in the proverb "Without Ceres and Bacchus, Venus is cold."[56]
Has Thais been back here long?

Pythias

Has she already left the soldier's?

Chremes

Long ago, ages! There was a huge argument between the two of them.

Pythias

She didn't tell you to come along with her?

---

56 For the Olympian deities Ceres, Bacchus, and Venus, see Appendix I p. 335. For Chremes, the meaning
of the proverb (by metonymy) is simply that partying (= the consumption of food and drink) leads to
heightened sexual desire (= Venus).

Chremes

                            Didn't say a thing—just nodded to me.   735

Pythias

What? That wasn't obvious enough to you?

Chremes

                           No, I didn't know what she meant.

Well, that is, until Thraso set my ignorant self straight by tossing me outside.

But there she is. I wonder how I beat her back here?

SCENE 16

Enter Thais returning from Thraso's house.

Thais

I'm quite sure he'll be here soon to take Pamphila away from me. Bring it on!

If he so much as lays one finger on her, I'll dig out his eyeballs right then and

    there!   740

I can put up with his stupidity and bluster as long as he's just all talk.

But if he starts converting any of that noise into action, he'll be very sorry!

Chremes

Thais, I've been here forever.

Thais

                      Chremes, my dear! I've been waiting for you.

Do you realize this whole disturbance was because of you?

And that this entire business has everything to do with you?

Chremes

                         Me? How could that be?

Thais

                                  It's because   745

I'm trying to reunite you with your sister. That's why I put up with this terrible

    treatment.

Chremes

Where is she?

Thais

          At my house.

Chremes

                What? *Your* house?

Thais

                     Enough of that:

She's been raised in a way the both of you can be proud of.[57]

Chremes

                         Really?

Thais

                         It's the plain truth.

---

57 I.e., she hasn't worked as a prostitute.

I'm giving her to you and I don't expect anything in return from you.

Chremes

I'm grateful to you, Thais, and I'll see you receive the reward you deserve.   750

Thais

Just make sure you don't lose her before you even get her from me, Chremes.

She's the one the soldier has come to take from me by force.

Pythias, go and get the little box with the keepsakes[58] in it.

Chremes

Thais, do you see he's—

Pythias

Where's the little box?

Thais

In the chest. Hurry, you're starting to annoy me.

Chremes

But look at the army he's bringing here with him!   755

Yikes!

Thais

You're not afraid are you, my dear friend?

Chremes

Oh nonsense!

Me afraid? No person alive could be less frightened!

Thais

That's just the spirit we need.

Chremes

I have a suspicion you have doubts about my manliness.

Thais

No, no! Look at it this way: you're dealing with a foreigner here.

He's far less influential than you. You're well-known here and have more friends. 760

Chremes

True, but isn't it foolish to confront trouble you could just avoid?

I'd prefer proactive prevention to reactive vengeance after the fact.

So you should go inside and bolt the door, and I'll run off to the forum.

I'd like to have some allies here for us in this mayhem.

Thais

Wait!

Chremes

It's better this way.

Thais

No, stay!

Chremes

I'll be right back.

---

58 These are items preserved from Pamphila's childhood that will secure her identity, i.e., the so-called "tokens of identification" stereotypical in recognition scenes of New Comedy.

Thais

                                    We don't need them, Chremes.   765

    Just tell him she's your sister, and you lost her as a little girl, and now you
        recognize her.

    (*re-enter Pythias*) Show him the keepsakes.

Pythias

                                      Here they are.

Thais

                                            Take them.

    If he gets violent, take him into court. Clear enough?

Chremes

                                    Perfectly.

Thais

    Make sure you speak with authority.

Chremes

                                  I will.

Thais

                                  Suck it up now!

    (*aside*) That's just about it! My protector here could really use some protection
        himself.   770

SCENE 17

Thraso and Gnatho return with Sanga and other slave-enforcers.

Thraso

    That I would take such blatant disrespect lying down, Gnatho!
    I'd die before that! Simalio, Donax, Syriscus! Forward march!
    First I'll storm the house.

Gnatho

                     Excellent!

Thraso

                            I'll carry off the girl as booty.

Gnatho

                                          Perfect!

Thraso

    Thais is in for some rough treatment.

Gnatho

                          Fabulous!

Thraso

                            Donax! Center-line with your crowbar!

    Simalio! Left-flank, Syriscus! You take the right!   775

    Bring up the others! Where is centurion Sanga and his platoon of pilferers?[59]

---

59 Sanga apparently is a cook (cf. 816). In ancient comedy, cooks are hired to cater parties on special
    occasions. As outsiders admitted to the home, they are stereotypically portrayed as thieves. Thraso's
    rag-tag band of warriors here is mock heroic.

Sanga

Present, sir!

Thraso

What, you worthless bum! Do you intend to do battle with that sponge you've got?

Sanga

Who, me? I know my general's fortitude and the ferocity of his soldiers.
There is no success to be had without bloodshed: how else would I staunch the
  wounds?

Thraso

Where are the others?

Gnatho

Others, damn it? There's only Sannio and he's on duty at home.   780

Thraso

Draw these men up! I'll be issuing orders to all from behind the frontline.

Gnatho (*aside*)

Now that's smart! He's positioned the troops for his own protection!

Thraso

This was a standard practice of Pyrrhus.[60]

Chremes

See what he's doing, Thais?
Wasn't I absolutely right about shutting up the house?

Thais

Though you might think he's a real man, the reality is he's a great big wimp.   785
You don't need to be afraid.

Thraso

What should we do?

Gnatho

If only you had a sling!
Then you could pick them off from way off and under cover. It'd be a rout!

Thraso

Look, there's Thais herself.

Gnatho

How long until we charge right in?

Thraso

Company halt!
A wise man should pursue all options before resorting to force.
For all we know, she may follow my orders without the use of force.

Gnatho

By the gods! 790

---

60 King of Epirus in northwestern Greece who invaded Italy in 280 BCE, where his limited and costly
    successes in particular battles resulted in his eventually losing the war (hence the term "Pyrrhic
    victory"). Menander (see Introduction pp. 3-4) died in 292/1 BCE, and so the reference here to Pyrrhus
    is Terence's doing.

The value of wisdom! I never spend time with you without walking away wiser!

Thraso

Answer me this first, Thais: when I gave you that girl,

Didn't you say I'd have the next few days with you alone?

Thais

So what?

Thraso

So what! You paraded your lover right under my nose!

Thais

Why's that any of your business?

Thraso

And then you had to sneak off with him!   795

Thais

I felt like it.

Thraso

Then give me Pamphila back—unless you'd prefer my taking her.

Chremes

She's not giving her back! If you so much as touch her, you—

Gnatho

Careful! Better shut up!

Thraso

I can't touch my own property? What do you mean?

Chremes

Your property, dirtbag?

Gnatho

Careful, careful now! You don't realize just who you're badmouthing.

Chremes

Keep out of this!

Do you understand your situation? If you start up any commotion today,   800

I'll see that you never forget this day, this place, or me!

Gnatho

Making an enemy of a great man like this! I feel sorry for you.

Chremes

Go away or I'll smash your head in today.

Gnatho

Is that so, you dog?

That's your attitude?

Thraso

Who do you think you are? What's your angle? What's the girl to you?

Chremes

I'll tell you. First of all, I declare she's freeborn.

Thraso

What?

Chremes
                                        An Athenian citizen.

Thraso
                                                        Ahh!   805

Chremes
And my sister.

Thraso
                    A barefaced lie!

Chremes
                              I hereby forbid you
To carry out any act of violence against her. Thais, I'm going to get our wet-nurse
    Sophrona
So she can come and look at these keepsakes.

Thraso
                                        You're forbidding
Me to touch my own property?

Chremes
                    Yes I am. (*exits*)

Gnatho
                                    Hear that? He's implicating himself in theft!
That's all you need.

Thraso
                Do you agree, Thais?

Thais
                          Find somebody else to answer your questions. (*exits*) 810

Thraso
What now?

Gnatho
                    Oh, let's go home. She'll come back to you soon enough on her own,
And begging.

Thraso
                Think so?

Gnatho
                          I'm absolutely sure of it. I'm an expert on how women think.
When you want them, they reject you; but when you reject them, they want you.

Thraso
                                                        Right.

Gnatho
Should I dismiss our troops?

Thraso
                        Whenever you want.

Gnatho
                                Sanga! Make like a real soldier

And set your heart's path toward hearth and home.   815
Sanga

My mind's been on my pots and pans for some time now.
Gnatho

                                                   Good man!
Thraso

                                                   Forward march!

SCENE 18

Thais returns from her house with Pythias.

Thais

Damn it, would you stop speaking in tongues with me?
"I know," "I don't know," "He went away," I wasn't there."
Whatever it is, just give it to me straight!
The girl's clothing is torn, she's crying, and won't say a word.   820
The eunuch's gone. Why? What happened? Speak up!
Pythias

It's too terrible for me to say. They're saying he wasn't really
A eunuch.[61]
Thais

                    Who was he then?
Pythias

                                        That Chaerea!
Thais

Which Chaerea?
Pythias

                                Phaedria's brother—the one who's an ephebe.[62]
Thais

What are you saying, you witch?
Pythias

                                            I made sure it was true.   825
Thais

What in the world does he have to do with us? Why was he brought to us?
Pythias

                                                                    I'm not sure,
But I think he may have fallen for Pamphila.
Thais

                                        Oh no! It's all over for me!
I'm screwed if what you say is true!
Is that why the girl's crying?

---

61 The Romans knew that eunuchs are in fact capable of achieving erections and engaging in sexual
intercourse if they are castrated after puberty.

62 Cf. n. 37 above.

Pythias
I think so.

Thais
Tell me, you worthless scum:

Didn't I warn you about this very thing when I left?   830

Pythias

What could I do? I put him in sole charge of her just like you told me.

Thais

Damn you! You put the wolf in charge of the lamb!

I'm so ashamed at having been fooled like this! What sort of a person does this?

Pythias

Mistress! Shhh, shhh, please! We're going to be okay!

There's our man in the flesh!

Thais
Where?

Pythias
Over there, to the left.   835

See him?

Thais
      Yes.

Pythias
Have him arrested immediately!

Thais

And then what would we do with him, idiot?[63]

Pythias
What do you mean, what would we do with him?

Just take a good look at him! Don't you see the shamelessness all over his face?

Am I right? And on top of that, such cockiness!

SCENE 19

Chaerea enters, still dressed as the eunuch.

Chaerea

Antipho's mother and father were both at home.   840

It seemed like they'd stayed there on purpose,

So that it would be impossible for me to go in without being seen.

While I'm standing outside their door, an acquaintance of mine shows up.

When I saw him, I hightailed it out of there as fast as I could

Into some abandoned alley, and then to another one,   845

And then to another. I was so worried

That someone would recognize me as I was scampering about!

But is that Thais I see there? It is! Now I'm in a pickle!

---

63 For the unclear legal situation, see Introduction p. 34.

What should I do? I'm not that worried—what can she do to me?

Thais

Let's approach him. Dorus! Greetings, my good man. Tell me now: 850
Did you run away?

Chaerea

                 Yes, mistress.

Thais

                            Are you proud of that?

Chaerea

No.

Thais

             Are you expecting to get off scot-free?

Chaerea

                             Forgive me this one offense.
If I commit another one, you can execute me.

Thais

Now was it my viciousness that made you so afraid?

Chaerea

                              No.

Thais

                             What was it then?

Chaerea (*pointing at Pythias*)

It was her. I was afraid she'd make false accusations to you about me.   855

Thais

What had you done?

Chaerea

                Nothing much.

Pythias

                    Oh? Nothing much, you shameless pig!
Raping a girl who's an Athenian citizen! You consider that
"Nothing much"?

Chaerea

            I thought she was a fellow-slave.

Pythias

A fellow-slave! I can barely keep from swooping down on you
And tearing out your hair, you mutant! And then he even comes to mock us!   860

Thais

Back off, crazy-woman!

Pythias

               What do you mean "crazy-woman"?
I'm sure I'd be fully justified in doing anything whatsoever to this convict!
Especially since he claims he's your slave.

Thais

Enough of this! Chaerea, this behavior doesn't become you.

Even if I completely deserved to be mistreated by you, 865
You had no right to behave like this.
My goodness, now I don't have a clue as to what I should do about this girl!
You've completely messed up all my plans,
And I don't think I can return her to her family.
That would have been the right thing to do and was what I wanted, 870
So that I'd get some long-term advantage for myself, Chaerea.

Chaerea

I hope from now on there will be a long-lasting bond between our families, Thais.
Often in cases like this one, a great friendship
Grows out of what was a very bad beginning.
Maybe this whole thing was the will of some god? 875

Thais

Goodness me, I'm certainly willing to accept that view of it all!

Chaerea

That's just what I hoped. And there's one thing you should know:
I did it out of love and I didn't intend to insult you.

Thais

I understand,
And it's for just that reason that I'm more disposed to forgiving you.
You didn't imagine I was so without human feelings 880
Or so naïve that I don't appreciate the power of love.

Chaerea

As the gods are my witness, I love you too, Thais!

Pythias

In that case, mistress, you really need to be on constant guard against him!

Chaerea

I wouldn't think of—

Pythias

I wouldn't trust you one single bit!

Thais

Stop that!

Chaerea

Now I really need your full support in this matter, 885
And I'm surrendering myself to your protection:
I hereby accept you as my patron.[64] Please, Thais!
I'll simply die if I can't marry her!

Thais

But what if your father—

---

64 The Roman social hierarchy was built around a rigidly stratified system of patrons and their dependent clients. In his outburst of joy here, Chaerea claims Thais as his emotional *patronus*, whereas in reality it is she who is seeking the formal, legal protections afforded by such a relationship (cf. 770 and Introduction pp. 32-33).

Chaerea

       Huh? Oh, he'll agree to it for sure
If she's a citizen.

Thais

      If you can just wait here a little while,   890
The girl's brother will be back in person shortly.
He went off to get the wet-nurse she had as a little baby.
You'll be here to witness her identification, Chaerea!

Chaerea

Of course I'll wait!

Thais

      In the meantime, wouldn't you prefer we
Wait for him inside instead of out here in front of the door?   895

Chaerea

I'd love it!

Pythias

    What in the world are you doing?

Thais

What's the matter?

Pythias

     Duh! Are you really thinking of welcoming
Him into our house after what he's done here?

Thais

           Why not?

Pythias

             Trust me,
He'll start up some ruckus again!

Thais

      Please be quiet!

Pythias

You don't seem to realize how shameless he is.   900

Chaerea

I won't do anything, Pythias.

Pythias

      I'll believe it
When I actually see it, Chaerea!

Chaerea

     Why don't you
Keep an eye on me yourself, Pythias?

Pythias

       I'd consider that keeping an eye out
For myself rather than keeping an eye on you! Gross! Get lost!

Thais (*sees Chremes approaching*)

Great! Her brother's here.

Chaerea
> Damn it all! Please, Thais,   905

Let's go off inside. I don't want him to see me in these clothes
Out here in public!

Thais
> Why? Are you shy after all?

Chaerea
Yes ... yes I am.

Pythias
> Really? He's a true virgin!

Thais
> Go ahead. I'll follow.

Wait here so you can bring Chremes inside, Pythias.

SCENE 20

Chremes enters with Sophrona.

Pythias
If only! If only some idea would pop into my head   910
About how I can pay back that lowlife Parmeno
Who passed off the faux-eunuch on us!

Chremes
> Move along now,

Sophrona.

Sophrona[65]
> I am moving.

Chremes
> Technically, yes—but I meant forward.

Pythias
Have you shown her the keepsakes already?

Chremes
> Each and every one.

Pythias
Well? What does she say? Does she recognize them?

Chremes
> Perfectly.   915

Pythias
Goodness, what wonderful news! I am so fond of that girl!
You two go inside. My mistress has been waiting for you there forever!
Oh, look! Our fine friend Parmeno is approaching.
Just look at him strutting about! So help me gods and goddesses,
I believe I've got just the thing to torture him to my satisfaction!   920

---

65 Her name means "Prudence" in Greek.

I'll go in and make sure about her identity,
And then I'll return to scare that lowlife to death!

SCENE 21

Parmeno enters.

Parmeno

I'm back to see how Chaerea's managing things.
If he's handled his affairs expertly, by the almighty gods,
Parmeno is in for some much deserved glory!   925
To downplay the fact that without any fuss or financial
Outlay I made possible what's usually
A very difficult and expensive affair
(seeing as the girl belongs to a greedy prostitute)—
There is this additional achievement I think I especially deserve a prize for: 930
I found a way for a young man to learn
All about the character and customs of prostitutes at an early age,
So that this newfound knowledge might inspire his eternal hatred of them!
Hookers! When they're out in public with their lovers
And daintily picking at their dinner, what could be more refined,   935
Better groomed or simply elegant?
But to get a picture of their dirty squalid life at home,
How disgustingly ugly they really are,
And how they greedily gobble up dark bread dipped in leftover gravy!
Knowing all this can be a young man's salvation!   940

Pythias (*aside*)

I swear I'll get my revenge for everything you've said or done, dirtbag!
You're not getting away with making fun of us!
(*so as to be heard*) Almighty gods! What a revolting deed! That poor young man!
Oh, and that wicked Parmeno who brought him here!

Parmeno (*aside*)

                                        What's this now?

Pythias

I felt so sorry for him! I ran out here so I wouldn't have to watch   945
The horrible punishments they said he'll get!

Parmeno

                              Holy Jupiter,
What's this commotion about? Did I really do it this time? I'll go up to her.
What's all this, Pythias? Who's getting punished?

Pythias

                              Like you don't know!
What nerve! You've just about finished off the young man
You passed off as the eunuch to trick us.

Parmeno

                              What do you mean? Tell me what happened. 950

Pythias

I will. Are you aware that the girl who was given to Thais today as a present is a
citizen?

And that her brother is from one of the very best Athenian families?

Parmeno

No, I wasn't.

Pythias

We just figured out her true identity. And that miserable bastard raped her!

When the brother found out what happened, seeing as he's very intense—

Parmeno

What'd he do?

Pythias

First he tied him up in a nasty way—   955

Parmeno

Tied him up?

Pythias

—even though Thais was begging him not to do it—

Parmeno

What?

Pythias

—and now he's threatening to inflict the standard punishment for adultery![66]

I've never seen that done and I never want to!

Parmeno

That's outrageous!

How could he do that?

Pythias

What do you mean "outrageous"?

Parmeno

What could be worse?

Who's ever heard of someone being arrested for adultery   960

In a whorehouse?[67]

Pythias

I don't know.

Parmeno

Here's something you do have to know, Pythias:

---

66 Chaerea can be considered an adulterer in the Greek sense of the word (*moechus*) in that he has had
    sex with another male citizen's dependent female; whether or not Chaerea is married to someone else
    is irrelevant. A wide range of punishments for adultery is attested in the ancient world, from, e.g.,
    the insertion of radishes into the offending male's anus to (under certain circumstances) execution on
    the spot, but it is not clear what Pythias means here in her fictitious account. At the end of Plautus'
    Miles Gloriosus ("The Braggart Soldier"), the lecherous soldier is threatened with castration for his
    adulterous ambitions.

67 For traditional Roman mores as they relate to prostitution, see Introduction p. 20.

I hereby proclaim that this is none other than my master's son!
Pythias

                                           Oh no,
Really? It's him?
Parmeno

            So Thais better not allow anything violent to be done to him.
But why don't I just go in and see for myself.
Pythias

                       Watch what you do in there, Parmeno!
You probably won't help him any, but just hurt yourself.   965
They think this whole thing was your idea.
Parmeno

                 Damn! What am I supposed to do then?
Where do I even start to ... hey, look! There's the old man coming back from the
    farm!
Should I tell him or not? Oh hell, I'll tell him, even though I'm sure
To get a major beating for it. I've got to, so Chaerea gets help.
Pythias

                     Good call.
I'm going in now. You tell him the whole story now, with all the details.   970

SCENE 22

*The father of Chaerea and Phaedrea enters from the wing leading
to the country.*

Senex[68]

The main advantage of having my farm so close by
Is that I never get bored with the city or the country.
When I've nearly had my fill of either, I switch places.
Is that our slave Parmeno? It sure is him.
Parmeno! Who are you waiting for outside the door here?   975
Parmeno

Who's that? Oh, master, I'm glad to see you're back home safe.
Senex

Who are you waiting for?
Parmeno (*aside*)

           Damn it! I'm so afraid, my tongue's tied!
Senex

                       Hey,
What's the problem? Why are you shaking? Are you okay? Answer me.
Parmeno

First of all, I'd like to consider the facts of this case.

---

68 Chaerea's father is never named, and is simply given the generic name "Old Man" (*senex* in Latin).

Whatever did happen … it wasn't my fault it happened! 980

Senex
What?

Parmeno
You have a right to know, and I should have told you before.
Phaedria bought a eunuch
To give her as a present.

Senex
Give who?

Parmeno
Thais.

Senex
He actually bought one? Damnation! For how much?

Parmeno
Twenty minae.

Senex
That does it!

Parmeno
What's more, Chaerea is in love with a musician in there. 985

Senex
No! What, in love? Does he even know anything about prostitutes at his age?
Is he here in town? If it's not one thing, it's another!

Parmeno
Don't look at me, Master. I'm not the instigator here.

Senex
Stop blathering about yourself. You convict!
As sure as I'm breathing, I'll …! But first I want an explanation of it all. 990

Parmeno
Chaerea was delivered to Thais here instead of the eunuch.

Senex
Instead of the eunuch?

Parmeno
Yes. And they arrested him for adultery
Inside here and tied him up.

Senex
This'll be the death of me!

Parmeno
Just look at how brazen these prostitutes are!

Senex
Is there any
Other harm or damage that you've conveniently left out? 995

Parmeno
That's all of it.

Senex

I should just burst right in there. (*goes inside*)

Parmeno

There's no question that I'm in for a major beating for this!
Even so, I had no choice in the matter, and I'm glad
That these women here are in for some trouble now thanks to me.
For some time now, the old man has been looking for an excuse   1000
To take some serious action against them—and now he's got it.

SCENE 23

Pythias enters from Thais' house.

Pythias

Goodness gracious me! This is the best thing that's happened to me in ages!
The way the old man came into our house just now all mistaken!
I was the only one who appreciated the humor in it since I knew what he was
    afraid of.

Parmeno (*aside*)

Now what's this about?

Pythias

I'm coming out to see Parmeno.   1005
Hmm! Where is he?

Parmeno (*aside*)

She's looking for me.

Pythias

Oh, there he is. I'll go up to him.

Parmeno

What is it, you fool? What are you after? Why are you laughing? Would you stop it?

Pythias

Oh goodness me, I'm exhausted! I almost died from laughing at you!

Parmeno

How's that?

Pythias

How's that! Well, it's just that I've never seen, and don't ever expect to see
Someone as stupid as you are again! Oh, words can't describe the fun we had   1010
At your expense inside! I actually used to think you were a very clever fellow!
Really! Did you have to believe everything I said?
Weren't you happy enough with having egged the young man on
To the deed without ratting the poor guy out to his father as well?
And how do you think he felt when his father saw him dressed in that outfit?   1015
Yes? Do you see that you've really had it now?

Parmeno

Damn! What are you saying, you bitch? It was all a lie? And you're still laughing!
You scum! Do you really think it's so cute to make fun of us?

Pythias

                                          Absolutely!

Parmeno

If you get away with this scot-free—

Pythias

                              Yes?

Parmeno

                          I sure as hell will pay you back!

Pythias

                                              Sure.
But your threats seem so future-oriented, Parmeno.   1020
You on the other hand will be strung up this very moment for causing a foolish
    young man
So much humiliation and then ratting him out. Both father and son want a piece
    of you.

Parmeno

I'm dead!

Pythias

            This will be your thanks for that gift you brought us. I'm out of here. (*exits*)

Parmeno

Damn! Given away and done in by my own stench, just like a skunk!

SCENE 24

Thraso and Gnatho enter.

Gnatho

What are we doing now? What's the plan? What do you hope to achieve here,
    Thraso?   1025

Thraso

What, me? I'm going to surrender to Thais and do what she tells me.

Gnatho

                                                        What!

Thraso

Why not? Hercules was Omphale's slave.[69]

Gnatho

                          Great reference!
(*aside*) I'd love to see her smash your head in with her sandal![70]
But that's her door creaking.

---

69 Omphale was a queen of Lydia, to whom Hercules was sentenced by Jupiter to serve as expiation for a
    murder he committed. In some Roman versions of the myth, Hercules is forced to wear woman's clothes
    and perform traditional women's work for Omphale.

70 This detail is not attested in extant accounts of the Hercules-Omphale myth, but the 2nd century CE
    Greek writer Lucian refers to a painting depicting such a scene. A famous marble statue found on the
    Greek island of Delos and dating to *ca* 100 BCE features Aphrodite (= Roman Venus: see Appendix I p.
    335) about to strike the lecherous pastoral god Pan with her sandal.

Thraso

Damn it all! What's this all about now?
I've never even seen this guy before. Why's he hightailing it out of there in such
a rush?   1030

SCENE 25

Chaerea enters from Thais' house.

Chaerea

Fellow Athenians! Is there anyone alive today who's luckier than me?
Absolutely no one, I'm sure! The gods have clearly made their powers manifest in
my case!
They've piled up so many blessings for me—and so out of the blue!

Parmeno (*aside*)

What's he so happy about?

Chaerea

Oh, Parmeno, my friend! Planner, starter, fulfiller
Of all my joys! Do you have any idea at all how happy I am right now?   1035
Do you know we found out Pamphila's a citizen?

Parmeno

So I heard.

Gnatho

And that she's engaged to me?

Parmeno

By the gods, that's great news!

Gnatho (*aside to Thraso*)

Did you hear what he said?

Chaerea

I'm also so glad that there's nothing but clear sailing ahead for my brother's affair!
We're all one happy family! Thais will fall under my father's sponsorship and
protection.[71]
She's put all her trust in us.

Parmeno

So Thais is all your brother's now?

Chaerea

Of course.   1040

Parmeno

That's another cause for celebration! The soldier will be booted out.

Chaerea

Go find my brother so he can hear the good news as soon as possible.

Parmeno

I'll see if he's home. (*exits*)

---

71 Cf. n. 64 above.

Thraso (*aside to Gnatho*)

Well, Gnatho, it's entirely clear that I'm eternally screwed!

Gnatho (*aside to Thraso*)

Couldn't be clearer.

Chaerea

Where do I start with my "thank you's"? Who deserves the most praise?

Is it the guy who came up with the plan or yours truly for daring to execute it? 1045

What about Fortune[72] herself? She was the helmsman of this ship,

She's the one who so conveniently crammed so many good things into one single day.

And then there's my delightful and easy-going father to thank!

Oh, Jupiter, preserve all these blessings for us!

SCENE 26

Phaedria enters from his house.

Phaedria

By the gods, I can hardly believe

What Parmeno just told me! But where's my brother?

Chaerea

Right here.   1050

Phaedria

I'm so delighted!

Chaerea

I'm quite sure of that! And no one deserves to have more love

Sent her way than Thais, dear brother! She's our family's biggest supporter!

Phaedria

Huh?

You don't have to praise her to me!

Thraso (*to Gnatho*)

Damn it all! The more hopeless it gets, the more I want her!

I beg you, Gnatho! All my hope is in your hands.

Gnatho

What do you want me to do?

Thraso

Bribe him,

Convince him, whatever, to allow me to play some small part in Thais' life.   1055

Gnatho

That won't be easy.

---

72 One of many abstractions that were personified in Roman religion (in contrast with Greek religion); there were temples dedicated to *Fortuna*, a goddess of "luck" in Rome and throughout Italy from an early date.

Thraso
> I know you can do it if you set your mind to it.
And if you pull it off, you can have any reward you want. Anything—it's yours.

Gnatho
> Really?

Thraso
> Yes, really.

Gnatho
> Okay. If I'm successful, I want your house to always be open to me
Whether or not you're there, and I want a permanent place at your dinner table,
No invitation necessary.

Thraso
> You have my word on that.

Gnatho
> I'm off to battle.

Phaedria
> Who's that talking there?   1060
Oh, it's Thraso.

Thraso
> Hello.

Phaedria
> Perhaps you're unaware of what's happened here.

Thraso
> I'm aware.

Phaedria
> Then why do I still see you hanging around this neighborhood?

Thraso
> I'm relying on your generosity?

Phaedria
> Do you know how reliable that is? Soldier! I hereby proclaim
That if I ever so much as meet you on this street again in the future, you are a dead
  man!
And don't even consider excuses about looking for someone or just passing through.

Gnatho
> Hey, no!   1065

Phaedria
> You've been warned.

Thraso
> It's not like you to be so arrogant!

Phaedria
> I am now.

Gnatho
> Just let me say a few things first. If you like what I have to say,
Do it.

Chaerea

We're listening.

Gnatho

Stand a little ways over there, Thraso. (*to Phaedria and Chaerea*)

First of all, I'd really like the both of you to understand

That whatever I propose to do here is proposed primarily out of self-interest.   1070

But if it benefits you as well, you'd be stupid not to do it.

Phaedria

Out with it.

Gnatho

I think you should accept the soldier as a rival.

Phaedria

What!

Accept him?

Gnatho

Think on it now. It's clear how much you enjoy living with her, Phaedria—

Or perhaps I should say *living it up* with her—

But you have so little to offer her, and Thais is someone who needs a lot.   1075

What could be better than financing your love affair in full at no expense to
  yourself?

And who in the world's more readily available for this purpose than Thraso?

First of all he's got the means and loves to lavish it.

On top of that, he's a fatheaded, dimwitted dolt who snores his way through life.

Thais could never fall in love with him, and he's easy to boot out when you
  want to.   1080

Phaedria

What shall we do?

Gnatho

And then there's the thing that I consider the most important of all:

There's no one alive who entertains guests so well and so lavishly.

Chaerea

It seems quite clear we can find some use for this man.

Phaedria

I agree.

Gnatho

Excellent choice. I have one additional request: let me join your clique.

I've been pushing that rock uphill for quite a while.[73]

Phaedria

You're in.   1085

---

73 The expression alludes to Sisyphus, who, as the result of cheating death, is eternally punished in the
  underworld by having to push a rock up a hill, only to have it roll back down once it reaches the summit.
  Gnatho here refers to both the tedium of flattering Thraso and the soldier's stupidity (cf. our expression
  "to have rocks in one's head").

Chaerea

Yes, it's our pleasure.

Gnatho

And in return, Phaedria and Chaerea, I serve you up Thraso,
For you to feed off of and on, and to provide you bounteous laughter.

Chaerea

I like it.

Phaedria

And he deserves it.

Gnatho

Thraso, come back here if you'd like.

Thraso

Please tell me how we're doing.

Gnatho

Well! They just didn't know who you are, so I revealed
The real Thraso to them by praising all your great deeds and your virtues.   1090
It was successful!

Thraso

Good work! I really owe you one.
I've never yet found a place where people didn't adore me.

Gnatho

Didn't I tell you the man simply exudes genuine Attic sophistication?[74]

Phaedria

He's exactly as you described him. Come on this way.

All

Farewell—and how about some applause?

---

74 Athenians, owing to the city's rich cultural traditions, were stereotypically assumed to be urban
sophisticates.

Appendix I:

Olympian Deities Mentioned in the Five Plays

Apollo (= Greek Apollo): the god of medicine, prophecy, poetry, music and other "civilized" arts. His chief oracle was at Delphi in Greece, to where pilgrims and city-states alike flocked for centuries to get a glimpse into the god's will as it pertained to their future by consulting the god's inspired priestess (the Pythia) and the temple priests.

Bacchus (= Greek Dionysus): also called Liber (an Italian fertility god in origin), the god of wine and intoxication. His cult followers, mostly females called Maenads, were thought to be liberated by an inspired madness that could include unpredictable and irrational behavior.

Ceres (= Greek Demeter): in origin an ancient Italian goddess of growth in general and grain in particular, and so, by metonymy, she often stands for food.

Diana (= Greek Artemis): in origin an Italian goddess of the moon, associated with the wilderness and hunting.

Hercules (= Greek Herakles): the hero and son of Jupiter (by Alcmena, to whom Jupiter appeared disguised as her husband Amphitryon) who became an Olympian god following the completion of his many labors. Men in Roman comedy very frequently swear by Hercules.

Juno (= Greek Hera): wife of Jupiter and goddess of marriage, sometimes identified with Lucina, a goddess of childbirth.

Jupiter (= Greek Zeus): the chief god in the pantheon, originally the Indo-European sky and weather deity, husband of Juno and a notorious philanderer.

Mars (= Greek Ares): god of war, he raped Rhea Silvia (a Vestal Virgin) who gave birth to Romulus (Rome's founder) and his twin brother Remus. He was also associated with wolves.

Neptune (= Greek Poseidon): originally an Italian god of water, he came to be a god of (esp.) the sea, horses, and bulls.

Venus (= Greek Aphrodite): the goddess of sex and love, incongruously and unfaithfully married to Vulcan.

Vulcan (= Greek Hephaestus): a god of fire, for which he often stands (by metonymy), portrayed as a handicapped blacksmith.

[The other three gods usually classified as Olympian—**Vesta** (= Greek Hestia), goddess of the hearth-fire, **Minerva** (= Greek Athena), goddess of handicrafts, **Mercury** (= Greek Hermes), god of boundaries, commerce and messengers—are not mentioned in the five plays translated here.]

Appendix II:

Currency Referred to in the Five Plays

drachma: a Greek silver coin. In the late Classical period, a skilled Athenian laborer made one *drachma* per day in wages.

mina: a Greek unit of currency, equivalent to one-hundred drachmas. Girls are typically sold (i.e., into prostitution) for twenty or thirty *minae* in New Comedy.

nummus: before *ca* 190 BCE, a *nummus* was the equivalent of two drachmas in the coinage of southern Italy.

Philip: a *Philippus* is a gold coin first minted by Philip II of Macedon (d. 336 BCE), the father of Alexander the Great; five *Philippi* = one *mina*.

talent: a very large sum, as an Athenian *talentum* = sixty *minae*.

Appendix III:

Correspondence between the Scene Numbers Used in the Five Plays and the Renaissance Act & Scene Numbers.

Menaechmi   (lines)

Prologue		1-76
Scene 1	Act I, Scene i	77-109
Scene 2	Act I, Scene ii	110-181
Scene 3	Act I, Scene iii	182-218
Scene 4	Act I, Scene iv	219-225
Scene 5	Act II, Scene i	226-272
Scene 6	Act II, Scene ii	273-350
Scene 7	Act II, Scene iii	351-445
Scene 8	Act III, Scene i	446-465
Scene 9	Act III, Scene ii	466-523
Scene 10	Act III, Scene iii	524-558
Scene 11	Act IV, Scene i	559-570
Scene 12	Act IV, Scene ii	571-674
Scene 13	Act IV, Scene iii	675-700
Scene 14	Act V, Scene i	701-752
Scene 15	Act V, Scene ii	753-875
Scene 16	Act V, Scene iii	876-881
Scene 17	Act V, Scene iii	882-888
Scene 18	Act V, Scene iv	889-898
Scene 19	Act V, Scene v	899-965
Scene 20	Act V, Scene vi	966-989
Scene 21	Act V, Scene vii	990-1049
Scene 22	Act V, Scene viii	1050-1059
Scene 23	Act V, Scene ix	1060-1162

Rudens (lines)

Prologue		1-82
Scene 1	Act I, Scene i	83-88
Scene 2	Act I, Scene ii	89-184
Scene 3	Act I, Scene iii	185-219
Scene 4	Act I, Scene iv	220-258
Scene 5	Act I, Scene v	259-289
Scene 6	Act II, Scene i	290-305
Scene 7	Act II, Scene ii	306-330
Scene 8	Act II, Scene iii	331-413
Scene 9	Act II, Scene iv	414-457
Scene 10	Act II, Scene v	458-484
Scene 11	Act II, Scene vi	485-558
Scene 12	Act II, Scene vii	559-592
Scene 13	Act III, Scene i	593-614
Scene 14	Act III, Scene ii	615-663
Scene 15	Act III, Scene iii	664-705
Scene 16	Act III, Scene iv	706-779
Scene 17	Act III, Scene v	780-838
Scene 18	Act III, Scene vi	839-891
Scene 19	Act IV, Scene i	892-905
Scene 20	Act IV, Scene ii	906-937
Scene 21	Act IV, Scene iii	938-1044
Scene 22	Act IV, Scene iv	1045-1190
Scene 23	Act IV, Scene v	1191-1204
Scene 24	Act IV, Scene vi	1205-1226
Scene 25	Act IV, Scene vii	1227-1264
Scene 26	Act IV, Scene viii	1265-1280
Scene 27	Act V, Scene i	1281-1287
Scene 28	Act V, Scene ii	1288-1356
Scene 29	Act V, Scene iii	1357-1423

Truculentus (lines)

Prologue		1-21
Scene 1	Act I, Scene i	22-94
Scene 2	Act I, Scene ii	95-208
Scene 3	Act II, Scene i	209-255
Scene 4	Act II, Scene ii	256-321
Scene 5	Act II, Scene iii	322-351
Scene 6	Act II, Scene iv	352-447
Scene 7	Act II, Scene v	448-481
Scene 8	Act II, Scene vi	482-550

Scene 9	Act II, Scene vii	551-644
Scene 10	Act III, Scene i	645-668
Scene 11	Act III, Scene ii	669-698
Scene 12	Act IV, Scene i	699-710
Scene 13	Act IV, Scene ii	711-774
Scene 14	Act IV, Scene iii	775-853
Scene 15	Act IV, Scene iv	854-892
Scene 16	Act V, Scene i	893-968

Adelphoe   (lines)

Prologue		1-25
Scene 1	Act I, Scene i	26-81
Scene 2	Act I, Scene ii	81-154
Scene 3	Act II, Scene i	155-208
Scene 4	Act II, Scene ii	209-253
Scene 5	Act II, Scene iii	254-264
Scene 6	Act II, Scene iv	265-287
Scene 7	Act III, Scene i	288-298
Scene 8	Act III, Scene ii	299-354
Scene 9	Act III, Scene iii	355-446
Scene 10	Act III, Scene iv	447-510
Scene 11	Act III, Scene v	511-516
Scene 12	Act IV, Scene i	517-539
Scene 13	Act IV, Scene ii	540-591
Scene 14	Act IV, Scene iii	592-609
Scene 15	Act IV, Scene iv	610-635
Scene 16	Act IV, Scene v	635-712
Scene 17	Act IV, Scene vi	713-718
Scene 18	Act IV, Scene vii	719-762
Scene 19	Act V, Scene i	763-775
Scene 20	Act V, Scene ii	776-786
Scene 21	Act V, Scene iii	787-854
Scene 22	Act V, Scene iv	855-881
Scene 23	Act V, Scene v	882-888
Scene 24	Act V, Scene vi	889-898
Scene 25	Act V, Scene vii	899-923
Scene 26	Act V, Scene viii	924-958
Scene 27	Act V, Scene ix	958-997

Eunuchus   (lines)

Prologue		1-45
Scene 1	Act I, Scene i	46-80
Scene 2	Act I, Scene ii	81-206
Scene 3	Act II, Scene i	207-231
Scene 4	Act II, Scene ii	232-291
Scene 5	Act II, Scene iii	292-390
Scene 6	Act III, Scene i	391-453
Scene 7	Act III, Scene ii	454-506
Scene 8	Act III, Scene iii	507-538
Scene 9	Act III, Scene iv	539-548
Scene 10	Act III, Scene v	549-614
Scene 11	Act IV, Scene i	615-628
Scene 12	Act IV, Scene ii	629-642
Scene 13	Act IV, Scene iii	643-667
Scene 14	Act IV, Scene iv	668-726
Scene 15	Act IV, Scene v	727-738
Scene 16	Act IV, Scene vi	739-770
Scene 17	Act IV, Scene vii	771-816
Scene 18	Act V, Scene i	817-839
Scene 19	Act V, Scene ii	840-909
Scene 20	Act V, Scene iii	910-922
Scene 21	Act V, Scene iv	923-970
Scene 22	Act V, Scene v	971-1001
Scene 23	Act V, Scene vi	1002-1024
Scene 24	Act V, Scene vii	1025-1030
Scene 25	Act V, Scene viii	1031-1049
Scene 26	Act V, Scene ix	1049-1094